ENGLAND

IN

PICTURE, SONG, AND STORY

WESTMINSTER HALL

"This my Palace of Westminster in the mighty heart of our Empire is the very cradle of our envied parliamentary institutions. Here is the anvil whereon our common law was forged to become the joint inheritance of the United States of America and our own community of peoples."—King George V to the two Houses of Parliament, Silver Jubilee, May 9, 1935.

ENGLAND IN PICTURE SONG AND STORY

by

J. W. CUNLIFFE

D. LIT. (UNIVERSITY OF LONDON)
LITT. D. (COLUMBIA UNIVERSITY)

PROFESSOR OF ENGLISH AND DIRECTOR EMERITUS OF THE
SCHOOL OF JOURNALISM OF COLUMBIA UNIVERSITY
IN THE CITY OF NEW YORK

AUTHOR OF "PICTURED STORY OF ENGLISH LITERATURE"

WITH

NOTES ON THE ILLUSTRATIONS

by

MARGARET BARNARD PICKEL

PH.D. (COLUMBIA UNIVERSITY)

D. APPLETON-CENTURY COMPANY

INCORPORATED

NEW YORK   LONDON

1936

PRINTED IN U. S. A.

DEDICATED

TO

J. E. C.

MY COMPANION

IN MANY ENGLISH JOURNEYS

FOR NEARLY FORTY YEARS

J. W. C.

JULY 24, 1936

PREFACE

It is a truism that the best way to learn about a country is to go and see it; and the next best is to study its history and read its literature. The present volume is an attempt to combine these three methods with the aid of modern processes of photographic reproduction. If the reader prefers to employ modern means of transport—steamship, railway, automobile, motorbus and airplane—the book may be no less useful in suggesting what to look for and what to read when one has found the places one likes best.

The plan followed is topographical and the visitor who does not want to take all England at one gulp may concentrate on a part or parts of it. Evidently the best places to learn about Celtic England are in Cornwall, Devon, and the Welsh border; and Wessex, whether the ancient Heptarchy or the more modern Wessex of Thomas Hardy, can best be studied in Dorsetshire and the adjoining counties. Surrey is the natural field for the lover of Meredith's poetry or Meredith's novels; and the country between London and Canterbury would be the chosen camping ground for the disciple of Chaucer or Dickens. The Shakespeare student would make straight for Warwickshire, and the admirer of the Romantic Revival would first visit the Lake District. But these are obvious and familiar instances. In many less known corners of England there are scenes celebrated by the novelist or poet and hallowed by historical or literary associations. The author's endeavor is to present these or recall them to the memory, and to help those who visit England, not for literary or historical study, but for sheer pleasure and mental recreation. It is intended for those who, whether students or tourists, will be glad to know where they will find scenes which will feed the imagination not only by their natural beauty but also by their association with the great men and the great events of the past.

In addition to the main text, the volume contains nearly four hundred pictures of scenes remarkable for natural beauty or historical association and portraits of the leading persons associated with them. Full notes are provided on the illustrations.

It is a pleasure to acknowledge indebtedness of various kinds —to Dr. Margaret Barnard Pickel for her assistance, not only in doing the Notes on the Illustrations but in many details of the main text; to Miss Enid Griffis for similar help and for preparing the manuscript for publication; to Macmillan and Company, Publishers, London, and to The Macmillan Company of New York, for permission to quote the lines by John Masefield, "On Malvern Hill," on page 257; to Macmillan and Company I am also obliged for the use of the quotations from the novels of Thomas Hardy in Chapters VI and VII and for the paragraph from Hugh Walpole's *Judith Paris* on page 357. I wish also to acknowledge the courtesy of Doubleday, Doran and Company, who hold the American rights for *Judith Paris,* and of Harper & Brothers, who hold similar rights for the novels of Thomas Hardy.

My obligations for the use of the copyright pictorial material are specifically acknowledged in the Notes on the Illustrations, but I wish in particular to thank my friend and college classmate Sir Christopher Needham for enabling me to obtain photographs of the Wythenshawe building project at Manchester and of other scenes in the North of England. In several instances, pictures have been taken specially for this volume by friendly photographers, among whom I would like to mention Mr. Cyrus F. Stimson, of the Smith College Art Department, Miss Alice Entwistle, of Clevedon, Somerset, and my niece, Miss Gertrude Price. The book would not be what I hope it is—or even what it really is—without the drawings made by Joseph Pennell for *English Cathedrals* (copyright by The Century Company of New York). For all these privileges I wish to record my sincere gratitude.   J. W. C.

CONTENTS

NOTES ON THE ILLUSTRATIONS

WESTMINSTER HALL   *Frontispiece*

King George rightly spoke of "this my Palace of Westminster", for it has descended by inheritance from one English sovereign to another since the time of Edward the Confessor. Constantly changed and extended, it was the regular royal residence in London until the time of Henry VIII. The Great Hall itself was added to the Palace by William Rufus and enlarged in the reign of Richard II. It was during the latter period that the King's Carpenter, Master Hugh Herland, designed and built the famous oak roof, in one span, which has held its place for over five centuries. Early in the twentieth century its timbers were found to be threatened with destruction by the death-watch beetle; a considerable portion of the ancient woodwork had to be removed and the original structure strengthened by a steel framework; these renovations were completed in 1923. For additional details see pp. 10, 64, and 71. On the steps at the back of Westminster Hall there is now a brass tablet at the spot on which King George stood to receive the loyal addresses presented by the two Houses of Parliament as shown in our illustration, reproduced from a copyright photograph by Fox Photos, London. In the centre of the Hall is another tablet marking the place where the royal coffin rested during King George's lying-in-state in January, 1936. At the head of the tablet is the Crown and at the foot a cross, and the inscription runs:

HIS MAJESTY
KING GEORGE
THE FIFTH
LAY IN STATE
HERE
FROM THE TWENTY-
THIRD OF JANUARY
UNTIL HIS BURIAL AT
WINDSOR ON THE
TWENTY-EIGHTH OF
JANUARY NINETEEN
HUNDRED AND THIRTY SIX.

Nearby are tablets recording the lying-in-state of King Edward VII and of W. E. Gladstone. The bodies of those who lost their lives in the wreck of the airship R 101 also lay in state in Westminster Hall, but there is no tablet to mark the spot.

LONDON STONE

PAGE
XXXViii

This ancient stone, since 1798 set in the south wall of the Church of St. Swithin (the weather saint), has been regarded with reverence for nearly two thousand years. It was formerly believed to be a prehistoric relic, but it is now thought to be more probably the "milliarium" of Roman London, from which the early colonists measured the distances along the roads they constructed. It is still, in a geographical sense, the centre of the Empire, and Jack Cade, the rebel leader, in Shakespeare's *2 Henry VI* (IV. vi) was right when he struck London Stone with his sword and exclaimed that now he was lord of the city. Reproduced from a print of 1791, showing the stone in its original place on the south side of Cannon St., a little to the west of its present position.

ix

ROMAN LONDON   2

Taken by permission from the reconstruction of Roman London from the southeast drawn by A. Forestier for the London Museum Catalogue, *London in Roman Times,* edited by R. E. M. Wheeler, Keeper and Secretary of the Museum (1930). The bridge stretches across the Thames at the point where London Bridge now stands. On the south side of the river (on the site of the present Southwark) is a Roman temple, possibly the shrine of the goddess Isis for which the jug found at Southwark and photographed on page 4 was intended. The bridge on the northern bank, seen a little higher up the river, crosses what is now the Walbrook (see pp. 3-4). Still higher up the river, on the same side, runs the Fleet. Various temples are shown, resting on the evidence of objects found upon these sites, and in the middle of the city is the great Basilica, which was the seat of government and contained the various government offices. The wall is seen marking the limits of the ancient city, which is more thickly populated on the original site of its foundation in the eastern half.

ROMAN JUG   4

This jug was found at Southwark and is now in the London Museum. It is about ten inches high and bears the inscription: LONDINI AD FANUM ISIDIS, "At the shrine of Isis in London"—the earliest contemporary use of the name of London that has come down to us. Our reproduction is from a photograph used by permission of the Museum authorities.

HADRIAN   4

Publius Hadrianus, born A. D. 76, Emperor of Rome 117-138, visited Britain in 122. This bronze head, which was found in the Thames near the third arch of London Bridge in 1834, was evidently from some statue in Roman London. It is now in the British Museum and is here reproduced from a photograph taken by the Museum Photographic Service.

FRANKS CASKET   6–7

This casket, also from the British Museum, is one of the most interesting monuments of Anglo-Saxon antiquity and has had an extraordinary history. As the inscriptions on it show, it was carved by a Northumbrian artist in the eighth century out of whalebone and was originally mounted in silver. Somehow it found its way to a monastery in the department of Haute-Loire in France and was later used as a work-box by a middle-class family of the neighborhood to keep needles and thread in. In 1856 it was discovered in the shop of a Paris dealer in antiquities by Sir A. W. Franks, who bought it and gave it to the Museum, of which he was then Keeper; it has since been called by his name. Our illustration shows the front panel with the silver mounting and lock missing. The scene on the left is taken from the story of Wayland the Smith, a famous artificer who was hamstrung and robbed of his magic ring by King Nithhad to prevent his escape from the kingdom. In revenge Wayland killed Nithhad's two sons and gave the King drinking cups made out of their skulls. He is seen on the extreme left with one of the cups in his right hand and the tongs in the other. Nithhad's daughter, Beaduhild, to whom her father gave the ring, broke it and brought it to Wayland to repair—to her own undoing. She is seen in the picture, accompanied by an attendant. More towards the centre is Wayland's brother capturing the birds whose wings Wayland used for his flight from the kingdom. The story is a familiar one in Anglo-Saxon literature and in German folklore generally. The right half of the panel pictures the three Magi bringing their offerings of gold, frankincense, and myrrh to the child Jesus, who is somewhat rudely drawn in the arms of the Virgin Mary, seated in a chair.

ANGLO-SAXON RINGS

These gold rings (now in the British Museum) are over a thousand years old; one (found at Laverstock, Wiltshire) bears the name of King Ethelwulf, the father of King Alfred, the other (found between Aberford and Sherburn, in Yorkshire) belonged to Ethelswith, King Alfred's sister.

ALFRED JEWEL

This is not only our most precious relic of the great English King but is also the oldest authentic portrait surviving from Anglo-Saxon times. It is a portrait of Alfred himself in colors set in gold and bears on its edge (shown in our illustration alongside the portrait) the inscription in Anglo-Saxon characters, "Alfred had me made". It is the handle of a bookmark or "æstil", a sort of pointer or ruler used for following the lines of manuscripts. It may have been used by Alfred himself or sent by him as a gift to some nobleman or church dignitary whom he wished to encourage in his educational plans. "Let all our youth be set to learning until they can read English well", he wrote in a circular letter sent to the leading men in his Kingdom. Perhaps he sent the book-mark with the letter. It was found in the marshes of Athelney, in Somersetshire, where Alfred gathered his forces for his final repulse of the Danes. It was also in this district that Alfred, according to the old story, was reproved by a cottager's wife for letting the cakes burn which she set him to watch as he sat by the hearth. The Jewel is in the Ashmolean Museum at Oxford.

THE TOWER OF LONDON

From a British Museum photograph of the print by the famous engraver, Wenceslaus Hollar of Prague (1607-1677), who established himself in Westminster and is commemorated by a tablet in St. Margaret's Church, recording the fact that he died in that parish.

CHAUCER

Reproduced from an early fifteenth century manuscript in the British Museum containing a poem by Chaucer's disciple, Thomas Occleve.

AN EARLY CAXTON

From a British Museum copy of *The Dicts or Sayings of the Philosophers,* the first dated book printed in England. The passage runs: "Here endeth the book named the dicts or sayings of the philosophers imprinted by me, William Caxton, at Westminster in the year of Our Lord, 1477, which book is lately translated out of French into English by the noble and puissant lord, Lord Anthony, Earl Rivers, Lord of Scales and of the Isle of Wight, Defender and Director of the Apostolic Seat of our Holy Father the Pope in this realm of England, and Governor of my Lord Prince of Wales; and it is so that at such time as he had accomplished this said work it pleased him to send it to me in certain quires to oversee . . ."

FIRST PRINTED ENGLISH BIBLE

From a British Museum copy of the translation which William Tyndale began to print in Cologne, but he was forced to flee to Worms, where he got out the New Testament in 1525. He was executed in Flanders in 1536, but Miles Coverdale completed the translation of the whole Bible which was printed at Zürich in 1535. The second edition, 1537, was the first complete Bible in English printed in England. The passage reproduced is the beginning of the first chapter of Genesis.

Houses of Parliament. Other "stairs" and "bridges" follow, for in the time of Elizabeth the Thames was the chief channel of communication between the cities of Westminster and London. York .House, originally built by Cardinal Wolsey when he was Archbishop of York, was seized by Henry VIII on Wolsey's death and later became part of the royal palace of Whitehall, now used as government offices. Other great houses of the Elizabethan nobility are indicated lower down the river: Durham, Russell, the Savoy (begun in the thirteenth century and given by Henry III to his wife's uncle, the Earl of Savoy, but swept away to make room for the approach to Waterloo Bridge; the Chapel of the Savoy, built in the early sixteenth century, is still in use). Somerset House was built by the Lord Protector of that name and was occupied by Elizabeth during the reign of her elder sister Mary; the present Somerset House, with its classical façade fronting the Thames above the Victoria Embankment, is an eighteenth century erection, now chiefly given to the registration of births, marriages, and deaths; but its left wing is King's College. Next, in Elizabethan times, came a lane leading (as it still does) to the Strand; then Arundel House—not the one where Lord Bacon died from his experimental stuffing of a fowl with snow —that is in Highgate. Milford Stairs is now marked by Milford Lane, but there is neither mill, nor ford, nor stairs. Leicester House gave its name to Leicester Square, and was in Elizabeth's time the residence of the Queen's favorite, frequented by Sir Philip Sidney and Edmund Spenser and many a lesser light of literature (see p. 28). So we arrive at Temple Stairs and make connection with the map of London on p. 20. "The way to Hampstead" is shown in the north and Gray's Inn between it and the river; further east are Islington, West Smithfield Market, and Ludgate. Old St. Paul's may be recognized by its square tower (see p. 39) and the outlines of the city wall may be followed on the map from Blackfriars by Cripplegate, Moorgate, Moorfields, Bishopsgate, and Aldgate to the Tower, near which there was a postern connecting the precincts of the city with the market of East Smithfield. Along the riverside from Blackfriars to Billingsgate various wharves may be noted; the most interesting are Queenhithe, once a famous fishmarket, now a general dock, and the Steel Yard (the site is now occupied by Cannon St. District Railway Station), from the middle of the thirteenth century to the time of Elizabeth the factory of the Hanseatic League and the centre of London trade with the Continent; Billingsgate was still a general market and was not devoted exclusively to fish (and the language of fishwives) till the end of the seventeenth century. London Bridge was in Elizabeth's time the only way of crossing on foot to the south side of the river. Southwark is marked and St. Mary Overy (now Southwark Cathedral). Between it and the Lambeth marshes lie the Bankside, the Bearbaiting houses, and the playhouses, though Shakespeare's Globe was not yet built when the map was made.

QUEEN ELIZABETH 23

Engraved by W. T. Fry from a portrait by Zucchero belonging to the Marquis of Salisbury. The Latin words, *Non sine sole iris,* mean "No rainbow without sunshine," and Iris was the messenger of the gods who descended from heaven to earth by the rainbow. The curious designs in the dress are symbolical, the serpent signifying wisdom, the eye insight, and the ear willingness to listen.

MIDDLE TEMPLE HALL 24

This old print, engraved by H. Melville from a drawing by T. H. Shepherd, shows the members of the Middle Temple at dinner in their famous Hall. The Minstrels' Gallery at the end was doubtless used in the performance of Shakespeare's *Twelfth Night,* which for students of literature is the most noteworthy incident in the history of the Hall, but it has many other memories for those interested in the development of the English Bar; many legal luminaries have sat at these tables and are now represented by portraits or coats of arms on the walls. The "high table" is still occupied by the Benchers or senior members of the Society; below them sit the younger barristers and the students. One table was given to the Inn by Queen Elizabeth, who had it made from an oak tree in the royal park at Windsor. Another is of wood from the timbers of the Golden Hind, in which Sir Francis Drake sailed round the world.

PENSIONERS' HALL and OLD PORCH, CHARTERHOUSE   25

These prints represent the Charterhouse buildings as they were when Thackeray went to school there. Little remains to connect the school with the Carthusian monks who occupied the site up to the time of the Reformation, when the last prior was put to death at Tyburn. The pupils and the masters have been removed to new buildings beautifully situated at Godalming in Surrey, but for the modern visitor the buildings here shown still retain the fragrance of their old associations.

THE GLOBE THEATRE   27

This view of the Globe Theatre with its flag flying and the Thames traffic in the background is taken from Visscher's map of London, 1616, of which the British Museum has a very fine copy, here reproduced. The octagonal shape shows that it is the second theatre as it was rebuilt in 1614. The first Globe, referred to by Shakespeare in *Henry V* as "this wooden O", was round in shape; it was burnt down in 1613.

WHITEHALL   29

Whitehall from the river with Lambeth Palace in the distance. Reproduced from a British Museum photograph of the seventeenth century engraving by Wenceslaus Hollar.

ST. JAMES'S PALACE   29

From a modern photograph. This ancient palace has been closely associated with the British Crown ever since the time of Henry VIII, who took it away from the "maidens that were leprous" to whom it was assigned as a hospital in the tenth century. His daughter, Queen Mary, died here. It was the birthplace of most of the children of Charles I. After the burning of Whitehall, in 1698, the Palace became the official residence of the sovereign in London, and ever since the English Court has been known as the Court of St. James's. Royal levees are still held here, and it is one of the places in London at which the accession of a new sovereign is proclaimed. In May, 1936, it was the scene of the proclamation of Edward VIII, "declaring His Majesty's Pleasure touching His Royal Coronation and the Solemnity thereof."

STATUE OF CHARLES I   31

About this statue adherents of the Stuart cause and admirers of the royal saint and martyr meet yearly on January 30, the anniversary of King Charles's execution, to honor his memory. In 1936, owing to the death of King George on January 20, they gracefully deferred the ceremony for a few weeks, but made up for the postponement by solemnly proclaiming Rupprecht, Crown Prince of Bavaria, as the rightful King of England. King Edward VIII evidently felt securely seated on the throne, for he lent the demonstrators the trumpeters of his own Household Foot Guards to assist in the proclamation of Rupprecht. Reproduced from an old print in the British Museum.

PAGE

PAGE

BRITISH MUSEUM READING ROOM   69

By permission of the Trustees of the Museum. The dome of the Reading Room is 140 feet in diameter and 106 feet high. There are seats for 458 readers in addition to the central dais for the operating staff. The volumes of the general catalogue seen round the outside of the dais number over 1000 and register about 5,000,000 books. Manuscripts and prints are housed in another part of the Museum building and the newspaper files are kept in a separate department at Colingdale, Hendon. The Library contains a copy of every printed book issued for sale since 1842, and many of its ancient literary treasures are unique.

LONDON COUNTY HALL FROM THE RIVER   70

From photographs reproduced by courtesy of the London County Council. These magnificent modern buildings on the south bank of the Thames below Westminster Bridge have cost more than the buildings of the Houses of Parliament across the river just above the bridge. They were begun in 1912 and have been subject to continual extension owing to the importance of the interests with which the Council has to deal. The new Waterloo Bridge is one of its most recent enterprises. Excepting Parliament, the Council may be said to be the most important democratic governing body in England, and it has taken the lead in working-class housing and other large social projects in which all political parties have had a share.

RICHMOND HILL and HAMPTON COURT   72

These and most of the other landscapes in this chapter illustrating the scenery of the upper Thames are from old prints.

POPE'S VILLA and TWICKENHAM FERRY   74

RUNNYMEDE and WINDSOR CASTLE   77

TOMBS OF WYCKHAM AND EDWARD III   79

From old prints. The enlargement of the head of Wyckham with its supporting angel was done by the British Museum Photographic Service.

ETON COLLEGE and STOKE POGES CHURCHYARD   81

LECHLADE BRIDGE AND CHURCH   82

CLIVEDEN   84

GREAT MARLOW   86

DORCHESTER BRIDGE AND CHURCH   88

The Abbey Church is the largest and in some ways the finest of English parish churches. In addition to its famous Jesse window, it contains an eighteenth century monument to a lady who died "the victim of excessive sensibility".

IFFLEY CHURCH   88

This, the best preserved of small Norman parish churches in England, was built in the twelfth century. The square tower and dog-tooth carving are characteristic. This view of Iffley and most of the views in the Oxford

gave were lost in the troublous times of the Wars of the Roses and the Reformation. In 1597 Sir Thomas Bodley paid for the restoration of the room over the Divinity School in which Duke Humphrey's books were kept. This room is still known as Duke Humphrey's Library and is shown in our illustration. Bodley's Bell still rings in the late afternoon to warn forgetful readers that it is time for them to go home.

The Radcliffe Camera is so named after its donor, a famous Court physician of the early eighteenth century. Its gallery provides one of the best points of view of Oxford and the country round about, and its dome, along with the adjoining spire of St. Mary's, is a conspicuous feature of the university city from the low hills which encircle it.

By courtesy of F. R. Mansbridge of the Cambridge University Press Department and of the Macmillan Company, New York. Lord Rutherford's photograph is by J. Palmer Clarke, Cambridge.

A drawing in pencil, done in 1919 by William Strang and now in the National Portrait Gallery.

Hardy's father was a joiner and contractor in a small way of business, and his mother, of about the same rank in life, came from the neighboring village of Melbury Osmond. This little cottage, charming in its simplicity, sufficed for their modest needs, and the novelist himself shared their simple tastes, even in the days of his prosperity. After his education and training as an architect in the neighboring town of Dorchester, he worked for a while in London and came back to his birthplace after he had abandoned architecture to write the novels which established his reputation. The simple monument in the lane adjoining the house bears the following inscription: "Thomas Hardy, O.M. was born in the adjacent cottage 2nd June 1840 and in it he wrote *Under the Greenwood Tree* and *Far from the Madding Crowd*. This monument is erected to his memory by a few of his American admirers. 1931". The monument was unveiled with an appropriate address by Dr. J. L. Lowes, Professor of English Literature at Harvard University. The plain shaft of stone befits not only Hardy's character but its natural situation on the edge of Egdon Heath.

Before going to the Grammar School at Dorchester founded centuries ago by one of his ancestors, Hardy attended a small dame school nearer to his birthplace. This childhood experience was used by Hardy for the setting of his first successful story, the romantic idyll *Under the Greenwood Tree*. The pleasant cottage and the magnificent tree beside it, shown in the illustration, according to local tradition suggested the title of the novel and the description of the house in which the heroine, the village schoolmistress, lived.

When Hardy felt himself sufficiently secure of the favor of the novel-reading public, he built himself a commodious house a mile or two out of Dorchester on the Wareham road. There the great novels of his maturity were written, the novelist lived there until his death, and it continued to be the home of Mrs. Hardy.

reproduced here, or the pen of Hardy, to give it glamor. The summer visitor, unless he is equally gifted, may see in it just natural beauty and charm.

RAINBARROW 184

Photograph by Cyrus F. Stimson, Art Department, Smith College, Northampton. Rainbarrow also has its elusive charm, not always obvious to the average observer. It is still wild, and the fox and the deer may be seen in the course of a morning walk, but it is the imagination of Hardy that has invested the neighborhood with its atmosphere of mystery.

THE QUIET WOMAN 184

This interesting inn sign of "The Quiet Woman" (with her head under her arm) is not near the site of the inn in *The Return of the Native* but some miles away at Halstock near Melbury Osmond, for some years the home of Hardy's mother and probably the original of Little Hintock in *The Woodlanders*. The headless woman is used as an inn sign in other parts of England, sometimes with the following lines underneath it:

A silent woman—how can that be?
Patient traveller, do not scoff;
Drawn from the very life is she,
And mute, because her head is off.

WOODSFORD FARM and WOODSFORD WEIR 186

The farm was photographed by Cyrus Stimson and the weir by Gertrude Price. The farm, with its thatched roof and old water wheel, is one of the most attractive scenes on the Frome and it is no wonder that it kindled Hardy's imagination. He describes the weir in *The Return of the Native* with an accuracy of detail that makes its identification beyond doubt.

T. E. LAWRENCE'S COTTAGE 188

Photograph by S. J. Herbert, Weymouth. The cottage is situated in one of the most secluded parts of Egdon Heath, deep in the woods. It is small and very simply furnished, the chief object of interest being a large, broad couch on which Lawrence could lie with his favorite books within easy reach. It is to be hoped that the National Trust, to which the property has been handed over, will be able to keep the interior as it was when Lawrence left it.

EGDON HEATH 189

Egdon Heath is a most difficult subject for the artist or photographer, but this photograph by Cyrus F. Stimson may convey something of the sense of expanse and mystery so well expressed by Hardy in his novel.

LAWRENCE'S GRAVE 189

Nothing could be simpler than the quiet grave without a headstone in Moreton graveyard on the edge of Egdon Heath. Photograph by Alice Entwistle.

SHERBORNE ABBEY CHURCH 190

This noble and well preserved church is a magnificent reminder of the splendor of the ancient historical kingdom of Wessex, two of whose rulers, Ethelbald and Ethelbert, are buried behind the high altar.

Salisbury is a more recent construction than most of the famous English cathedrals (the see was removed from Old Sarum in 1220), but it makes up for its comparative lack of antiquity by its unity of design; the whole structure, except the spire, having been put up within forty years, a most unusual record in ecclesiastical building. Its graceful proportions are familiar all the world over through reproductions of the Constable painting and a closer view of its harmonious detail confirms the impression conveyed in Henry James's phrase, "a blonde beauty" among cathedrals.

To scholars the Cathedral is most famous for its Chapter House and for the manuscript of the Exeter Book which it contains. This precious relic of Anglo-Saxon literature has been for over eight hundred years part of the Library of the Cathedral, to which it was presented by Leofric, Edward the Confessor's personal friend and trusted counsellor and Bishop of Exeter.

Except for the tower of Winchester Gaol, a comparatively modern building, on which the black flag was hoisted to announce the death of Tess of the D'Urbervilles, this old print (1812) presents exactly the same prospect as is described by Hardy when he tells how Angel Clare and Liza Lu climbed the West Hill of Winchester on that fatal morning.

The Turneresque view of Tintagel engraved by W. Finden realizes the impression created for English readers by Malory's *Morte d'Arthur* and Tennyson's *Idylls of the King* perhaps better than an actual visit made by automobile or charabanc to the ancient rock fortress about which so many legends have gathered.

This old print by J. Greig from a drawing by Prout, 1811, also brings to the eye a better idea of what Glastonbury was than a personal visit under modern conditions. Except for the church tower, the picturesque surroundings of the ancient Pilgrim's Inn shown in the engraving have disappeared, but the twentieth century tourist may still stay at the Inn and even occupy the room in which the last Abbott of Glastonbury spent the night before his execution at the top of the neighboring Tor.

The space chained off in the front of the foreground encloses the place before the high altar where King Arthur and Guinevere are supposed to have been buried.

In a recent article on the progress of archæology, Stanley Casson has an interesting note on the builders of Avebury and neighboring long barrows, which he regards as communal burial grounds or family vaults: "To about the year 2000 B.C. must be attributed that most ancient of all British large-scale monuments, Avebury Circle. It seems to have been built about the time that the first big invasion of our island took place—that called the invasion of the "Beaker Folk", a continental people from Holland and Germany who entered in two waves along the eastern and southern coasts. These were the first users of metal in our islands and, to judge by their remains, a strongly built, round-headed people whose physiognomy was that of the "John Bull" of the caricatures. Excavations in the last few years have shown that these people had reached Avebury and that the Circle must have been made about the time of their arrival. But, as a monument, Avebury continues the Atlantic tradition of big stone building that had gone on for several centuries in the west. The "Beaker Folk" soon amalgamated with the indigenous Neolithic people. From this blend developed the "British Bronze Age." Further excavation since this note was published (1933) indicates that some at any rate of the remains in and about Avebury belong to the Bronze Age. H. G. Wells places part of the action of *The Secret Places of the Heart* in the neighborhood of Avebury and gives a fine description of the remains.

STONEHENGE FROM THE EAST and FROM THE WEST 216

From photographs taken by H.M. Office of Works.

SIR FRANCIS DRAKE 220

Reproduced from a British Museum copy of a Dutch chart published by Hondius about 1595. The inscription reads: "The living image of the most valiant knight Francis Drake, together with a delineation of his wonderful voyage which he began from England on the Ides of December, 1577, and happily accomplished on the fourth Kalend of October, 1580."

THE ARMADA 222

The inscription at the top reads: "The right hand of the Most High saved us". "Differo, dissipo", "I scatter abroad and overwhelm", probably refers to Psalm XVIII, 13-15. The gathering of the troops which Queen Elizabeth reviewed at Tilbury is indicated on the right hand side of the engraving, and Calais is shown on the opposite shore. The original print was published in George Carleton's *A Thoughtful Remembrance of God's Mercy in the Deliverance of the Church and State in the Reigns of Elizabeth and James I* (1624).

THE ARK ROYAL 222

From a contemporary woodcut in the British Museum. This was the flagship in Queen Elizabeth's navy at the time of the repulse of the Armada and was commanded by Lord Howard of Effingham, with Sir Francis Drake as one of the subordinate commanders. It was Drake's device of the burning fire-ships steered into the midst of the Armada as it lay at anchor off Calais that caused the dispersal of the Spanish fleet and its ultimate destruction as it attempted to make its way home northwards around the coasts of Scotland and Ireland.

ROMAN BATH 226

This photograph of the Roman Bath, with the Abbey Church in the background and the reflection of the pillars in the water of the Bath, was supplied by Mr. John Hatton, Director of the Spa at Bath, and is reproduced by permission of the Bath Corporation.

THE CIRCUS, BATH 228

This photograph of the left half of the famous Bath Circus comes from the same source as the last picture. The Circus was planned by the elder Wood, who devised the arrangement of three crescents as arcs of the same circle, each facing one of three openings. Our photograph thus presents one third of the whole design. In the Circus there dwelt at one time or another the following distinguished persons at the numbers indicated:

PAGE

7-8 William Pitt, Earl of Chatham, M.P. for Bath; 13 David Livingstone; 14 Lord Clive; 22 Major André; 24 Thomas Gainsborough; 27 Sir Edward Parry.

WIDCOMBE MANOR 228

By the kindness of Mr. John Hatton this photograph was taken specially for this book with the permission of the owner, Mr. Horace Annesley Vachell.

WELLS CATHEDRAL, WEST FRONT 229

CHEPSTOW CASTLE 232

From an old print. The Norman keep dates from the eleventh century but most of the Castle is Edwardian, dating from the fourteenth century. The distinguished Anglican divine, Jeremy Taylor, was imprisoned here under the Commonwealth and by way, perhaps, of poetic justice, Henry Marten, the Regicide, spent within its walls the twenty years between the Restoration and his death.

RAGLAN CASTLE 232

Raglan is beautifully situated a little above the Wye Valley between Tintern and Monmouth and, although sadly battered in the Civil War, is still a magnificent ruin.

TINTERN ABBEY 234

Our reproduction is from a print dated 1784, so that it shows the Abbey as Wordsworth saw it.

MONNOW BRIDGE 234

This picturesque old tower still provides access to the Monmouth main street and has the unique distinction of being the only tower of its kind in England built upon a bridge.

GEOFFREY OF MONMOUTH'S WINDOW 236

This fine old window, now part of a building used as a national school, according to local tradition gave the light in which Geoffrey in 1136 completed his Latin *History of the Kings of Britain,* now more noted for the fables than for the facts it contains; but according to modern archæologists the room called "Geoffrey's Study" has no more claim to authenticity than the tall exploits of early British heroes which he related.

HEREFORD CATHEDRAL 238

The Cathedral contains a famous *Mappa Mundi,* a medieval map made by Richard of Haldingham early in the fourteenth century. In this "map of the world" Jerusalem is shown at the centre of the earth's surface and Paradise at the top.

LUDLOW 238

TITLE PAGE OF *COMUS* MS. 240

This is a facsimile from the original manuscript at Bridgewater House. It is a stage copy, probably in the handwriting of Henry Lawes, whose name appears at the end of the dedication of the printed edition of 1637. This first page of the manuscript reads (with modernized spelling): "A masque represented before the Right Honorable the Earl of Bridgewater

Lord President of Wales and the Right Honorable Countess of Bridgewater, at Ludlow Castle the 29th of September 1634. The chief persons in this representation were: The Lord Brackley, The Lady Alice [Egerton], Mr. Thomas Egerton. Author Jo. Milton."

Shaw celebrated his eightieth birthday on July 25, 1936, by attending a revival of *St. Joan* at the Malvern Festival. The Festival started as a tribute to the genius of Shaw and the 1936 season included two other plays of his, *On the Rocks* and *Pygmalion*.

A photograph reproduced by permission of The Macmillan Company, New York.

A drawing by William Rothenstein from *Poems 1908-1919* by John Drinkwater, by permission of Houghton Mifflin Co.

Malvern is beautifully situated among hills which have been famous from the time when William Langland slept upon them to dream his wonderful allegory of social wrongs, "Of all the wealth of the world and the woe also." It was from weariness of walking that the author of *The Vision of William concerning Piers the Plowman* fell asleep; and six centuries later the unwearied G.B.S. made the Malvern Hills once more famous by tramping over them while his plays were being acted at the Festival below. The National Trust is combining with local efforts to save Malvern Hill from the building speculator.

Drawn by Joseph Pennell for *English Cathedrals*. The Cathedral is seen from the river Severn.

The restoration took place in 1864; before that time part of the house was used as a butcher's shop; the building at the right is the old Swan and Maidenhead Inn.

Kenilworth was the seat of Robert Dudley, Earl of Leicester, the early favorite of Queen Elizabeth, who gave him the title and the estate. It was the scene of many revels on the occasion of the Queen's visit in 1575, when Leicester pressed his suit for her hand with great vehemence and with costly entertainments at which Shakespeare may have been present as a spectator in his childhood.

The register of this church contains the entries of Shakespeare's baptism and burial which give us important biographical facts. He and his wife and his children were buried either in the church or in the churchyard, and the bust on his tomb, reproduced on p. 277, is perhaps the best surviving guide to his personal appearance.

The house in Stratford, which Shakespeare bought when he had established his fame in London and in which he died, was pulled down in 1759 by an irate proprietor who was troubled by the numerous sightseers that applied for admission and had a quarrel with the assessors about its taxable value. This reproduction rests upon the authority of Wheeler's *Stratford* and the house is perhaps drawn from recollection or even from imagination. The Guild Chapel, adjoining the house, is a faithful representation, and beyond it is the Guildhall. In the upper story of the latter was the old Grammar School of which Shakespeare was probably a pupil; the school is now held in the former almshouses, extending still further to the right.

Shakespeare must often have passed over this bridge both in his carefree youth and in ripe manhood, when he had made his fortune, taken New Place, bought the Stratford tithes and, as a successful burgess, earned the right to be buried in the chancel of Trinity Church. The bridge was built by Sir Hugh Clopton, who made additions to the church and thus gave his name to one of the chapels.

Shakespeare seems to have been curiously indifferent to the perpetuation of his works in printed form except for his poems, *Venus and Adonis* and *Lucrece*. He sold his plays to the theatre company of which he was a member, and though individual plays appeared, often in stolen and surreptitious copies, the collection made by his fellow players or some enterprising bookseller did not appear until seven years after his death. The First Folio, as it is called, has perhaps caused more textual controversy than any other book in the English language. It has increased enormously in value, so much so that the Bodleian Library, which sold its copy of the First Folio when the Second Folio came out, was obliged to buy the copy back three centuries after its first publication at a cost of some thousands of pounds, raised by public subscription. The Droeshout portrait printed on the title page perhaps possesses more claims to authenticity than the bust, which may be merely a conventional figure, but it cannot be said that either gives very much clue to the appearance of the poet in the living flesh.

YORK MINSTER   280

The great glory of York Minster is its glass, which was made in the neighborhood and is among the oldest in England. As a memorial to the women who gave their lives in the War the famous Five Sisters window was restored in 1925.

WHITBY ABBEY   282

LINDISFARNE GOSPEL MS.   282

This manuscript is believed to have been written in the Lindisfarne Monastery before the end of the seventh century. It consists of the Latin (Vulgate) version of the four Gospels, and the passage here reproduced from the unique British Museum manuscript is the beginning of the Gospel of St. John.

DURHAM CATHEDRAL   284

Durham, like Lancashire and Cheshire, is a County Palatine, originally charged with the defence of the Border, and the diocese was co-terminous with the County; the Bishop's peculiar responsibilities and powers were almost as weighty as his spiritual functions and for many centuries after the foundation of the Cathedral in 995 it was "Half church of God, half castle 'gainst the Scot." Its commanding position and magnificent towers are strikingly represented in the drawing by Joseph Pennell for *English Cathedrals* which is here reproduced.

BEVERLEY ABBEY   286

Beverley Minster was founded by John of Beverley, Bishop of York, who was buried in the monastery in 721. Miracles wrought at his tomb led to his canonization and brought many pilgrims of high rank, including crowned heads, to make offerings at his shrine. Though much restored, the church still vies with the cathedrals in architectural grandeur.

BOLTON PRIORY   286

According to tradition, Bolton Priory in Wharfedale was founded in the twelfth century to commemorate the death at the Strid of the "Boy of Egremont," who was the son of Lady Alice de Romilly, the daughter of the founder. In attempting to leap the rocky channel of the Wharfe, here about two yards wide, the child missed his footing because the hound hung back on the leash in fear of the boiling waters below. This romantic story, though it has perhaps no historical foundation, has won a permanent place in literature by Wordsworth's poetic version of the legend.

LINCOLN CATHEDRAL and PETERBOROUGH CATHEDRAL   288

Drawn by Joseph Pennell for *English Cathedrals*.

SOMERSBY CHURCH and SOMERSBY RECTORY   290

TENNYSON IN OLD AGE   291

HADRIAN

This statue (two metres high) of Hadrian in Greek dress was found at Cyrene and is now in the British Museum. It is interesting to compare it with the bust of Hadrian (also in the British Museum) which was found near London Bridge and is reproduced on p. 4.

COINS OF THE ROMAN EMPERORS FOUND IN BRITAIN

If we take these coins in order from the top of the page, the first bears the head, name and titles of Vespasian (Emperor 70-79). The obverse represents the reestablishment of the Roman power in Britain under Agricola during Vespasian's reign. See p. 391.

The second coin is that of Hadrian (Emperor 117-138). At the beginning of his reign he visited Britain and carried out the elaborate works described on the previous page. The obverse of the coin commemorates his visit.

The third coin also bears the head of Hadrian and on its obverse has the figure of Britannia which adorns the copper coins of Great Britain to this day.

The fourth coin bears the portrait and name of Septimus Severus (Emperor 193-211). The obverse commemorates the Roman victories in Britain during his occupation of the throne.

The last coin bears the name and lineaments of Magnentius (Emperor 350-353) and is of interest because the obverse testifies to the fact that he was a Christian Emperor. The central monogram, formed of two Greek capital letters, stands for Christus, and the letters Alpha and Omega, the first and last in the Greek alphabet, refer to the verse in the Book of Revelation: "I am Alpha and Omega, the beginning and the ending, saith the Lord, which is, and which was, and which is to come, the Almighty." After the adoption of Christianity as the state religion under the Emperor Constantine, the monogram often formed the upper part of the standards of the Roman legions.

SECTIONS OF ROMAN WALL

The uppermost drawing shows a section of the outer ditch (on the right), the Wall, the rampart south of the Wall, the other ditch, with the small mound of earth excavated from it, and the second rampart. The drawing was done by the Reverend John Collingwood Bruce a year or two before the publication of the first edition of his great work, *The Roman Wall*. His predecessor, W. Hutton, in his *History of the Roman Wall*, gives a similar profile of the Wall and vallum as it appeared in 1722, taken from Bishop Warburton. Hutton writes, in his account of his walk along the Wall near this point in 1801: "I now travel over a large common, still upon the Wall, with its trench nearly complete. But what was my surprise when I beheld, thirty yards on my left, the united works of Agricola and Hadrian, almost perfect. I climbed over a stone wall to examine the wonder; measured the whole in every direction; surveyed them with surprise, with delight, was fascinated and unable to proceed; forgot I was upon a wild common, a stranger, and the evening approaching. I had the grandest works under my eye of the greatest men of the age in which they lived and of the most eminent nation then existing; all which had suffered but little during the long course of sixteen hundred years. Even hunger and fatigue were lost in the grandeur before me. If a man writes a book upon a turnpike road, he cannot be expected to move quick, but, lost in astonishment, I was not able to move at all." This was at Port Gate, eighteen miles from the Wall's end and fifteen and a half miles from Newcastle.

The next section is near Carrawburgh, a few miles further west. The sections are drawn on a scale of seventy-five feet to the inch; the Wall has, in these parts, disappeared, but is restored in the drawing from sketches made at other points where the Wall remains standing. The ramparts, which are composed of earth or mingled not infrequently with masses of stone, stand six or seven feet above the neighboring ground. They are about twenty-four feet away from the ditch between. The ditches vary in size; the north ditch in Hutton's time averaged about thirty-six feet wide and fifteen feet deep; the southern ditch was about thirty-four feet across the top and nine feet deep. At some points the northern ditch is still deep enough for a farmer and his plow to disappear in it from view.

The third is still further west, at Bradley, in the hill district near Borcovicus, which is thirty miles from Newcastle. The drawing, after Warburton, shows the relation between the Wall and the vallum. The Wall follows the crest of the hill and uses its precipitous slope to the north as a means of defence. The ditch and its accompanying ramparts follow the valley at a considerable distance to the south. As shown in the section, the perpendicular height of the base of the Wall is seven hundred and fifty feet from the ground level. From the top to the bottom of the hill, where the vallum is built, is about a quarter of a mile.

Still further west, between the Tipalt and the Solway, the country is characterized by small hills, which the Wall ascends on one side and descends on the other. Here, as in the fourth profile, the Wall, which for most of its length stands above the vallum, is below it and so commanded by the earthen ramparts. This gives the vallum the advantage of height in resisting a foe from the south.

These two copyright photographs of the Roman Wall were taken by Gibson and Son, Hexham, Northumberland, and are here reproduced by courtesy of the London and North Eastern Railway Co.

This plan and sketch represent the same ruins as are photographed on p. 400.

The belief that Dea Coventina was a water deity is confirmed by this representation of her attendants as Naiads or water nymphs. Each of them holds a goblet in her upraised hand and in the other a flagon from which a stream of water is flowing. This view is further confirmed by the discovery of the large cistern referred to in the lines of the text below the illustration.

The recumbent figure sculptured on this votive tablet, also found in the Carrawburgh excavations, is probably Coventina. The inscription beneath states that the tablet was dedicated to the goddess Coventina by Cosconianus, prætor of the first cohort.

LONDON STONE

CHAPTER I

LONDON

LONDON is the inevitable Mecca for the pilgrim in pursuit of commercial, literary, historic, or scenic interest. As, in the ancient world, all roads led to Rome, so in modern England, almost all main roads go to (and from) London. If you were at Berwick-on-Tweed on the Northern Border and wanted to go by rail to Penzance in the far West, your best way would be southeast through London. Even in the early centuries of the Christian era, Londinium was "the commercial centre of Roman Britain and the point from which the main roads radiated." The Roman road to the West country underlies the thoroughfare now called Holborn and Oxford Street, and where the Marble Arch now stands at the northeast corner of Hyde Park, it intersected the road to the North anciently known as Watling Street. The way by which the Roman legionaries and colonists passed from London to Westminster was the way of the modern traveler along Fleet Street and the Strand. By this way the kings of England, since the crowning of William the Conqueror and his Norman successors at Westminster, have passed to assure the citizens of London of the continuance of their ancient rights and privileges. Along the same thoroughfare I saw the American doughboys march on their way to the battlefields of France and President Wilson drive through crowds of cheering citizens "to make the world safe for democracy."

PREHISTORIC LONDON. If the imaginative reader wished to cast his thought still deeper "in the dark backward and abysm of time," he might conjure up a phantasmagoria of the Old Stone Age, when the hippopotamus, the rhinoceros, and the

ROMAN LONDON

mammoth roamed the valley of the Thames, for their teeth and bones have been dug up from the sites of the Old Bailey, Waterloo Place, and Pall Mall, and the flint implements of palæolithic man have been found underneath Piccadilly Circus. In the Neolithic Age (about 3000-2000 B.C.) there was a village or string of villages higher up the river, in the neighborhood of Hammersmith, but there is no evidence of any settlement on the actual site of the City of London.

About where Westminster Bridge crosses the Thames, there was probably in those far back days a ford, neighboring an island in the river marshes later known as Thorney, the Isle of Thorns, which became the site of Westminster Abbey, consecrated, according to tradition, by the first Bishop of London in 616. At this ford, as is commonly supposed, Julius Cæsar was opposed by the British leader Cassivellaunus at the second Roman invasion of Britain in B.C. 54. Cassivellaunus set sharpened stakes in the river bed and on the northwestern bank to impede the progress of the Roman legionaries. But C. E. Montague puts this encounter at the scene of his novel *Rough Justice,* higher up the river, and gives us a lively picture of the Roman cavalry "splashing and stumbling across, the men on foot panting up the steep bank, dripping wet; and then the Britons above, turning tail of a sudden—changed from a defiant, yelling front into scampering figures huge and clear on the sky-line."

When the Romans seriously undertook the conquest of Britain in B.C. 43, their armies crossed the Thames somewhere below the site of London, which they probably made their temporary headquarters. It was obvious that the site was admirably suited for a bridge and a trading centre. It was at that period about the head of tide-water, and it was the lowest point at which both banks of the Thames afforded a firm landing. Instead of the soft alluvial soil below that point, there was at Southwark a gravel ledge, faced on the northern side of the river by two gravel-capped hills. These were separated at that time by a stream later called the Walbrook, the brook by the

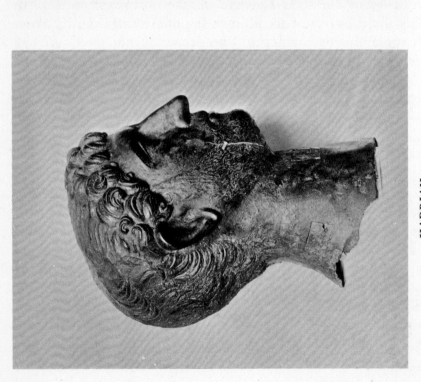

ROMAN JUG

HADRIAN

wall, which at the time of the foundation of the Roman city marked its western limit. Walbrook is still the name of the street leading from the Mansion House, the official residence of the Lord Mayor of London, southwards towards the Thames. A little further west the Fleet Brook ran where a great sewer now flows under Farringdon Street and New Bridge Street to empty itself into the Thames under Blackfriars Bridge; boats could pass upon the Fleet as far as where the Holborn Viaduct now crosses it. There was another small tributary to the Thames which the old Roman road crossed further west; it was later called Tye Bourne and gave its name to a famous place of execution for London criminals. Still later, Tyburn Lane changed its name to Park Lane, running along the east end of Hyde Park and still one of the most fashionable of London streets.

LONDINIUM finds its first historical record in the *Annals* of Tacitus, A.D. 61. At that time it had not yet reached the dignity of a colony, but it was already the principal mercantile centre, and a "great mart of trade and commerce." In the revolt against the Roman power led by the British queen Boadicea, London (not yet fortified) was abandoned by the Roman general and laid desolate by the rebels. But the reëstablishment of Roman authority restored the city's commercial supremacy and for three centuries or more it was a centre of Roman power and influence. The city was enclosed by walls, one running parallel with the Thames close to the shore. This has disappeared in the course of centuries, but part of the northern wall may still be seen in the street called London Wall, and there is another fragment preserved in the yard of the General Post Office. Tacitus says that the Britons were quick to acquire the Roman language, dress, culture, luxuries, and vices, and evidence in support of this statement may be found in the Guildhall, the London, and the British Museums. There is a Roman bath still on view in Strand Lane, but more considerable signs of the Roman occupation may be found at St. Albans, Silchester (near Reading) and Bath, where there was less disturbance by subsequent building.

ANGLO-SAXON LONDON. After the Roman withdrawal owing
to the break up of the empire in the beginning of the fifth century, London sank into decay. The Roman province of Britain
fell back into the tribal conflicts which had preceded the coming of Cæsar, complicated after a while by the arrival of a
new set of adventurers. One group, the Angles, was to change
the name of Southern Britain to England; another group, the
Saxons, took possession of London, and gave names to the neighboring counties of Essex, Middlesex, and Sussex. A third group,
the Jutes, founded the kingdom of Kent, whose overlord Ethelbert, marrying a Frankish princess, restored communication
with the Continent through Christian missionaries, and made
Canterbury—the city of the men of Kent—the ecclesiastical
capital of England, though in later years the Archbishop, as

FRANKS CASKET — LEFT HALF

ANGLO-SAXON RINGS   ALFRED JEWEL

FRANKS CASKET — RIGHT HALF

Primate of the English Church, had his official residence in London at Lambeth Palace. The Venerable Bede, who died in 735, records in his History of the English Church that at the beginning of the seventh century London was still an emporium of many people coming by land and sea, and to this date he ascribes the establishment of the bishopric of London, at St. Paul's Cathedral Church. But when the first Bishop of London was promoted to the see of Canterbury, his East Saxon flock relapsed into heathenism. After weary years and even centuries of inter-tribal strife, London fell into the hands of the Scandinavian marauders known to the English as the Danes. The heroic determination of Alfred, King of Wessex, for a time stemmed the tide, and even recovered London; but it is noteworthy that the most precious relic of the great king was found in the marshes of Athelney more than a hundred miles away. In the century after his death, the Danes not only retook London, but put their own king on the throne. It was on the tidal reach of Westminster that King Canute (according to an old story) had his throne placed and bade the waves not wet his feet, in order to reprove the flattery of his courtiers. The last of the Anglo-Saxon kings, Edward the Confessor, built a great palace at Westminster and made the Abbey into a royal chapel.

Castrum Royale Londinense.   vulgo   the TOWER.

NORMAN LONDON. William the Conqueror realized the importance of London, and after his first success at the coast, made haste to assure the citizens of his goodwill, granting them a charter in which he confirmed the Bishop and the portreeve (or Mayor) in their offices, along with their subordinates. "And I will that every man be his father's heir, after his father's day; and I will not endure that any man offer any wrong to you." But at the southeast corner of the city wall, where may have stood even from British times a fort, perhaps restored by King Alfred, William built a Norman keep or castle, which is still one of the most impressive parts of the Tower of London. The Conqueror doubtless intended it to keep the citizens of London in subjection, but in the course of centuries the fortress became a prison in which some of the most romantic victims of English history were confined—Wallace, the Scottish patriot in the fourteenth century; the Duke of Clarence and the "little princes" of the House of York in the fifteenth; the two of Henry VIII's Queens who were beheaded, Anne Boleyn and Catherine Howard; the Protestant martyrs, Cranmer, Ridley, and Latimer; Lady Jane Grey, Elizabeth before she was Queen, her favorites, Essex and Sir Walter Raleigh; the Royalist leaders, Strafford and Laud. In more recent years the Tower housed Jacobite prisoners and the spies of the Great War; lighter sides of Tower life are its housing of the Crown jewels and the quaint name and picturesque costume of its warders, the Beefeaters, who gave title and color to Gilbert and Sullivan's opera, *The Yeomen of the Guard.*

CHAUCER was born in Thames Street and lived most of his life in or about London, near the Tower or London Bridge, at Westminster or Windsor, in the performance of various duties as collector of Customs, member of Parliament, and an officer of what we should now call the Board of Works. The most remarkable architectural achievement of his time was Westminster Hall, begun three centuries before and finished in 1399, the year before Chaucer's death. Immediately after its completion, it served as the scene of the deposition of the reigning monarch, Richard II, and subsequently as the scene of some of the most famous trials of English history. William Wallace, Sir Thomas More, the Earl of Essex, Strafford and his master Charles I were condemned to death here; the Seven Bishops in the seventeenth century and Warren Hastings in the eighteenth were here acquitted. At George V's Silver Jubilee in May, 1935, the King and Queen drove in state to Westminster Hall to receive congratulatory addresses there from both Houses of Parliament. (See Frontispiece.)

Chaucer gives us a lively and amusing picture of the life of the fourteenth century, not only in London, but at home and abroad in the Europe of his day. No other poem in the wide range of English literature affords such a complete insight into contemporary life as the Prologue to the *Canterbury Tales.* The Tabard Inn, at Southwark, where the characters gathered for their pilgrimage to Canterbury, has disappeared, but Chaucer's pilgrims still live in their quaint costumes, their no less quaint manners, their piquant sayings, and fresh and natural views of life. Then arose the phrase "Merry England," which the Elizabethan poets recalled with longing. Chaucer's London apprentice was a gay bird:

> At every bride-ale would he sing and hop;
> He loved the tavern better than the shop,
> For when there any riding was in Cheap
> Out of the shop thither would he leap;
> And till that he had all the sight y-seen
> And dancèd well, he would not come again.

Belonging to the same period was the perhaps equally fictitious figure of Sir Richard (popularly called Dick) Whittington, thrice Lord Mayor of London and one of the richest merchants of his day, though he had begun as a poor apprentice, his only capital a pet cat, which he sold for a large sum where cats were needed owing to a plague of rats and mice.

CHAUCER

AN EARLY CAXTON

FIRST PRINTED ENGLISH BIBLE

FIRST "GREAT BIBLE"

THE INTRODUCTION OF PRINTING was the principal event of London life in the fifteenth century. William Caxton was born in Kent, but spent many years as Governor of the English Guild of Merchant Adventurers in Flanders, where he acted as scrivener, or copyist, to the sister of Edward IV, Margaret Duchess of Burgundy. So it came about that the first book printed in English was done at Bruges. In his preface to this book,—a translated compilation of French romances, called the *Recuyell of the Histories of Troy*—Caxton tells us that in his work as a copyist his pen was worn, "my hand weary and not steadfast, mine eyes dimmed with over much looking on the white paper, and my courage not so prone and ready to labor as it hath been." He felt old age coming upon him and therefore learned "at my great charge and dispense to ordain this said book in print." A year later he brought the first press over to London and set up his sign of the "Red Pale"—a heraldic shield with a red bar down the middle—on a house in the Almonry at Westminster. He was a practical business man and quite conscious of the importance of the fact that "all the books of this story here imprinted as you may see were begun in one day and also finished in one day." If it pleased any man to buy copies, he said, "all imprinted after the form of the present letter, which be well and truly correct, let him come to Westminster in the Almonry at the Red Pale, and he shall have them good cheap." But he was also anxious to give the people useful and beneficial books. He printed two editions of Chaucer —the second because he had found a better text,—other books of poetry and history, and many translations from the classics.

WESTMINSTER ABBEY retains nothing of the Saxon churches built on its original site and only the foundations of the Norman church begun by Edward the Confessor. Henry III in the thirteenth century undertook an entire reconstruction, which was continued during the two following centuries. To the thirteenth century belongs in the main the Chapter House, in which the House of Commons met from the time of Edward III until

CAXTON'S HOUSE AT WESTMINSTER

WESTMINSTER ABBEY, WEST FRONT

WESTMINSTER ABBEY, NAVE

1547. The great nave, begun in the thirteenth century, was completed in the fifteenth. The fourteenth century Jerusalem Chamber, adjoining the west entrance to the nave, was the scene of the death of Henry IV as recounted by Shakespeare in *2 Henry IV,* Act IV. The Assembly of Divines who drew up the Presbyterian Westminster Confession met here in 1643-8, and when the Revised Version of the Bible was prepared in the nineteenth century, the committee of scholars in charge of the Old Testament sat in this Chamber.

The body of Edward the Confessor, on his canonization in the twelfth century, was placed in a shrine before the high altar, and removed in the thirteenth century to a special chapel, behind the altar. East of this again was built, early in the sixteenth century, the Henry VII Chapel, which is the most magnificent example of the English Perpendicular style. Washington Irving wrote of it: "On entering, the eye is astonished by the pomp of architecture and the elaborate beauty of sculptured detail. The very walls are wrought into universal ornament, incrusted with tracery, and scooped into niches crowded with the statues of saints and martyrs. Stone seems, by the cunning labor of the chisel, to have been robbed of its weight and density, suspended aloft as if by magic, and the fretted roof achieved with the wonderful minuteness and airy security of a cobweb."

The Poet's Corner, which is sought by every visitor to the Abbey who is interested in English literature, is to be found at the southeast corner of the south transept. The tomb of Chaucer, which first attracts attention, was placed there about a century and a half after the poet's death; in front of it are the graves of Tennyson, Browning, and Denham, and adjoining it that of Drayton. Nearby is Spenser's monument, surrounded by memorials to Milton, Gray, Coleridge, Shakespeare, Burns, Gay, and Goldsmith. Not far away are inscriptions or busts to Addison, Sir Walter Scott, Thackeray, and Ruskin. Macaulay and Dickens lie in graves beneath our feet. That of Dickens still bears fresh flowers of remembrance, and many linger by the place where rest the ashes of Thomas Hardy.

WESTMINSTER ABBEY, HENRY VII CHAPEL

CHAUCER'S TOMB

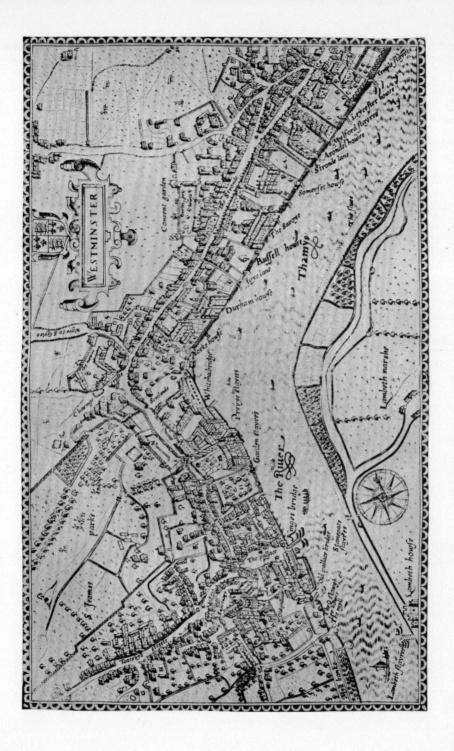

THE LONDON OF ELIZABETH was more seriously minded than Chaucer's London, having passed through the struggles of the Protestant Reformation with the Puritan Revolution impending. The Elizabethan apprentice was not so frivolously minded as his medieval predecessor—less given to singing and dancing, and more inclined to celebrate a holiday by raiding the London houses of ill-fame and sacking a theatre or two. The merchant adventurers did not go forth with any such paltry cargo as Whittington's pet cat, but with ships well provided with manufactured goods. The Italian financiers who had given Lombard Street its name, and the German merchants known as the Hanseatic League, who had had a wharf of their own on the Thames, came no more to conduct London's commerce. The London bankers and traders did their own business in the Royal Exchange erected for them by Sir Thomas Gresham, whose statue survived two fires to figure still in front of the bell tower with his crest, a gilded grasshopper, above it. Queen Elizabeth opened the original Exchange in 1570 and encouraged the East India and other trading companies, which carried English goods to all the known markets of the world and introduced English commerce into countries hitherto almost unknown.

The Queen interested herself also in education and was responsible for the re-organization, on an old monastic foundation, of the famous Westminster School, whose pupils have a daily service in the Abbey all to themselves, and enjoy the privilege of attending the Coronation ceremony there. They still keep up the performance of an annual Latin play, and one of the first headmasters, Nicholas Udall, wrote for them the first English regular comedy, *Ralph Roister Doister*. The school has a long list of distinguished alumni, including the poets Ben Jonson, Cowley, Dryden, Cowper and Southey; the philosopher Locke; Sir Christopher Wren, greatest of English architects; and Gibbon the historian. Another famous Elizabethan foundation was the Merchant Tailors' School, which nourished the greatest of English epic poets, Edmund Spenser, and Samuel Richardson, the first English novelist. It now stands on the site

QUEEN ELIZABETH

of the Charterhouse School, celebrated by Thackeray in *The Newcomes,* whose hero is a pupil in his childhood, and in his old age becomes a pensioner on the ancient monastic foundation. Beside Thackeray, its alumni list includes the cavalier poets, Lovelace and Crashaw, Roger Williams of Rhode Island, Steele and Addison, and John Wesley. Older than any of these as an educational foundation is the Blue Coat School of Christ's Hospital, with Lamb, Coleridge and Leigh Hunt as its most famous pupils. It formerly occupied the present site of the General Post Office, but has now been removed to Sussex, as the Charterhouse School has to Surrey.

No English educational institutions, not even the colleges of Oxford and Cambridge, have had on their rolls more distinguished names than the London Inns of Court, the legal foundations at which English advocates are "admitted to the Bar" after "eating their dinners" and passing the necessary examinations. In the reign of Elizabeth these halls of learning played an important part in the development of the English

MIDDLE TEMPLE HALL

PENSIONERS' HALL, CHARTERHOUSE

OLD PORCH, CHARTERHOUSE

drama. It was in their own Great Hall that the Gentlemen of
the Inner Temple acted the first English tragedy, *Gorboduc,*
written by two of their number; the Queen was present and at
her request the performance was repeated in her palace at
Whitehall. Other early tragedies were acted at Gray's Inn and
enlisted the services of one of its most renowned members,
Francis Bacon. In its hall Shakespeare's *Comedy of Errors* was
acted as part of the Christmas festivities of 1594, and on Feb-
ruary 2, 1602, *Twelfth Night* was acted in the hall of the
Middle Temple. Both these halls were built in the early years
of Elizabeth's reign and are admirable examples of Elizabethan
construction and decoration.

In 1593-4 Shakespeare was living in the parish of St.
Helen's, Bishopgate, conveniently near to the earliest London
theatres, The Theatre and the Curtain, which had been built
outside the city walls, at Shoreditch, in order to escape the
interference of the civic authorities; afterwards he lodged a
little further West, at the corner of Monkwell and Silver
Streets. When the lease of The Theatre ran out, it was moved
across the river to the Bankside and rebuilt under the new name
of the Globe; many of Shakespeare's plays had their first production here, or at the covered or "private" theatre at Blackfriars, near which Shakespeare, in his later years, owned a
house. All these have now given place to modern buildings.
The probable site of the Globe Theatre is now occupied by a
large brewery.

Shakespeare was a country boy who sought fortune in London in his early manhood, and went back to his home town
for his last years; he gives us in the two parts of *Henry IV* the
liveliest pictures of London tavern life and of the country
life he loved. The other great poet of the time, Edmund Spenser, was a Londoner who was driven to seek fortune in Ireland
and looked back to London from what he regarded as exile in
a savage wilderness. In a marriage song he wrote for the two
daughters of the Earl of Worcester, he says:

THE GLOBE THEATRE

At length they all to merry London came,
To merry London, my most kindly nurse
That to me gave this life's first native source,
Though from another place I take my name,
A house of ancient fame.
There when they came, whereas those bricky towers,
The which on Thames broad agèd back do ride,
Where now the studious lawyers have their bowers,
There whilom wont the Templar Knights to bide,
Till they decayed through pride.
Next whereunto there stands a stately place
Where oft I gainèd gifts and goodly grace
Of that great lord which therein wont to dwell,
Whose want too well now feels my friendless case.

The "stately place" on the riverside was Leicester House, which afterwards passed into the hands of Elizabeth's other ill-fated favorite, Essex. In Elizabeth's London, with its narrow and dirty streets, as unsafe as they were insanitary, the Thames was the main thoroughfare, both from bank to bank and up and down the river. A row of noblemen's palaces on the northern shore found ready access by water to the row of theatres, bear gardens and other houses of entertainment across the river, lower down, on the Bankside.

STUART LONDON. The theatres have disappeared so completely that it is hard to fix their sites, and few traces of the palaces remain. The noblest of them was Whitehall which as York House had been the London seat of the Archbishop of York until, on the death of Cardinal Wolsey, it was seized by Henry VIII, who married Anne Boleyn in Whitehall, and died there. The Elizabethan Banqueting House was burnt down in the reign of her successor, James I, who erected a more magnificent hall on plans drawn by Inigo Jones. From the beginning of Charles I's reign the new Banqueting House was used for the performance of the masques which were the favorite court amusement of the time. In it was acted the most magnificent example of this form of dramatic entertainment, *The Triumph of Peace,* which was offered to the King and Queen

WHITEHALL

ST. JAMES'S PALACE

by the combined efforts of the Inns of Court in 1634 at a cost
of £21,000—equal to over a million dollars in modern value.
The smoke of the torches used at this and other masques threatened serious damage to the paintings by Rubens and other great
artists hung in the Banqueting House and a new and larger hall
was built for the purpose. The Banqueting House is the only
part of the vast palace which has survived, and is known prin-
cipally by the modern passerby along Whitehall as the building from which Charles I stepped through a window to the
scaffold on which he was beheaded. He had walked that morning through the Park from the neighboring palace of St. James,
which has given to the English Court the name it still bears.
"Nothing in his life Became him like the leaving it." A Puritan
poet, Andrew Marvell, wrote of his behavior on the scaffold:

> He nothing common did or mean
> Upon that memorable scene,
>   But with his keener eye
>   The axe's edge did try;
> Nor called the gods, with vulgar spite
> To vindicate his helpless right,
>   But bowed his comely head
>   Down as upon a bed.

A curious memorial of the bitterness of faction in those times
is the bronze equestrian statue of Charles I, which now occupies
one of the noblest sites in London, at Charing Cross, where
the traffic of the Strand flows by Trafalgar Square. It was originally cast for a Royalist nobleman to adorn his own grounds,
but owing to the troubles of the time was never put up. When
the Parliamentary party gained control, it was sold to a brazier
to be melted down. He did a lively trade in mementoes of the
royal martyr, supposed to be manufactured out of the metal,
but after the Restoration revealed the fact that he had buried
the statue and kept it intact. He gave it to Charles II, who set
it up where it has stood for nearly three centuries, looking down
Whitehall toward the scene of his father's execution.

The Statue of K. CHARLES I.
at Charingcross in Brasse

PURITAN LONDON. Except in literature, the Puritans perhaps destroyed more works of art than they created. Macaulay, himself something of a Puritan, says they put down bear-baiting, not because of the pain it gave to the bear, but because of the pleasure it gave to the spectators; and the giving and receiving of pleasure seems an essential part of art. But it must not be supposed that an objection to legitimate pleasures was characteristic of the Puritan temper. The Regicide Colonel Hutchinson is an instance to the contrary, for he took pleasure, not only in his garden but in "paintings, sculpture, and all liberal arts"; he was also a lover of music. The last-named delight was shared by Oliver Cromwell and by John Milton, though both had perhaps more of the stern than of the gentle in their disposition. The English metropolis has never been without admirers of royalty, but in the troublous times before the Commonwealth, the sympathies of the citizens and its officers were mainly with the Parliamentarians, and the London trainbands did much—and the resources of the London merchants and bankers perhaps did more—to enable the Roundheads to win the Civil War. Cromwell was a Huntingdon squire, who became a country member of the House of Commons, but he was married at St. Giles, Cripplegate, lived and died in the Palace of Whitehall, and was buried in Westminster Abbey. At the Restoration his body was dug up, and the head cut off at Tyburn, and exposed at Westminster Hall. His statue now turns its back on the House of Commons, which he sent about its business no less summarily than any modern dictator.

MILTON was a Londoner, born in Bread Street, Cheapside, about midway between St. Paul's Cathedral and St. Mary-le-Bow, where there is a memorial to him, placed originally in the neighboring church of All Hallows, in which Milton was baptized. He went to St. Paul's School, founded by Dean Colet a century earlier, and a contemporary portrait gives us a good idea of the kind of boy he was—something like the young John the Baptist he described in *Paradise Lost:*

MILTON, AGED 10

When I was yet a child, no childish play
To me was pleasing; all my mind was set
Serious to learn and know, and thence to do
What might be public good; myself I thought
Born to that end, born to promote all truth,
All righteous things.

After seven years' education at Christ's College, Cambridge, Milton retired to his father's house in the country at Horton, some twenty miles out of London, where he wrote *L'Allegro* and *Il Penseroso, Arcades, Comus,* and *Lycidas.* He was recalled from travels on the Continent by the outbreak of the Civil War, thinking it base "to be traveling for amusement abroad while my fellow citizens were fighting for liberty at home." He joined the Honorable Artillery Company, the oldest of English military organizations, but soon found that he could serve the Puritan cause better with the pen than with the sword. He took a "pretty garden-house" in Aldersgate Street and from 1643 to 1647 he was living in various houses in the City. As Latin Secretary to the Commonwealth (1649-52) he had an official residence in Scotland Yard, Whitehall. After the fall of the Puritan administration he came back to the City and retiring into obscurity (for some time he was in fear of his life), he was able to complete *Paradise Lost.* During the plague years of 1665-6 he took refuge a few miles away at the village of Chalfont St. Giles, where the cottage in which he began *Paradise Regained* is preserved as a Milton Museum. He returned to the City to finish *Paradise Regained* and was buried at St. Giles, Cripplegate. The house in which Milton died was near the last resting places of three other stalwart Nonconformists—John Bunyan, George Fox, and Daniel Defoe. The first and last mentioned lie in the old Nonconformist Burial Ground called Bunhill Fields, and George Fox in the Friends' Burial Ground near by. Across the road is John Wesley's Chapel, with his statue in front of it and his grave at the back. Next to the chapel is the house in which he died.

MILTON'S COTTAGE

CHALFONT ST. GILES

CHARLES II AND SAMUEL PEPYS. After the Restoration the Banqueting House was the setting of those scenes of royal debauch which Pepys has described in his Diary. But beside addiction to sensual pleasure, Pepys and his master had serious interests which should not be forgotten. Pepys in his soberer hours was a diligent Secretary of the Admiralty, as the latest instalment of his diary, unknown till 1935, makes abundantly clear; and he was also a member of the Royal Society for the Advancement of Science, which Charles founded and encouraged by attendance at its meetings. Both were interested in parks and pleasure grounds, Pepys more particularly in the cherry gardens three miles down the river. Charles combined his interest in science and in landscape gardening at Greenwich Park and Greenwich Observatory, which fixes for all nations the zero meridian of longitude and the official mean time of Great Britain. But the main interest of Charles was in laying out St. James's Park, feeding the birds in the pond he had made for them, and flirting with Nell Gwynn, who lived just over the wall of the avenue which skirts the Park and is still called the Mall. This Charles had constructed for the then fashionable game of "pall-mall," which seems to have required almost as much space for its exercise as the modern games of cricket and golf which, it is said, it resembled. At the foot of the Mall there were the popular "Spring Gardens"— there is still a street there of that name, just by the Admiralty Arch. In Charles II's time the "New Spring Gardens" were laid out on the Surrey side higher up the river and immediately became a fashionable resort. They are frequently mentioned by the diarists and dramatists of the time, but are better known to the modern reader under the name of Vauxhall Gardens, which they bore from 1785 until their abolition in 1859. Boswell describes them as "peculiarly adapted to the taste of the English nation; there being a mixture of curious show, gay exhibition, music vocal and instrumental, not too refined for the general ear—for all which only a shilling is paid—and though last, not least, good eating and drinking for those who

CHARLES II PEPYS

GREENWICH PARK

choose to purchase that regale." As many as 16,000 persons at
once were entertained there, and 15,000 lamps were used to
illuminate the grounds. There were numerous small pavilions
and recesses where refreshments (including champagne and
ice!) were served.

Over the two main events of his reign—the GREAT PLAGUE
and the GREAT FIRE—Charles II had no possible control. The
Plague in six months swept off a hundred thousand Londoners
—one-third of the total population. The fire laid every building
low between the Tower and the Temple—from Pudding Lane
to Pie Corner, as the chronicler of the time phrased it. It destroyed 13,200 houses and 87 churches, but it was a blessing
in disguise. The old streets were narrow and dirty, nests of
infection; the old houses were of wood and a constant fire-
menace. Driven out to live in tents and shacks on the Fen north
of London Wall—known as Moorfields and Finsbury Fields—
the citizens began to extend their homes in that direction instead of spreading out east and west, as had been the custom
up to that time. Sir Christopher Wren, the great architect of
the period, wished to rebuild the city on a new and more scientific plan; he was not allowed to have his way in this, and
had to devote his energies to the building of St. Paul's. His
first difficulty was to get the ruins of the old structure out of
the way—they were still in some places 200 feet high—without
loss of life. Pepys thought it "strange how the sight of stones
falling from the top of the steeple do make me sea-sick, but
no hurt, I hear, hath yet happened." Wren's next difficulty was
to get the royal approval of his plans without offending the
King's brother James, who wished to have the new cathedral
constructed in such a fashion as to fit it for the Roman rite, in
case the nation reverted to Catholicism; the discussion about
the addition of side-chapels to his plan is said to have driven
Wren to tears. After much struggle and heartburning, some
ten years after the Fire, the new structure was begun, and
twenty-two years later was so far advanced that service could be

OLD ST. PAUL'S (1620)

ST. PAUL'S FIFTY YEARS AGO

held in the choir. Nearly twenty years passed before the Cathedral could be reported as finished, and even then much was
left to be done for the carrying out of his original plans, some
of which still remain unexecuted. Wren lived to be over ninety
years of age and was buried in the cathedral he had created;
at the north transept portico, there is an inscription to his memory, ending with the words, "Si monumentum requiris, circum-
spice." (If you seek his monument, look around you.) In a
long life of extraordinary energy Wren accomplished many
other important architectural works. In London alone, he built
fifty-two churches, restored the Temple, built the central tower
of Westminster Abbey, and planned the two western towers,
which were completed after his death. Wren also rebuilt Temple Bar, until 1878 one of the most familiar objects of the
City, whose western boundary it marked at the point in the
Strand where the Lord Mayor still meets the newly crowned
sovereign. As a memorial to the Fire he built at the point
where it began a Doric column 202 feet high called the Monument, of which Pope wrote (in allusion to an inscription ascrib-
ing the origin of the fire to Catholic incendiaries) :

> Where London's column, pointing at the skies,
> Like a tall bully, lifts the head and lies.

CLUBS AND COFFEE HOUSES. Coffee was introduced into
England under the Commonwealth, and during the eighteenth
century gradually displaced to some extent the use of beer by
all classes, wine by the gentry, and gin (recently brought in
from Holland) by the London slum-dwellers, whom it de-
bauched by its cheapness, offering the opportunity of being
"drunk for a penny, dead drunk for twopence." There were
soon five hundred coffee houses in London, affording for a
few pence the social opportunities of a modest club. Newsletters
and the newspapers and periodicals then coming into vogue
were lent to all customers without charge or read aloud for
the common advantage; there was political discussion, a great
deal of gossip and considerable literary activity. Sir Richard

DEFOE PILLORIED AT TEMPLE BAR

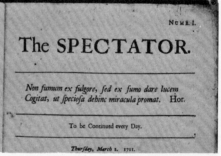

A LONDON COFFEE-HOUSE

STEELE

ADDISON

Steele, opening a new chapter in literary history with the first number of *The Tatler,* promised that "all accounts of gallantry, pleasure, and entertainment shall be under the article of White's chocolate house; poetry under that of Will's Coffee house; learning, under the title of Grecian; foreign and domestic news, you will have from Saint James's coffee house; and what else I have to offer on any other subject shall be dated from my own apartment." Washington Irving suggests that at his white cottage at Hampstead Steele wrote "many numbers of *The Spectator,*" but he seems to have done much more work at the coffee houses mentioned; and when Addison joined forces with Steele in editing *The Tatler,* a letter box in the shape of a carved lion's head was set up at Button's Coffee House for the receipt of contributions. In a short street running from Covent Garden to Drury Lane (still known as Russell Street) there were three or four coffee houses which were the meeting place of literary coteries, like the Mermaid Tavern of Elizabethan times, where Shakespeare and Jonson matched their wits against each other.

From the coffee houses sprang the clubs, the connection being so close that it is sometimes difficult to mark the transition. The Cocoa Tree Club which at the time of the Rebellion of 1745 was a center for Jacobite partizans took its name from a chocolate house of Queen Anne's reign. It was on St. James's Street, off Piccadilly, and on the same street were also to be found Brooks's, the leading Whig Club, and White's, the leading Tory Club. These differed little from their modern London representatives—the Carlton, the National Liberal, and the Reform Clubs—except that in the eighteenth century they were less given to politics and more given to gambling, often for high stakes. The political organizations are less interesting than the literary clubs whose modern representative is the Athenæum on Pall Mall, now the principal club thoroughfare. An early progenitor of this type of organization was the Kit Cat Club, to which belonged Addison, Steele, and the celebrated artist of the time Sir Godfrey Kneller, who painted the portraits of

POPE

SWIFT

CONGREVE

GAY

the other members; the room in which they met was provided by the publisher, Jacob Tonson, and Christopher (Kit) Cat supplied the mutton pies—and the name of the Club. No less famous was the Scriblerus Club, founded by Dr. Arbuthnot in 1713, and including also Pope, Swift, Congreve, and Gay. The Literary Club, founded in 1764 by Dr. Johnson and Sir Joshua Reynolds, had an equally distinguished membership—Boswell, Goldsmith, Burke, Garrick, Gibbon, and Adam Smith, the first English political economist. The notable point about these clubs was the personality of their members, not the magnificence of their place of meeting. Dr. Johnson said of Burke that no one could take shelter with him from a sudden shower without recognizing that he was in the presence of an extraordinary man. This was true of the other members whose portraits are reproduced on the following pages. There is a successor of the Literary Club existing in London today, no doubt with very comfortable quarters, but who knows who are its members?

DR. JOHNSON was born at Lichfield and came first to London in his infancy, being brought by his mother to be "touched" by Queen Anne for the scrofula or "king's evil," for which the royal touch was supposed to effect a miraculous cure. In Johnson's case it was unsuccessful, for he suffered all his life from defective eyesight and a nervous twitching of the limbs. When he came again to town as a young man in search of fortune, it was on the assurance of a friend that "by spending threepence in a coffee house, he might be for some hours every day in very good company; he might dine for sixpence, breakfast on bread and milk for a penny, and do without supper." As to the last item of the program he was not disappointed, but for the rest he was often in extreme poverty. He tells us that one night he and Richard Savage, another literary adventurer who was as impecunious as himself, walked round St. James's Square for several hours in want of a lodging; but they kept up their spirits and "resolved they would stand by their country." He was a fervent admirer of London and expressed his devotion in

JOHNSON

BOSWELL

GOLDSMITH

BURKE

REYNOLDS

GARRICK

GIBBON

ADAM SMITH

verse, prose, and conversation. He said to Boswell: "The happiness of London is not to be conceived but by those who have been in it. I will venture to say, there is more learning and science within the circumference of ten miles from where we now sit, than in all the rest of the kingdom." When Boswell interposed with the remark, "The only disadvantage is the great distance at which people live from one another," Johnson crushed him with the rejoinder, "Yes, Sir; but that is occasioned by the largeness of it, which is the cause of all the other advantages."

Johnson was frequently offered country preferment, but he would not "leave the improved society of the capital, or consent to exchange the exhilarating joys and splendid decorations of public life, for the obscurity, insipidity, and uniformity of remote situations." He found "the full tide of human existence" at Charing Cross and did not like to get far away from it. The faithful Boswell has preserved for us an exact list of his London lodgings and houses in order of time, and we know where each of his great works was written. Of all these only the house in Gough Square has been kept as it was, and the attic may still be seen where he worked at the Dictionary with half a dozen amanuenses. According to tradition, one of his favorite resorts was the neighboring Cheshire Cheese in Fleet Street, which still keeps the atmosphere of an eighteenth century coffee-house.

CHARLES LAMB was a more complete Londoner than Dr. Johnson and the memory of both is closely associated with the Temple. Johnson lived at No. 1 Inner Temple Lane, and Lamb at No. 2 and No. 4, but the site is now covered by the modern pile called Dr. Johnson's buildings. Lamb was born at No. 2 Crown Office Row, which is still standing, and lived there until he went to Christ's Hospital School; the building has gone, but the old-world charm of the school and its scholars, with their quaint costume, a long blue coat, knee-breeches, and yellow stockings, is preserved in two of Lamb's best essays. From

The Stair Way.

Dr Johnsons House in Gough Square.

Herbert Railton.

school he entered the service of the South Sea Company (of unhappy memory) and then of the East India Company, but the old South Sea House, and the old India House (where Lamb was a clerk up to the age of fifty) have both disappeared. So has the house near High Holborn, where the tragedy happened which changed the whole course of Charles Lamb's life; his sister, Mary, in a sudden fit of insanity, killed her mother, and her care was henceforth her brother's first thought. They went back to the Temple, where they had grown up together, and Lamb wrote cheerfully to his friend Manning: "I am going to change my lodgings, having received a hint that it would be agreeable, at our Lady's next feast. I have partly fixed upon most delectable rooms, which look out (when you stand a-tip-toe) over the Thames and Surrey Hills, at the upper end of King's Bench Walks in the Temple. There I shall have all the privacy of a house without the encumbrance, and shall be able to lock my friends out as often as I desire to hold free converse with my immortal mind; for my present lodgings resemble a minister's levee . . . I shall be as airy, up four pair of stairs, as in the country; and in a garden, in the midst of that enchanting, more than Mahometan paradise, London, whose dirtiest drab-frequented alley, and her lowest-bowing trades-man, I would not exchange for Skiddaw, Helvellyn, James, Walter, and the parson into the bargain."

Lamb used to meet Coleridge and Southey at the Salutation and Cat Tavern in Newgate Street. At St. Andrew's Church (said to be the largest of Wren's parish churches) between Holborn Viaduct and Holborn Circus, Mary Lamb was brides-maid and Charles best man at Hazlitt's first marriage, and Lamb was present at Hazlitt's death at 6 Frith Street, Soho. When the days of his clerkship were coming to a close, Lamb took Colebrook Cottage at Islington, and was very proud of it, "never having had a house before." It faced the New River, into which Lamb's friend George Dyer walked after paying his first call; the stream has now been covered over, and a pleasant avenue of trees has been interposed between Lamb's old home

Yours ratherish unwell

Chs Lamb.

(64 Duncan Terrace) and Colebrook Row. Lamb's last years were spent in the London suburbs of Enfield and Edmonton, and he and Mary lie buried in the same grave in Edmonton Churchyard.

KEATS went to school at Enfield and served his medical apprenticeship at a surgeon's house at 6 Church Street, Edmonton. It was presumably to the latter address that the reviewer of *Endymion* in *Blackwood's Edinburgh Magazine* (probably John Lockhart) wished the poet to return when he gave Keats the famous "back to your gallipots" advice: "It is a better and a wiser thing to be a starved apothecary than a starved poet: so back to the shop, Mr. John, back to 'plasters, pills, and ointment boxes.' " Keats was born in Finsbury, lived in Cheapside, and studied at Guy's Hospital on the other side of London Bridge, but the part of London that we naturally associate with him is Hampstead, where he lived in Wentworth Place and fell in love with Fanny Brawne, who lived next door. The two houses are now thrown together and form the Keats Memorial, in which a remarkable collection of relics of the poet is preserved. It was at the Vale of Health in Hampstead Heath that Keats used to visit his friend Leigh Hunt, where he met Shelley; and it was on a walk in this direction that he met Coleridge, who was living with his friends, Mr. and Mrs. Gilman, at Highgate. The two poets shook hands as they parted, and as Coleridge and his companion resumed their walk, Coleridge said "There is death in that hand." Within a year Keats found that he was suffering from consumption and went to Rome, to die there within a few months.

Coleridge stayed in Highgate for the last eighteen years of his life, and was buried there. He had other connections with London: he was a scholar at Christ's Hospital with Lamb, and in the year in which he met Keats delivered his famous course of lectures on Shakespeare in the hall of the London Philosophical Society. But his more significant connections were with Wordsworth in Somerset and in the Lake District.

KEATS HOUSE AT HAMPSTEAD (FRONT)

KEATS HOUSE AT HAMPSTEAD (REAR)

KEATS IN HIS ROOM (SEVERN)

QUEEN VICTORIA IN 1837

A FORESTIER
Cimiez 1897

Victoria R I 1897

Thomas Carlyle (Chelsea, 1865)

CHELSEA has historical monuments connected with Sir Thomas More, two wives of Henry VIII, the Princess Elizabeth, James I, and Charles II; but for most moderns the literary and artistic associations of Cheyne Walk (named after an eighteenth century lord of the manor) are more significant. At No. 16, Dante Gabriel Rossetti lived for eighteen years, and for a short time had Algernon Swinburne and George Meredith as lodgers; it was here that he kept a menagerie in the garden and proposed to buy a white elephant he saw advertised in the papers, so that he might teach it to clean the windows and thus advertise his paintings. Another eccentric painter of real genius, J. M. W. Turner, spent his last years at No. 119. George Eliot died at No. 4. But the great glory of Cheyne Walk is that for nearly half a century Thomas Carlyle lived at No. 5 (now No. 24 and a Carlyle Museum). When they took possession in July, 1834, Mrs. Carlyle wrote: "We have got an excellent lodgement, of most antique physiognomy, quite to our humor: all wainscoted, carved, and queer-looking, roomy, substantial, commodious, with closets to satisfy any Bluebeard, a china closet in particular that would hold our whole worldly substance converted into china! Two weeks ago there was a row of ancient trees in front, but some crazy-headed Cockneys have uprooted them. Behind we have a garden (so called in the language of flattery) in the worst order, but boasting of two vines which produced two bunches of grapes in the season, which 'might be eaten,' and a walnut tree from which I have gathered almost sixpence worth of walnuts." There Carlyle constructed the padded room in which he could write in peace and preach the Gospel of Silence in fifty volumes. There he received visits from John Stuart Mill, Tennyson, the Brownings—and in fact all the great writers of the early Victorian era. It was there that in his lonely and embittered widowhood Carlyle gave vent to those sarcastic and ill-tempered judgments of his contemporaries that are faithfully reported by his friend J. A. Froude, the author of the official Biography, thus giving rise to a controversy of which the echoes lasted till the present day.

CARLYLE'S HOUSE AT CHELSEA

THE FRONT DOOR

THE GARDEN

THE GARDEN DOOR

Faithfully yours

Charles Dickens

DICKENS READING "THE CHIMES" TO HIS FRIENDS

THE LONDON OF DICKENS is twofold. There is the actual London in which Dickens suffered the humiliations of his childhood, fell in love, got married, wrote novels, edited magazines, made and acted plays, gave recitals from his own works, labored and amused himself with a feverish activity, separated from his wife and retired from London to Gad's Hill, where he was stricken to death while writing at his desk. And there is the London which was the creation of his imagination and was perhaps more real to him—certainly more real to millions of his readers—than the London of actual fact. Which was the real Doctors' Commons, the one in which Charles Dickens worked as a shorthand writer, or the one in which David Copperfield wasted his time? The former has disappeared from the face of the earth, the latter still lives in the minds of men. So with the Marshalsea Prison in which Charles Dickens visited his father, and the adjoining King's Bench Prison in which David Copperfield visited Mr. Micawber; both prisons have gone, but both still live in *David Copperfield, Little Dorrit* and *Barnaby Rudge*. Old Hungerford Market, where the boy Charles Dickens pasted labels in a blacking factory, is lost in the foundations of Charing Cross Railway Station, but the warehouse of Murdstone and Grinby, in which David Copperfield washed bottles, is still familiar to thousands on both sides of the Atlantic. The thousands recall the denunciations Traddles delivered at Aunt Betsey as the Government, or Mr. Dick as the Opposition (as the case might be), but they have forgotten the debates that Charles Dickens reported for a dozen years, night after night, in the Press Gallery of the House of Commons—"predictions that never come to pass, professions that are never fulfilled, explanations that are only meant to mystify."

With the eye and the pen of genius Dickens portrayed for us the variegated features of the London scene of his time; and in himself and in his writings he embodied the characteristics of the Victorian spirit—especially its humanitarian idealism degenerating into sentimentality.

PARLIAMENT. The Victorians found no solution for the problems of industrialism—and their successors are still seeking—but they had enough political prescience to recognize that democracy was inevitable. At the very beginning of the Victorian era the knell was sounded of a landed aristocracy managing national affairs in its own interest by means of a hereditary House of Lords and a House of Commons it controlled by corruption and "pocket boroughs." The very dukes recognized the fact when they saw the broken windows of the most popular of their number, the victor of Waterloo—Wellington's windows, broken by a London mob. When another London mob pulled down the palings of Hyde Park in 1866 because they were forbidden to assemble there for a reform demonstration, the middle class saw that a further extension of the franchise was necessary; and the enfranchisement of the agricultural laborer followed, peacefully enough, twenty years later. When the ancient Palace of Westminster, with St. Stephen's Chapel (where the Commons had met since 1547) and the old House of Lords, was swept away by the fire on October 18, 1834, it was already realized by the discerning that the new Houses of Parliament would need a new kind of members. The be-wigged and knee-breeched legislators of the old régime made way for the silk-hatted and black-coated members of the Victorian middle class; and these in their turn gave place to the business-like tweeds and even the cloth caps of Labor Members before the century ended. The Victorian poet laureate paid a tribute to the Queen and to the English policy of opportunism in graceful Tennysonian accents:

> Her court was pure; her life serene;
>   God gave her peace; her land reposed,
>   A thousand claims to reverence closed
> In her as mother, wife, and Queen.
> And statesmen at her council met
>   Who knew the seasons when to take
>   Occasion by the hand, and make
> The bounds of freedom wider yet.

HOUSES OF PARLIAMENT

WESTMINSTER HALL (TRIAL OF WARREN HASTINGS)

How London Is Governed. A baffling and yet endearing characteristic of the English people is their willingness to tolerate an ancient anomaly if it does not cause extreme inconvenience—and sometimes even if it does. So the boundaries of the City of London have not been changed at all since 1550, and even now do not go far beyond the Roman walls of fifteen hundred years ago. The City (strictly so called) has an area of a little over a square mile and a population of less than fourteen thousand, its buildings being mainly churches, banks, offices, warehouses and stores. The City authorities maintain their ancient privileges of meeting the reigning sovereign at Temple Bar, conducting the Lord Mayor's show, and giving to His Majesty's Government an annual banquet at which important speeches are delivered. But the City is only the nucleus of the Greater London of the Metropolitan Police District, which has an area of a little more than six hundred square miles, and a population of over eight millions. This includes all parishes wholly within fifteen miles of Charing Cross and also those of which any part is within twelve miles.

Only the City proper is governed by the City of London Corporation with its councillors, aldermen, and Lord Mayor. The rest of the larger London is divided into 28 independent boroughs, each with a mayor and council of its own. These are combined for certain purposes in the London County Council, established in 1888. There are numerous other authorities for special purposes. The Port of London Authority controls the Thames for seventy miles below Teddington Lock; above that point the authority is the Thames Conservancy Board. In so far as the Thames supplies London with water, the Metropolitan Water Board is in charge; but the swans on the river belong to the King.

In spite of these complexities London has managed to carry out numerous improvements in modern times. Old London Bridge was the only bridge across the Thames estuary until 1750, when old Westminster Bridge was completed. The present London Bridge dates from 1831, and Westminster Bridge

OLD WESTMINSTER BRIDGE

OLD WATERLOO BRIDGE

from 1862; of the other bridges the most graceful was Waterloo Bridge, built by Rennie in 1811-17, and about to be replaced by the London County Council.

To the same period belonged Regent Street, which has recently been altered, not for the better from the esthetic point of view. Queen Victoria Street, the Holborn Viaduct, Aldwych, Kingsway, Shaftesbury Avenue, Victoria Street and Victoria Station are all achievements of the Victorian era; to the same period belong the widening of the Strand and Fleet Street, the building of the British Museum and of the Law Courts, and the construction of the Victoria Embankment. All these things should be remembered in mitigation of the shortcomings of the Albert Memorial and the adjoining expanse of academic and imperial buildings, all of the Victorian or Edwardian régime. To the present reign must be credited the London County Hall and many magnificent hotels and palaces of commerce.

Buckingham Palace, built in the eighteenth century for the Duke of Buckingham, was bought by George III and given by him to Queen Charlotte to replace Somerset House, formerly the Queen's residence. Since it became the town residence of the sovereign about a hundred years ago, it has undergone repeated alterations, especially of the front facing St. James's Park, where a crowd now gathers daily to witness the changing of the guard.

NEW WATERLOO BRIDGE

BRITISH MUSEUM READING ROOM

LONDON COUNTY HALL — FROM THE RIVER

LONDON COUNTY HALL

CHAPTER II

UP THE THAMES TO OXFORD

THE ROYAL PARKS and palaces near London extended further and further west in the course of centuries. The English sovereigns from the time of William the Conqueror, and perhaps even earlier, were too afraid of the power of the citizens of London to reside in their midst. The Tower of London, adjoining the eastern wall, was a palace before it was a prison, but the first William, who built it, preferred to be further away from the city at the Palace of Westminster which his predecessor, Edward the Confessor, had erected, partly, no doubt, that he might superintend his favorite project of rebuilding Westminster Abbey, where his tomb may still be seen. The Palace of Westminster was the principal royal residence until Henry VIII, on the fall of Wolsey, seized and enlarged the palace of Whitehall which the ambitious Cardinal had designed for his own use as Archbishop of York. Henry's children and the Stuart sovereigns lived at Whitehall till it was burnt down in 1698, and William III moved the Court to the neighboring palace of St. James; there it stayed till the reign of William IV. But the third William made for himself a second palace at Kensington, where Queen Victoria was born, and Buckingham Palace, on her accession, became the official London residence of the royal family.

As wealth and comfort increased and communication improved, successive sovereigns developed a taste for hunting parks and pleasure gardens further to the West. St. James's Park, Hyde Park, and Kensington Gardens were all at first private parks or gardens belonging to the sovereign, the first two going back to the time of Henry VIII, the last to the acquisition of Kensington Palace by William III. Kew Gardens

RICHMOND HILL

HAMPTON COURT

are made up of the grounds of Kew Palace and of a hunting lodge attached to the ancient palace of Sheen, built by Edward III and rebuilt by Henry VII, who gave it the name of Richmond in compliment to himself as Earl of Richmond in Yorkshire. Edward III, Henry VII, and Queen Elizabeth died there. The palace has entirely disappeared, and so has another famous building at the entrance to Richmond Park, the Star and Garter Hotel, which often appears in Victorian and early nineteenth century novels; the latter site is now occupied by a hospital for disabled soldiers and sailors of the Great War. Richmond Hill nearby, with its municipal park and terrace gardens, still commands one of the finest views in England, celebrated by Scott in the *Heart of Midlothian,* and by Thomson in *The Seasons:*

Enchanting vale! beyond whate'er the Muse
Has of Achaia or Hesperia sung!
O vale of bliss! O, softly swelling hills!
On which the power of cultivation lies,
And joys to see the wonders of his toil.
Heavens, what a goodly prospect spreads around,
Of hills and dales, and woods, and lawns, and spires,
And glittering towns, and gilded streams, till all
The stretching landscape into smoke decays.

Hampton Court and Bushy Park adjoining it (also Crown property) lie a few miles higher up the river than Richmond, with which they vie in natural beauty. Hampton Court has the additional attraction of a great palace, with its ancient glories still intact and accessible to the public, though some of the smaller rooms are occupied by royal pensioners. It was one of the most ambitious building projects of Cardinal Wolsey, who intended it for his own private residence, but before his plans were quite completed found it expedient to make a present of it to Henry VIII. It was a favorite resort of subsequent sovereigns: James I held here the conference of divines at which the Authorized Version of the Bible was planned; Charles I

POPE'S VILLA

TWICKENHAM FERRY

was imprisoned here by the Puritans; William III fell from his horse while riding in the Park and died in the palace. In Queen Anne's reign Pope made Hampton Court the scene of his satiric poem *The Rape of the Lock:*

> Close by those meads, for ever crowned with flowers,
> Where Thames with pride surveys his rising towers,
> There stands a structure of majestic frame,
> Which from the neighboring Hampton takes its name.
> Here Britain's statesmen oft the fall foredoom
> Of foreign tyrants and of nymphs at home;
> Here thou, great Anna! whom three realms obey,
> Dost sometimes counsel take—and sometimes tea.
> Hither the heroes and the nymphs resort,
> To taste awhile the pleasures of a court;
> In various talk the instructive hours they passed,
> Who gave the ball, or paid the visit last;
> One speaks the glory of the British queen,
> And one describes a charming Indian screen;
> A third interprets motions, looks, and eyes;
> At every word a reputation dies.
> Snuff, or the fan, supply each pause of chat,
> With singing, laughing, ogling, and all that.

Pope had a villa at Twickenham on the Thames between Richmond and Hampton Court, and was buried in Twickenham Church, where he erected a monument to his parents and to himself. The villa has given place to a more modern structure and the famous grotto lives only in Pope's description of it in a letter to his friend Edward Blount (June 2, 1725): "I have put my last hand to my works in my gardens, in happily finishing the subterraneous way and grotto: I there found a spring of the clearest water, which falls in a perpetual rill, that echoes through the cavern day and night. From the river Thames, you see through my arch up a walk of the wilderness, to an open temple, wholly composed of shells, in the most rustic manner; and from that distance under the temple, you look down through a sloping arcade of trees, and see the sails on the river passing suddenly and vanishing, as through a perspective glass. When you shut the door of this grotto, it becomes, on the instant, from a luminous room, a camera obscura; on the walls of which, all objects of the river, hills, woods and boats, are forming a moving picture in their visible radiations: and when you have a mind to light it up, it affords you a very different scene: it is finished with shells interspersed with pieces of looking-glass, in angular forms; and in the ceiling is a star of the same material; at which, when a lamp (of an orbicular figure, of thin alabaster) is hung in the middle, a thousand pointed rays glitter, and are reflected over the place. There are connected to this grotto by a narrower passage two porches, one towards the river, of smooth stones, full of light and open; the other toward the garden, shadowed with trees, rough with shells, flints, and iron ore. The bottom is paved with simple pebble, as is also the adjoining walk up the wilderness to the temple, in the natural taste, agreeing not ill with the little dripping murmur, and the aquatic idea of the whole place."

A few miles higher up the river lies Runnymede, the flat marshy field where King John was forced by the barons to seal Magna Charta. Near it is Cooper's Hill, which gave Sir John Denham's famous poem its title and suggested one of the most famous apostrophes to Father Thames:

> My eye, descending from the hill, surveys
> Where Thames amongst the wanton valleys strays;
> Thames, the most loved of all the ocean's sons,
> By his old sire, to his embraces runs,
> Hasting to pay his tribute to the sea,
> Like mortal life to meet eternity. . . .
> O could I flow like thee, and make thy stream
> My great example, as it is my theme!
> Though deep, yet clear, though gentle, yet not dull,
> Strong without rage, without o'erflowing full.

The last two lines, which have been particularly admired, were added by the author as an afterthought, in the second edition.

RUNNYMEDE

WINDSOR CASTLE

WINDSOR CASTLE is the most famous of all the royal palaces and the furthest from London—forty-five miles by water from London Bridge. It was probably the gift by Edward the Confessor of the land about it to the monks of Westminster Abbey that induced William the Conqueror to acquire it from them, though he may well have been impressed by the natural advantages of the site for a place of defense and also by the beauty of the surrounding country. A description of Thames scenery of more than a century ago attempts to do justice to Windsor Castle in these words: "This princely and magnificent residence of the British Monarchs is situated on the summit of a hill, which commands the most beautiful, rich, and luxuriant prospects. The silver Thames flows beneath it, and by its serpentine course through the vale which its waters fertilize, heightens and completes the unrivalled scene." William built the first castle within four years of his accession on its present site and plan, laid out the parks, and took steps to preserve the deer and other game. Subsequent sovereigns made use of the Castle for various purposes, chiefly as a fortress, and King John lodged in it before going down to Runnymede to seal the Great Charter of English liberties. Edward III, who was born at Windsor, took down a good part of the Castle and rebuilt it in its present form, the work being executed under the direction of William of Wyckham, on a salary of a shilling a day. This may seem low pay even for the fourteenth century, but William became Bishop of Winchester and the founder of Winchester College and New College, Oxford; on the inner wall of one of the towers, he had cut the words *Hoc fecit Wyckham,* "This made Wyckham," and when the King objected that he was claiming too much credit for himself, he said the inscription meant not that he made the building but that the building made him. Edward III instituted here the noble order of the Knights of the Garter, whose banners still hang in St. George's Chapel, mainly built by Edward IV. Nearly every English sovereign had a hand in Windsor Castle—Henry VII, Henry VIII, Edward VI, Mary, Elizabeth, and so on down to Victoria, whose

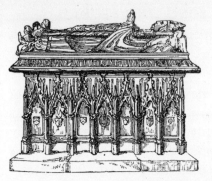

WYCKHAM'S TOMB AT WINCHESTER

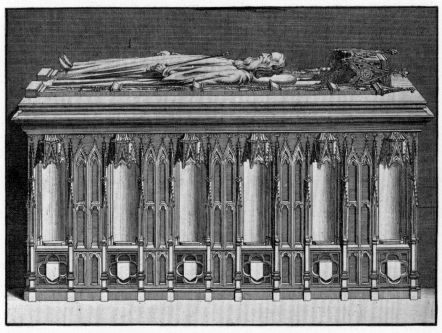

EDWARD III'S TOMB AT WESTMINSTER

hand was heavy upon it; but the original design of the Conqueror has defied alteration and the lapse of time.

ETON COLLEGE is, so to speak, next door to Windsor, being less than a mile on the other side of Windsor Bridge. It was founded by Henry VI to provide for ten "sad priests," four lay clerks, six choristers, twenty-five poor scholars, and twenty-five poor men. These are now represented by seventy "collegers," who are neither poor nor sad, being selected by competition from the best England has to offer; but the majority of the pupils are "Oppidans," who pay large fees, and live in "houses" over which the masters preside. Eton has long been regarded as the leading English public school—not "public" in the American sense—quite the contrary—and its pupils include many names known to history. It was Wellington who is reported to have said that the battle of Waterloo was won on the playing fields of Eton—certainly not in the classrooms, a cynic added later. Adjoining the Playing Fields is the Poet's Walk, commemorating another distinguished pupil, Thomas Gray, who wrote the *Ode on a distant Prospect of Eton College*:

> Ye distant spires, ye antique towers,
>   That crown the watery glade,
> Where grateful Science still adores
>   Her Henry's holy Shade;
> And ye, that from the stately brow
> Of Windsor's heights the expanse below
>   Of grove, of lawn, of mead survey,
> Whose turf, whose shade, whose flowers among
> Wanders the hoary Thames along
>   His silver-winding way.

In the Eton College Library is the original manuscript of Gray's *Elegy written in a Country Churchyard,* associated with Stoke Poges Church, not many miles off, where Gray himself is buried. The *Ode,* from which the first stanza is quoted above, is said to have been written in his mother's garden, about a mile away.

ETON COLLEGE

STOKE POGES CHURCHYARD

LECHLADE BRIDGE AND CHURCH

SHELLEY would not be everyone's choice for the laureate-
ship of the Thames. Every movie fan is familiar with 50 Wim-
pole Street as the house from which Robert Browning rescued
Elizabeth Barrett, but who knows from what London address
Shelley eloped with Harriet Westbrook or who cares that he
first met Mary Godwin in Old St. Pancras Churchyard, by
the graveside of her mother, Mary Wollstonecraft? Yet the
Thames made more impression upon Shelley's mind and did
more to mold his genius than was the case with any of the
older poets whose smooth-flowing and more familiar tributes
have been already quoted. Shelley wrote his first important
poem of any length, *Alastor,* "under the oak-shades of Windsor
Great Park; and the magnificent woodland was a fitting study
to inspire the various descriptions of forest scenery we find in
the poem." So wrote Mary Godwin, with whom he was enjoy-
ing a season of quiet happiness in the summer of 1815, between
his final break with Harriet Westbrook the previous year and
her suicide in the Serpentine the year following. Mary Godwin
writes further: "He rented a house on Bishopgate Heath, on
the borders of Windsor Forest, where he enjoyed several months
of comparative health and tranquil happiness. The later summer months were warm and dry. Accompanied by a few friends,
he visited the source of the Thames, making a voyage in a
wherry from Windsor to Cricklade. His beautiful stanzas in
the churchyard of Lechlade were written on that occasion."
As, in comparison with Gray's *Elegy written in a Country
Churchyard,* Shelley's lines are little known, they may here be
given at some length:

> The wind has swept from the wide atmosphere
> Each vapor that obscured the sunset's ray;
> And pallid Evening twines its beaming hair
> In duskier braids around the languid eyes of Day:
> Silence and Twilight, unbeloved of men,
> Creep hand in hand from yon obscurest glen.

CLIVEDEN

They breathe their spells towards the departing day,
Encompassing the earth, air, stars, and sea;
Light, sound, and motion own the potent sway,
Responding to the charm with its own mystery.
The winds are still, or the dry church-tower grass
Knows not their gentle motions as they pass.

Thou too, aereal Pile! whose pinnacles
Point from one shrine like pyramids of fire,
Obeyest in silence their sweet solemn spells,
Clothing in hues of heaven thy dim and distant spire,
Around whose lessening and invisible height
Gather among the stars the clouds of night.

The dead are sleeping in their sepulchres:
And, mouldering as they sleep, a thrilling sound,
Half sense, half thought, among the darkness stirs,
Breathed from their wormy beds all living things around,
And mingling with the still night and mute sky
Its awful hush is felt inaudibly.

Thus solemnized and softened, death is mild
And terrorless as this serenest night:
Here could I hope, like some inquiring child
Sporting on graves, that death did hide from human sight
Sweet secrets, or beside its breathless sleep
That loveliest dreams perpetual watch did keep.

Shelley returned to the Thames valley to write his next poem, *The Revolt of Islam,* in the neighborhood of Bisham Wood, near Great Marlow, during the summer of 1817. It is his first mature and yet passionate setting forth of the revolutionary ideals which inspired both his poetry and his life. It is dedicated to Mary Godwin in stanzas of which the first two may be quoted:

So now my summer task is ended, Mary,
And I return to thee, mine own heart's home;
As to his Queen some victor Knight of Faëry,

GREAT MARLOW

Earning bright spoils for her enchanted dome;
Nor thou disdain, that ere my fame become
A star among the stars of mortal night,
If it indeed may cleave its natal gloom,
Its doubtful promise thus I would unite
With thy belovèd name, thou Child of love and light.

The toil which stole from thee so many an hour,
Is ended,—and the fruit is at thy feet!
No longer where the woods to frame a bower
With interlacèd branches mix and meet,
Or where with sound like many voices sweet,
Waterfalls leap among wild islands green,
Which framed for my lone boat a lone retreat
Of moss-grown trees and weeds, shall I be seen:
But beside thee, where still my heart has ever been.

In later years Mary gave a fuller account of the conditions under which the poem was written: "During the year 1817 we were established at Marlow in Buckinghamshire. Shelley's choice of abode was fixed chiefly by this town being at no great distance from London, and its neighborhood to the Thames. The poem was written in his boat, as it floated under the beech-groves of Bisham, or during wanderings in the neighboring country, which is distinguished for peculiar beauty. The chalk hills break into cliffs that overhang the Thames, or form valleys clothed with beech; the wilder portion of the country is rendered beautiful by exuberant vegetation; and the cultivated part is peculiarly fertile. With all this wealth of Nature which, either in the form of gentlemen's parks or soil dedicated to agriculture, flourishes around, Marlow was inhabited (I hope it is altered now) by a very poor population. The women are lacemakers, and lose their health by sedentary labor, for which they were very ill paid. The Poor-laws ground to the dust not only the paupers, but those who had risen just above that state, and were obliged to pay poor-rates. The changes produced by peace following a long war, and a bad harvest, brought with them the most heart-rending evils to the poor. Shelley afforded

DORCHESTER BRIDGE AND CHURCH

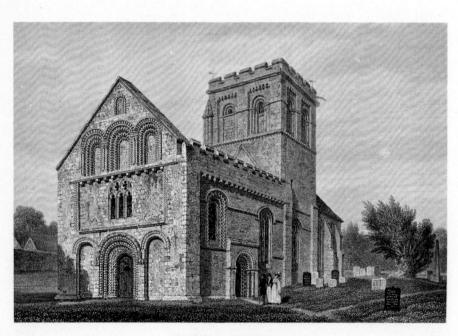

IFFLEY CHURCH

what alleviation he could. In the winter, while bringing out his poem, he had a severe attack of ophthalmia, caught while visiting the poor cottages. I mention these things—for this minute and active sympathy with his fellow-creatures gives a thousandfold interest to his speculations, and stamps with reality his pleadings for the human race."

Marlow is one of the loveliest of the many lovely reaches of the Thames between Eton, where Shelley went to school and got into trouble for rebelling against "fagging," and Oxford, from which he was promptly expelled for the authorship of a pamphlet entitled *The Necessity of Atheism*. When his defiance of prevailing conventions and his revolutionary opinions resulted in his permanent exile to Italy, his mind often went back with pleasure to the Thames valley. "My thoughts for ever cling," he wrote, "to Windsor Forest and the copses of Marlow."

ABOVE WINDSOR in the Thames valley are many notable places—Henley, famous for its regatta; Reading, famous for biscuits, seeds, and the Roman remains of Silchester. "You arrive at Silchester Ruins" (says G. M. Boumphrey in his recent work *Along the Roman Roads*) "along green lanes, and are confronted by a great wall of flint and stone, still from 10 to 20 feet high, and overgrown with trees and bushes and brambles. This wall runs right round a space of 100 acres, an irregular shape, about 800 yards each way. Four gaps show where the four great gateways were, at North, South, East and West; and at the South Gate there are still slight traces of the bastions that flanked it. Inside the walls are quiet fields of springing corn or plough, with nothing at all to show that a few feet below the surface lie long lines of walls, and the remains of mosaic floors." Dorchester and Iffley, still higher up the river, have also antiquities well worthy of a visit, but they are most easily reached from Oxford. In and about Oxford there is a great deal to see and a great deal to talk of.

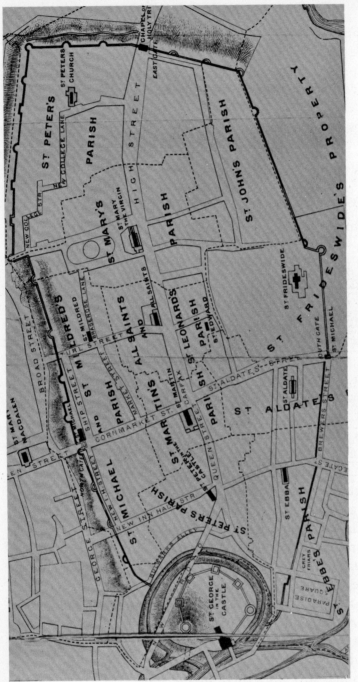

MAP OF OLD OXFORD

CHAPTER III

OXFORD

OXFORD is an ancient city, and the first thing to realize about it is that it is older than the University that has made it famous. As the historian J. R. Green put it, Oxford had centuries of civic life before ever a student appeared in its streets. There are pleasing legends about beginnings of the university in Anglo-Saxon times or even earlier, but there is no definite mention of it as a seat of learning before the twelfth century. The Anglo-Saxon Chronicle mentions "Oxnaford" along with London as a stronghold in the hands of Edward, son of King Alfred, in 912. There are many other references to the town in Anglo-Saxon times, and an Anglo-Saxon mound was the foundation of a Norman castle, which stood at the West gate of the town from the time of William the Conqueror, and of which one tower is still standing. Even in Anglo-Saxon times the town probably had a protective rampart of turf surrounding it, surmounted by a wooden palisade, and in the thirteenth century Henry III had it renewed with stone. "The wall enclosed a small rectangular space, measuring about half a mile from east to west, and a little more than a quarter of a mile from north to south, with a central street about thirty-six feet above the level of the river. The two tall towers of the Castle and St. Michael's guarded the western and northern approaches. On the north side was a deep ditch with water running through it, called Canditch; but, as ground became valuable, this was gradually filled up, and it is now represented by Broad Street" (Charles W. Boase in the Historic Towns Series). The main streets crossed at the "four ways" of Carfax (*Quatre voies*). From that point—still the centre of the modern city—we may walk along Cornmarket Street to the site of the North Gate by

MAGDALEN BRIDGE

THE HIGH STREET

St. Michael's Church, which has incorporated (and restored) the old watchtower which stood on the old city wall. Above the gate was the Bocardo prison in which the Protestant Martyrs, Ridley, Latimer, and Cranmer, had their last meal before they were burnt outside the wall at a spot still marked in what is now Broad Street. It was here, and not at the Memorial in Magdalen Street, that the prophetic words of Latimer were spoken: "Be of good comfort, Master Ridley, and play the man. We shall this day light such a candle by God's grace in England as I trust shall never be put out." It was here too that Cranmer thrust into the flame the hand that had signed his recantation.

Passing by Broad Street to New College Street and through the College Gate into the College Garden, we find a noble survival of the city wall, carefully preserved (according to a fourteenth century contract) by the College authorities. Pursuing our way through New College Lane and Queen's Lane to the High Street, we are quickly where the East Gate stood, just above Magdalen Bridge. Leaving the High by King Street we find further traces of the old walls in Merton Fields and arrive at the site of the South or Water Gate at the corner of Christ Church above the Grand Pont (now called Folly Bridge) across which there was (and is) a road leading to Abingdon. Five minutes' walk up the hill will bring us back to Carfax. Or we may go west by Brewers Street to the Castle tower and mill, past the site of the great Franciscan monastery of which Roger Bacon was a member; he was buried nearby and there is a tablet to him on the remains of the old city wall. It was during his time that Henry III granted the Franciscans "for the greater quiet and security of their habitation, that they might enclose the street that lies under the wall from the Watergate (Southgate) in St. Ebbe's to the little postern in the wall toward the castle, but so that a wall with battlements, like to the rest of the wall of Oxford, be made about the dwelling, beginning at the west side of Watergate, and reaching southward to the bank of the Thames, and extending along

VIEW FROM ABINGDON ROAD

VIEW FROM THE MEADOWS

the bank westward as far as the land of the Abbot of Bec in the parish of St. Bodhoc, and then turning again to the northward till it joins with the old wall of the borough, by the east side of the small postern." The four gates were not pulled down till 1771.

The scattered allusions to Oxford as a seat of learning in the twelfth century are succeeded in the thirteenth by definite recognition of the university by the established authorities—the Pope and the King. These two powers were at odds in the years preceding Magna Charta (1215—a date every English schoolboy remembers), and King John, in defiance of ecclesiastical authority, hanged three Oxford scholars who were concerned in the accidental shooting of a woman while the students were practising archery. The result was a papal interdict which reduced the city to such straits that it agreed not only to submit to ecclesiastical authority, but to offer masses for the slain, to remit half the house rents of the scholars for the next ten years, to provide a hundred of them with food and ale, and to establish a yearly payment of money for the use of poor scholars. This was the first conspicuous defeat of the city in the protracted struggle between "town and gown," in the course of which, says J. R. Green, "the University found Oxford a busy, prosperous borough, and reduced it to a cluster of lodging houses. It found it among the first of English municipalities, and it so utterly crushed its freedom that the recovery of some of the commonest rights of self-government has only been brought about by recent legislation." There were repeated clashes between the citizens and the students; the citizens won in the hand-to-hand combats, being more numerous, but the power of the Church and the Crown always redressed the balance in favor of the University. Bishop Grostête in 1240 made the fines paid by citizens the nucleus of a loan fund for students, who paid no interest but deposited books, plate or other property as security; some such system, supported by voluntary contributions instead of fines, may still be found in many American colleges. Another (and less honorable) college tra-

ST. MARY'S CHURCH

dition is that of disorder and defiance of the authorities in celebration of some festival or athletic victory. There are many examples in the history of Oxford, but the classic instance is that of St. Scholastica's Day in 1355. It was a holiday, and some Oxford clerks, drinking in a Carfax tavern, sent for the vintner and found fault with the wine. He replied with "snappish words and saucy language" and one of the students broke his head with a quart pot (*cum quarta caput ejus fregit,* as the Latin chronicle of the time puts it). The landlord went out in a temper and called on his friends and neighbors to help him. They rang the bell of the town church of St. Martin and the scholars rang the bell of the university church of St. Mary. Then a riot began in which forty of the students were killed and their Inns and Halls pillaged. The city was put under an interdict, the Mayor and Bailiffs sent to prison, and the citizens obtained pardon only by paying a heavy fine on the spot and binding themselves to do annual penance on St. Scholastica's Day (with more payments) at St. Mary's Church—an observance which was maintained till 1825. Jurisdiction over wine, ale, and bread; control of the markets; the cleansing and paving of the streets (at the expense of the citizens) ; regulation of public order, even when no student was involved, passed to the university Chancellor. For over five centuries the city was "practically governed by the University. The University thrived on her own misfortunes." (Rashdall, *The Universities of Europe in the Middle Ages.*)

The city recovered its rights with the passage of the Municipal Corporations Act of 1835, and with its ancient powers and dignities restored it came into more amicable relations with the University. Some of the dons took an interest in the government of the city and even became members of the City Council. In the present century greater prosperity came to Oxford with the establishment of automobile and other industries within its borders, and its crowded streets and busy factories have made it as of old, a thriving municipality in its own right, and not merely an appanage of the University and a resort for tourists.

MERTON COLLEGE LIBRARY

NEW COLLEGE FROM THE GARDEN

THE COLLEGES. It was no doubt the public disorder for which the students were, at least in part, responsible that led to the foundation of colleges. The university authorities themselves complained that serious crimes were committed by students who lived in no hall but were mere roomers in private houses—*chamber-dekens,* passing their days in sleep and their nights in riot and debauchery. In 1264 the royal chancellor, Walter de Merton, founded the first college to train students for the service of God in Church and State—a phrase still familiar in the documents and addresses of Yale and other American colleges which regard the university as a nursery for national leadership. Merton College doubtless adopted some of its features from the monastic foundations which were rich and powerful in the Oxford of that day; but it was expressly provided that it was to be a secular institution; no "religious" (monk or friar) was to be admitted. The community was to consist of a body of poor students living together under the authority of a few seniors (later called Fellows) and a Warden, and an allowance of a shilling a week was made to each scholar to provide him with food; this was the origin of the system of scholarships and fellowships still in vogue at English colleges and universities. University College and Balliol College were founded about the same time. Merton was the model for the first college at Cambridge, Peterhouse, founded a few years later, and from the Cambridge college of Emmanuel John Harvard carried the plan of the English college to the New World.

At Oxford, Exeter College, Oriel, and Queen's were founded in the first half of the fourteenth century, and in the second half William of Wyckham fortified the college system by the foundation of New College, its scholars to be drawn entirely from the public school of Winchester he established at the same time. Eton and King's College, Cambridge, were founded by Henry VI in the fifteenth century on Wyckham's plan. Wyckham was the first to plan his college buildings round a quadrangle and he also began at New College the tutorial system so closely associated with Oxford's name and fame.

Of the fifteenth century colleges Lincoln was intended to controvert the heresies of Wyclif, a Balliol don who had the Bible translated into English, was a vigorous pamphleteer against the papal supremacy, and has been saluted as "the morning star of the Reformation." All Souls was designed to pray for the souls of the English soldiers slain in the French wars, the Archbishop of Canterbury having it somewhat on his conscience that, in order to protect the revenues of the Church (see Shakespeare's *Henry V*, Act I), he had sent a great many fellow subjects, gentle and simple, to an untimely end. It still enjoys the distinction of being the only college (in England, and probably in the world) without students, with the exception of four Bible-clerks, provided (it is said) to save the Warden from attending daily chapel oftener than he is inclined; it has, however, a very distinguished body of non-resident fellows; it is also famous for the excellence (and strength) of its home brewed ale. Magdalen, the last of the fifteenth century colleges, was, like All Souls, modeled on New College; its founder, William of Waynflete, was a protégé of Wyckham's, and like him Bishop of Winchester. The archi-episcopal founder of All Souls began life as a Fellow of New College.

The close connection between the Church and the University is unmistakable, not only in the medieval period, but for centuries after. Up to 1871 every student had to declare his acceptance of the doctrines of the Church of England. Before the Reformation the University transacted its business, kept its books, its money, and its archives, and held its meetings and conferred degrees in the university church of St. Mary, where the annual university sermon is still preached and the principal benefactors of the university remembered in a special service beginning with the verse from the Apocrypha: "Let us now praise famous men and the fathers who begat us." The only important university building erected in this early period was the Divinity School, above which was built a Library to contain the books presented to the University by Humphrey, Duke of Gloucester. This now forms the central portion of the

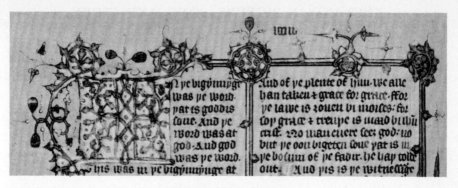

WYCLIFFITE BIBLE

ALL SOULS COLLEGE

Bodleian, where the readers sit "in little cells and curtained cages" if they prefer a medieval atmosphere to the more modern resources of the Radcliffe Camera and still more recent extensions.

It seems natural to associate this earlier Oxford with the clerk of Chaucer's Prologue, lean as his own horse, with threadbare cloak, and not much money in his pockets, entirely given to prayer and meditation:

> Of study took he most care and most heed.
> Not one word spoke he more than there was need,
> And that was said in form and reverence,
> And short and quick, and full of high sentence.
> [Fragrant] with moral virtue was his speech,
> And gladly would he learn and gladly teach.

We have been encouraged to look back to the medieval period as a kind of Golden Age, but it is well to consider also the other side of the shield. The low-lying situation of Oxford among the marshes of the Thames was in itself unhealthy and the lack of sanitation made the city subject to fever. The filthiness of the streets was even more dangerous than the frequent quarrels of the students, not only with the townsmen but among themselves. Erasmus, who came to Oxford to learn Greek at the end of the fifteenth century, contrasts the general dirtiness with the cleanliness of the Low Countries from which he came. "The floors are in general laid with a white clay, and are covered with rushes, occasionally removed, but so imperfectly that the bottom layer is left undisturbed, sometimes for twenty years, harboring expectorations, vomitings, the leakage of dogs and men, ale-droppings, scraps of fish, and other abominations not fit to be mentioned. The island would be much more salubrious if the use of rushes were abandoned. More moderation in diet, and especially in the use of salt meats, might be of service, more particularly were public ediles appointed to see the streets cleaned from mud, and the suburbs kept in better order."

BODLEIAN LIBRARY

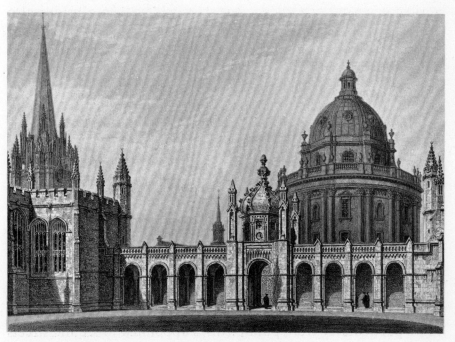

RADCLIFFE CAMERA

HENRY VIII   CARDINAL WOLSEY

CHRIST CHURCH HALL

THE REFORMATION. Oxford accommodated itself to the religious conflicts of Henry VIII's reign as well as it could. Wolsey is said to have begun his career as a Fellow of Magdalen, and it is certain that he took a lively interest in the affairs of the University, revising the statutes and establishing new lectureships. His most princely benefaction was the erection of Cardinal College, named after himself, on the site of the old Priory of St. Frideswide. When the Cardinal fell, the King took over the benefaction, and gave it his own name, but afterwards changed his mind and called it Christ Church, combining an academic and an ecclesiastical foundation and the College chapel with a Cathedral Church, in which he placed the throne of the Bishop of Oxford. Thus the Dean of the College became also the Dean of the Cathedral. It became the largest, the richest, and usually the most fashionable of the Oxford colleges. It has the oldest and biggest bell, taken from Osney Abbey, the largest quadrangle, and the finest dining hall, built by Wolsey in 1529, with an enormous kitchen, vast fireplaces and a huge gridiron.

The Tudor period was responsible for many changes, of which the most important was the substitution of classical learning for the medieval philosophy supposed to be derived from Aristotle. But it was also responsible for a social change of which the advantages were more doubtful. The colleges which had been founded for the benefit of poor scholars became the resort of the sons of the rich. Bishop Latimer said plainly to Edward VI, "There be none now but great men's sons in colleges, and their fathers like not to have them preachers," and in the same reign a Royal Commission directed that pains should be taken "to prevent rich men from taking advantage of the founders' bounty." If such pains were taken, they were of no avail, for we find Harrison complaining in 1586 that the colleges "were erected by their founders, at the first, only for poor men's sons, whose parents were not able to bring them up unto learning; but now they have the least benefit of them, by reason the rich do so encroach upon them. And so far hath this inconvenience spread itself that it is in my time a hard matter for a poor man's child to come by a fellowship, though he be never so good a scholar and worthy of that room."

Queen Elizabeth and the early Stuart kings, with their love of classical learning, frequently visited Oxford, and the University naturally took the side of King Charles in his quarrel with Parliament. Most of the colleges melted their silver plate in contribution to the royal treasure chest, and are therefore worse off in that respect than the Cambridge colleges, which were more Puritan in their sympathies. After the battle of Edgehill (1642) Charles occupied Oxford, fortified it, and made it his headquarters, London being in the hands of Parliament all through the Civil War. Oxford surrendered to the Parliamentary forces by the King's command in 1646, the University was "reformed," four hundred students and fellows who refused to submit to the authority of Parliament were expelled, and Cromwell became Lord Protector of the Realm and Chancellor of the University. While the war lasted, Oxford remained loyal to the Crown, and the Royalist newspapers at Oxford replied to the Parliamentary journals published in London. After the Restoration, Charles II was holding his Court at Oxford in 1665, when the first issue of the official *Gazette* was published. So it happened that the first number of the oldest English newspaper which still continues to appear was published at Oxford and called the *Oxford Gazette*.

THE ROYAL SOCIETY. Some years before the founding of the Royal Society in 1662 under Charles II, as already noted, informal meetings of a group of scientists had been held in London. Under the Commonwealth this group was split into two by Cromwell's appointment of some of the members, who were Puritan sympathizers, to academic positions at Oxford. One of these, Dr. John Wilkins, became the Warden of Wadham College, and the diarist Evelyn makes this note of a visit he paid there on July 13, 1654: "We all dined at that most obliging and universally curious Dr. Wilkins, at Wadham. He was the

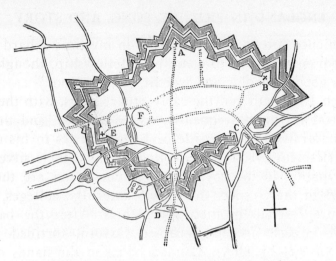

FORTIFICATIONS OF OXFORD 1643–6

A—St. Giles' Church. B—Holywell Church. C—Magdalen Bridge. D—Grand Pont
(Folly Bridge). E—St. Thomas'. Church. F—Oxford Castle.

Numb. 1

The Oxford Gazette.

Published by Authority.

Oxon, Nov. 7.

THis day the Reverend Dr. *Walter Blandford*, Warden of *Wadham Colledge* in this University, was Elected Lord Bishop of this See, vacant by the death of Dr. *Paul*, late Bishop here.

Oxon, Nov. 12. This day His Majesty in Council, according to the usual custom, having the Roll of Sheriffs presented to him, pricked these persons following, to be Sheriffs for the succeeding year, in their respective Counties of *England* and *Wales*.

Berks. Basil Brent, *Esquire*.

fieur *de Cannillac* having been put to death by the Commissioners of the *Grands Jours* : It seems they have laid some new Taxes or Impositions on those parts, There are Troups marching against them, and it is thought they will soon be reduced. my Lord *Aubigny* Lord Almoner to her Majesty, having lain sick some time here of an Hydropsie attended with a Flux, is this week dead.

Paris, Nov. 18. The Mareschal *de Turenne* arrived here on Sunday last from the Frontiers, whence he brings account that the Succors intended against the Prince of *Munster* had passed in small parties, and that they had been received at *Maestricht* by Monsieur *Beverning* in the name of the States General.

first who showed me the transparent apiaries, which he had built like castles and palaces, and so ordered them one upon another, as to take the honey without destroying the bees . . . He had above in his lodgings and gallery a variety of shadows, dials, perspectives, and many other artificial, mathematical, and magical curiosities, a waywiser, a thermometer, a monstrous magnet, conic and other sections, a balance on a semi-circle; most of them his own, and that prodigious young scholar's Mr. Christopher Wren." Wren was Professor, first of Astronomy, then of Geometry, and it was a common belief of his contemporaries that if he had not turned his attention to architecture, he might have rivalled the fame of the great Cambridge mathematician of the time, Isaac Newton.

Some jealousy and ill-feeling met the Oxford attempt to substitute the method of investigation and experiment advocated by Francis Bacon for the traditional arguments from abstract principles derived from the medieval conception of Aristotelianism. Dr. Sprat, another Wadham scholar, in 1667 wrote a *History of the Royal Society* to prove that experiments are not injurious to the universities. Dr. John Wallis, appointed Savilian Professor of Geometry by Cromwell in 1649, came out boldly in defense of the new studies. "Our business was (precluding matters of theology and state affairs) to discourse and consider of philosophical inquiries, and such as related thereunto: as Physick, Anatomy, Geometry, Astronomy, Navigation, Staticks, Magneticks, Chymicks, Mechanicks, and Natural Experiments; with the state of these studies and their cultivation at home and abroad. We then discoursed of the circulation of the blood, the valves in the *venæ lacteæ,* the lymphatic vessels, the Copernican hypothesis, the nature of comets and new stars, the satellites of Jupiter, the oval shape of Saturn, the spots in the sun and its turning on its own axis, the inequalities and selenography of the moon, the several phases of Venus and Mercury, the improvement of telescopes, the grinding of glasses for that purpose, the weight of air, the possibility or impossibility of vacuities, and Nature's abhorrence

WADHAM COLLEGE

BOTANIC GARDEN

thereof, the Torricellian experiment in quicksilver, the descent of heavy bodies and the degree of acceleration therein, and divers other things of like nature."

Still another Oxford scientist and a leading member of the Royal Society was Robert Boyle, whose epitaph gravely records that he was the "Father of Chemistry and brother of the Earl of Cork." A more enduring title to fame, perhaps, is that he was the correspondent of Spinoza.

PEPYS (also a member of the Royal Society) was a Cambridge man, though late in life he received a diploma from Oxford in acknowledgment of the gift to the university of a portrait of Wallis by Kneller. Pepys visited Oxford in 1668, and did indeed go to the new Botanic Garden, but otherwise he showed more of the eagerness of the modern tourist to see everything in a day, than of a serious scientist. "9th June we came to Oxford, a very sweet place: paid our guide [on the journey] £1.2s.6d.; barber, 2s.6d.; book, Stonehenge, 4s.; boy that showed me the colleges before dinner, 1s. To dinner, and then out with my wife and people and landlord, and to him that showed us the schools and library, 10s.; to him that showed us All Souls College and Chichele's picture, 5s. So to see Christchurch with my wife, I seeing several others very fine alone before dinner, and did give the boy that went with me 1s.; strawberries, 1s.2d.; dinner and servants, £1.0s.6d. After coming home from the schools, I went with the landlord to Brazen-nose College, to the butteries, and in the cellar find the hand of the Child of Hale [John Middleton, the giant, servant at Brasenose, who died 1623], butler 2s. Thence with coach and people to Physic [Botanical] garden, 1s. So to Friar Bacon's Study, I up and saw it and gave the man 1s.; bottle of sack for landlord, 2s. Oxford mighty fine place and well seated, and cheap entertainment."

Anthony Wood, who published his *History and Antiquities of the University of Oxford* in 1674, notes under date May 3, 1669: "Monday was the first day that the flying coach went from

Oxon to London in one day . . . They entered into the coach
at the tavern door against All Souls College precisely at 6 in
the morning and at 7 at night they were all set down in their
inn at London."

In 1688 the Fellows of Magdalen College had their share
in the glorious Revolution. Magdalen, like most of the Oxford
colleges, was predominantly Tory and Royalist, but the Fellows were not for the divine right of kings when it was exercised to deny the rights of the Fellows. James II ordered them
to elect as President of Magdalen a Catholic and a man of
bad character. They refused, and elected one of their own number. James voided the election, came to Oxford, called the
Fellows before him, bullied them, and commanded them to
elect his candidate. They again refused, and were expelled from
their positions. But in the end the Fellows came back to their
old academic chairs, and it was the King who lost his throne.
The Fellows of Magdalen still celebrate the day when their
predecessors were "restored" and drink an annual toast to the
motto *jus suum cuique*—"to every man his own."

SAMUEL JOHNSON was a student at Pembroke College
1728-31, but left without a degree owing to his father's in-
solvency. The University later gave him first a Master's, and
then a Doctor's degree, and he was ever a most loyal and grateful Oxonian. In 1730 John Wesley, who had been a student
at Christ Church and was a Fellow of Lincoln, founded the
Society of Methodists, who bound themselves to certain religious observances. In 1768 six students were expelled for attending conventicles and consorting with reputed Methodists.
They had preached in a barn to a mixed multitude, talked of
"drawing nigh unto God," frequented the house of Hewet, a
stay-maker who was known to offer extempore prayer, and had
been heard to say "they must sit down and wait for the Spirit."
Boswell was inclined to defend them as poor harmless crea-
tures, but Johnson said the academic authorities were right.
"Sir, that expulsion was extremely just and proper. What have

JOHN WESLEY

CHARLES WESLEY

GEORGE WHITEFIELD

BENJAMIN INGHAM

they to do at a University, who are not willing to be taught, but will presume to teach? Where is religion to be learnt, but at a University? Sir, they were examined, and found to be mighty ignorant fellows." BOSWELL: "But was it not hard, Sir, to expel them, for I am told they were good beings?" JOHNSON: "I believe they might be good beings; but they were not fit to be in the University of Oxford. A cow is a very good animal in the field; but we turn her out of a garden."

The idea that the University was a close preserve restricted to members of the Church of England was not merely a point of view; it was the law and became the fact. It led in the nineteenth century to the expulsion of Shelley and to the withdrawal of Newman; and in the eighteenth it was on this account that the gates of Magdalen College were for ever shut against Gibbon, the historian—not because of the skepticism of his later years, but because as a boy of sixteen he became a Roman Catholic. This no doubt affected the acid tone of Gibbon's description of the University in his *Memoirs,* though it does not invalidate the facts he alleges. Most of the university professors, he says, "have for these many years given up altogether even the pretence of teaching." The duty of instruction was left in the hands of the tutors or fellows of the various colleges, where the students' maintenance was provided "at their own expense or at that of the founders, and the stated hours of the [dining] hall and chapel represent the discipline of a regular and, as it were, religious community." The fellows of Magdalen as he found them about the middle of the eighteenth century "were decent easy men who supinely enjoyed the gifts of the founder; their days were filled by a series of uniform employments; the chapel and the hall, the coffee-house and the common room, till they retired, weary and well satisfied, to a long slumber. From the toil of reading, or thinking, or writing, they had absolved their conscience; and the first shoots of learning and ingenuity withered on the ground, without yielding any fruits to the owners or the public. As a gentleman-commoner, I was admitted to the society of the fellows, and

MAGDALEN COLLEGE PARK

ST. JOHN'S GARDEN

fondly expected that some questions of literature would be the amusing and instructive topics of their discourse. Their conversation stagnated in a round of college business, Tory politics, personal anecdotes, and private scandal: their dull and deep potations excused the brisk intemperance of youth: and their constitutional toasts were not expressive of the most lively loyalty for the house of Hanover." Altogether, though Gibbon, on account of the delicacy of his childhood, was a studious youth and eager to learn, he found the fourteen months he spent at Magdalen College "the most idle and unprofitable of my whole life."

DURING THE EIGHTEENTH CENTURY Magdalen vied with St. John's in the beauty of its surroundings and the lassitude of its students. Nicholas Amhurst, who was expelled from St. John's in the first half of the century, reported of the members of that foundation that "he saw, though he could not agree they had a vast deal of learning, that they had very good linen; not abundance of wit, indeed, but very rich lace, red stockings, silver-buttoned coats, and other things which constitute a man of taste in Oxford." Andrew Lang, a nineteenth century graduate of Merton College, says, "It is easy to understand that men find it a weary task to read in sight of the beauty of the groves of Magdalen and of St. John's. When Kubla Khan 'a stately pleasure-dome decreed,' he did not mean to settle students there, and to ask them for metaphysical essays and for Greek and Latin prose compositions. Kubla Khan would have found a palace to his desire in the gardens of Laud, or where Cherwell, 'meandering with a lazy motion,' stirs the green weeds, and flashes from the mill-wheel, and flows to the Isis through meadows white and purple with fritillaries.

> And here are gardens bright with sinuous rills,
> Where blossoms many an incense-bearing tree;

but here is scarcely the proper training-ground of first-class men!"

It must of course be realized that these eighteenth century criticisms and these conditions refer to the Oxford of the past, not that of the present. A Bill throwing the universities open to Nonconformists was passed by the House of Commons in 1834 but rejected by the Lords. In 1843 when an honorary degree was conferred upon the American ambassador, who happened to be a Unitarian, the undergraduates made such a riot that the Vice-Chancellor had to put an end to the proceedings. The reform was actually carried in 1871, and perhaps the complete modernization of the University may be dated from the admission of women to degrees in 1920.

Reformation of methods of teaching and habits of study may be said to have begun with the establishment of the distinction between honor and pass students in 1802. The pass student, if he has had a good training at school, may get his degree without any very close application to study, and give most of his attention to athletics, and other "extra-curricular" activities, as they might be called in an American college. The student who wants to take a good place in the honors list must work, and work hard. Some colleges now take only honors men, and the pass student plays a continually smaller part in the life of the University, though he still counts financially, as he is usually not in receipt of a scholarship and pays all his fees. But this reformation of learning and teaching has come slowly. Professor Goldwin Smith, who was a demy (a scholar receiving half as much as a fellow) of Magdalen College in 1842-5 wrote in his *Reminiscences* (1911) : "My Magdalen, like my Eton, was a relic of the past. It had forty Fellowships, thirty Demyships or Scholarships, and a revenue of forty thousand pounds a year, besides its rich dower of historic beauty. It took no Commoners, and its educational output in my time was eight or ten undergraduate Demys and one Gentleman-Commoner, who, being under the phantom authority of the nonagenarian President, lived in a licence beyond even the normal licence of his class . . . It was with keen regret that I left Magdalen; my heart has always turned to its beauty, and often the sound of its sweet bells has come to me across the ocean. Reformed it had, in justice to the University and the nation, to be; and I had to bear a hand in the process; but I was helping to destroy a little Eden in a world where there are not many of them."

An Oxford college has a life of its own. The university professors give a few lectures but no student is required to attend them. Each college has its own teaching staff, though some colleges combine courses for the sake of economy; still, the college student may eat, sleep, study and be taught within his own college walls, attend his college debating society, row in the college boat, play for the college teams, read in the college library—few undergraduates give more than a cursory glance to the Bodleian. One college may pride itself on its prowess on the river, another on its devotion to learning. Oriel College numbered among its fellows most of the leaders of the new High Church party known to the nineteenth century as the Oxford movement. Keble began it with his sermon on "national apostasy," preached in July, 1833, in the university church of St. Mary's, of which Newman was Vicar. It was a church hallowed with memories of the Protestant leaders Wyclif, Cranmer, Ridley, Latimer, and John Wesley, and when Newman resigned the pulpit, from which he had so often held the Oxford of his day spellbound with his eloquence and spiritual fervor, it was to be received into the Catholic Church, of which he long after became a Cardinal.

CHRIST CHURCH, combining a college and a cathedral, was the home of orthodoxy, Toryism, and fashion in the seventeenth century, when it expelled William Penn for nonconformity and John Locke, the philosopher, for his political opinions. In the nineteenth century it had among its members four English prime ministers, Sir Robert Peel, W. E. Gladstone, Lord Salisbury, and Lord Rosebery. Ruskin was one of its "gentlemen-commoners" and C. L. Dodgson (Lewis Carroll) one of its dons. The Alice of *Alice in Wonderland* was the daughter of Dean Liddell, whose Greek lexicon classical students still use.

CHRIST CHURCH STAIRCASE

SIR ROBERT PEEL

LORD SALISBURY

W. E. GLADSTONE

LORD OXFORD (H. H. ASQUITH)

BALLIOL COLLEGE in the second half of the nineteenth century took a distinct lead under the mastership of Benjamin Jowett, counting among its alumni such statesmen as Lord Lansdowne, Lord Oxford (H. H. Asquith), Lord Milner, Lord Curzon and Viscount Grey. Among its poets were Southey, Calverley, Swinburne, Arthur Hugh Clough, and Matthew Arnold. The last-named celebrated Oxford both in prose and verse. Perhaps nothing ever said about Oxford is so well known as his salutation of the "Beautiful city! so venerable, so lovely, so unravaged by the fierce intellectual life of our century . . . spreading her gardens to the moonlight and whispering from her towers the last enchantments of the Middle Age . . . home of lost causes, and forsaken beliefs, and unpopular names, and impossible loyalties!" and yet "ever calling us nearer to the true goal of all of us, to the ideal, to perfection—to beauty."

Arnold's *Scholar Gypsy* is a song to Oxford woods and hills, Oxford streams—"the stripling Thames at Bablock-hithe"—and Oxford flowers:

> the frail-leafed white anemone—
> Dark bluebells drenched with dews of summer eves—
> And purple orchises with spotted leaves.

Thyrsis is a lament for Clough, Arnold's poet-friend and fellow student, and it is composed in the same mood of recollection of the fields and streams about Oxford:

> I know the wood which hides the daffodil,
>   I know the Fyfield tree,
> I know what white, what purple fritillaries
>   The grassy harvest of the river-fields,
>   Above by Ensham, down by Sandford, yields,
> And what sedged brooks are Thames's tributaries;
>
> I know these slopes; who knows them if not I?—
>   But many a dingle on the loved hill-side,
>   With thorns once studded, old, white-blossomed trees,
>   Where thick the cowslips grew, and far descried
>   High towered the spikes of purple orchises,

SHELLEY

ARNOLD

MORRIS

SWINBURNE

> Hath since our day put by
> The coronals of that forgotten time;
>   Down each green bank hath gone the ploughboy's team,
>   And only in the hidden brookside gleam
> Primroses, orphans of the flowery prime.
>
> Where is the girl, who by the boatman's door,
>   Above the locks, above the boating throng,
>   Unmoored our skiff when through the Wytham flats,
>   Red loosestrife and blond meadow-sweet among
>   And darting swallows and light water-gnats,
>   We tracked the shy Thames shore?
> Where are the mowers, who, as the tiny swell
>   Of our boat passing heaved the river-grass,
>   Stood with suspended scythe to see us pass?—
> They all are gone, and thou art gone as well!

EXETER COLLEGE has a fine chapel with a tapestry (The Star of Bethlehem) done by William Morris from designs by Burne-Jones, members of the Pre-Raphaelite Brotherhood who were both undergraduates here. Another member of the Pre-Raphaelite Brotherhood who later became famous as a critic of Renaissance art was Walter Pater, a student at Queen's and for many years a fellow of Brasenose College. Oscar Wilde, whose contributions to art were of a more dubious character, was a demy of Magdalen.

A word should also be said of the Modern History School at Oxford, with which were associated such distinguished names as J. A. Froude, J. R. Green, Mark Pattison, William Stubbs, E. A. Freeman, S. R. Gardiner, and T. F. Tout.

MODERN OXFORD thinks less of its past and more of the future than it used to do. It has Socialist dons and Pacifist students. Was it not the Oxford Union which started the recent crusade in the American colleges against militarism? Women were admitted to the university examinations without degrees in 1884 and to full rights in 1920. Another feature of Oxford life of special interest to Americans is the presence of the

RUSKIN

NEWMAN

PATER

GALSWORTHY

Rhodes Scholars, of whom the great majority come from the United States. To quote from a manual entitled *Oxford of Today,* written by the Rhodes Scholars of the past for those of the future, admission to the University of Oxford is now "open to all, irrespective of age, sex, creed, color, nationality, or station" who can fulfil the requirements for entrance.

OF SPORTS at Oxford the most important thing to be said is that intercollegiate athletics interest the students more than the inter-university contests. The rival university of Cambridge is met on neutral ground in London during the vacations; intercollegiate matches are practically the only contests during term time. "There are fewer spectators in the stands and more athletes in the fields at Oxford or at Cambridge than at any other university in the world." The university boat race is rowed every year over a course on the Thames just above London, between Putney and Mortlake. The spectators include thousands who have no interest in either university, and few undergraduates are present. What interests the average undergraduate is the series of races between the colleges rowed in term time at Oxford and called "Torpids"—on account of the slow pace of the boats used, heavy eight-oared shells with fixed seats. In *Oxford of Today,* from which the above quotations are made, these races are described by R. P. Coffin from his own experience as a Rhodes Scholar: "What the Thames lacks in breadth it has happily supplied in length—for from the site of the Old Mill that ground its grist for 700 years at Iffley there is better than a mile of weirless water upstream to the old lodging place of Roger Bacon on Folly Bridge. So the sport is cut to fit the river. Each afternoon, for six consecutive days, three divisions of college Torpids, composed of about a dozen boats each, row over this mile. The boats start 150 feet apart, and pursue one another up to the head of the row of college barges by Christ Church meadow; that is to say, the medium lucky boats and the medium unfortunate row through to the end. The very good or the hopeless crews finish their

IFFLEY MILL

FOLLY BRIDGE

work anywhere this side of the end. When a boat closes the gap ahead, it rams the stern of its prey until the coxswain in the stricken craft throws up his hand to acknowledge the bump. If he is overproud and neglects to confess defeat, it is best to sink him and his galley-slaves; then you are sure of the bump. It does not pay to hesitate, for there is the boat behind to serve you as you would serve others. It is not an easy thing to make a bump; many an over-lapped boat has slipped away to safety by a supreme wrench of the tiller in the nick of time; coxswains are full of wiles from long practice in hugging shores and dodging pursuers.

"When a bump is made, both bumper and bumpee drop out of the race. So some boats may have only a hopeless gap to pursue to the end of the course. Next day the bumper and bumpee exchange places. Thus the better boats work their way to the top of their divisions, while the weaker drift, bumped to ignominy, towards the tail of the procession. In the day's race, the lowest division rows first; and so on to the top division; the gaps being bridged by the head boat of the third division rowing the course a second time as the bottom boat of the second division, and the head boat of the second, rowing as bottom boat of the first. That boat which leads all after the closing race is Head of the River—which means glory immortal and year-long fame. Junior common rooms are hung with tiller trophies of headships of yesterday. One college is said to have been accustomed to close its grace before dinner with the words —'By grace of God, first on the River!' "

CHAPTER IV

THE HOME COUNTIES

THE HOME COUNTIES (so called by all Londoners) are Kent, Surrey, Middlesex, Essex, and Hertford. About all these, the transatlantic visitor has the same kind of doubt as beset the English traveler going from New York to New England—that he could not tell where the suburbs of New York City ended and the State of Connecticut began. But each of the Home Counties has not only its own boundaries but its own characteristics —quite apart from its nearness to London.

KENT is the county traversed by most travelers on their way between England and the European Continent, and the fact that its cliffs look across the Channel to the shores of France has vitally affected the history of Kent and the character of its inhabitants. Ancient tradition connects its coast with the legendary names of King Arthur, Hengist and Horsa, and we know that in Roman times the port of Dubræ (Dover) was the landing place from Bononia (Boulogne) and the beginning of Watling Street, which led through Canterbury to London. It was in Kent that the Anglo-Saxon marauders made their first settlement on British soil in the Isle of Thanet, then separated from the mainland by a navigable channel defended by the old Roman forts of Rutupiæ (Richborough) and Regulbium (Reculver). The Roman Durovernum became Canterbury (Cantwarabyrig), the borough of the men of Kent, and there the Saxon king Ethelbert received the Roman missionaries headed by St. Augustine in 597. Every subsequent attack on England, from the Norman Invasion to the Great War, was directed in the first instance at Kent, and at the beginning of the nineteenth century, during the crisis of an expected Napo-

DOVER CASTLE

SHAKESPEARE'S CLIFF

leonic invasion, Wordsworth addressed "to the Men of Kent" his well known patriotic sonnet:

> Vanguard of Liberty, ye men of Kent,
> Ye children of a soil that doth advance
> Her haughty brow against the coast of France,
> Now is the time to prove your hardiment!
> To France be words of invitation sent!
> They from their fields can see the countenance
> Of your fierce war, may ken the glittering lance,
> And hear you shouting forth your brave intent.
> Left single, in bold parley, ye of yore,
> Did from the Norman win a gallant wreath;
> Confirmed the charters that were yours before;—
> No parleying now! In Britain is one breath;
> We all are with you now from shore to shore:
> Ye men of Kent, 't is victory or death!

The "dear, white cliffs of Dover" have for centuries been the last bit of England seen by the traveler to the East, or the first glimpse of his native land caught by the returning exile. Shakespeare immortalized one of them, and made it his own, for it is now known as "Shakespeare's cliff." The lines in *King Lear* could hardly have been written except from personal experience of standing on the edge of the cliff and looking out to sea:

> Come on, sir; here's the place: stand still. How fearful
> And dizzy 'tis to cast one's eyes so low!
> The crows and choughs that wing the midway air
> Show scarce so gross as beetles: half way down
> Hangs one that gathers samphire, dreadful trade!
> Methinks he seems no bigger than his head:
> The fishermen that walk upon the beach
> Appear like mice; and yond tall anchoring bark
> Diminished to her cock; her cock, a buoy
> Aimost too small for sight: the murmuring surge
> That on the unnumbered idle pebbles chafes
> Cannot be heard so high. I'll look no more,
> Lest my brain turn and the deficient sight
> Topple down headlong.

GAD'S HILL PLACE, KENT

CANTERBURY CATHEDRAL FROM THE SOUTHWEST

By the modern reader and frequenter of the movies, the Dover cliffs are perhaps more commonly associated with the attack of Miss Betsey Trotwood upon intrusive donkey-riders and the painful journey of little David Copperfield from his London lodgings to his Aunt's cottage. It is possible for the modern tourist to follow the steps of the weary little traveler along the Old Kent Road from London through Greenwich to Rochester where he may visit the ancient cathedral and Eastgate House, an Elizabethan mansion haunted by memories of Edwin Drood. Near Rochester are also to be found Cooling Marshes, where Dickens laid the opening scenes of *Great Expectations,* and Gad's Hill Place, where the novelist went to live in 1857 and where he died in 1870. Dickens first saw the great house as a child in the course of a country walk with his father, who told him that if he "were to be very persevering and to work very hard" he might some day come to live in it. Nearly half a century later Dickens bought the place and spent on it most of the money he made on his American tour of 1867-8, which really brought Dickens to his death through the overstrain of recitals from his own works.

In the neighboring town of Chatham, Dickens lived as a child with his spendthrift father, the prototype of the immortal Micawber. It was at Chatham that David Copperfield sold his jacket to the dreadful old man and refused to go away until he had obtained 1s-4d of the 1s-6d promised him for the sale. Canterbury, "with its old houses and gateways and the stately gray Cathedral, with the rooks sailing round the towers" is unforgettably associated by readers of *David Copperfield* with the Micawber family, Uriah Heep and his mother, Agnes Wickfield and her father, Dr. Strong and his too youthful wife, just as Dover is associated with Aunt Betsey Trotwood and Mr. Dick.

Of the earlier history of Canterbury Cathedral something has already been said in connection with the coming of St. Augustine, to whom King Ethelbert gave the site on which a Roman basilica had once stood for the foundation of the leading

CANTERBURY CATHEDRAL FROM CHRIST CHURCH GATEWAY

church of Saxon England. Augustine's church was burnt down the year following the coming of William the Conqueror, and Lanfranc, the first Norman Archbishop, undertook a reconstruction which was continued by his successors in the next century. But for a long time the prestige of the cathedral church was outdone by that of the adjoining Benedictine monastery which St. Augustine had founded and in which he and his episcopal successors were buried. It was the quarrel between Henry II and Archbishop Becket, and the assassination of the latter in his own cathedral which gave the metropolitan church its preëminence. Hurriedly interred in the crypt, Becket's body was later removed to a magnificent shrine behind the high altar, where (as the ecclesiastical chronicler says) "he celebrated his first mass, where he was wont to prostrate himself with tears and prayers, where God for his merits had performed so many miracles, where poor and rich, kings and princes, had worshiped him, and whence the sound of his praises had gone forth into all lands." It was by no arbitrary choice that Chaucer made the shrine of St. Thomas the destination of his pilgrims, for the murdered archbishop had become "the most famous intercessor in all Europe." So, after a brief acknowledgment of the merits of far-off shrines sought by pilgrims in other lands Chaucer says:

> And specially from every shirès end
> Of Engèland, to Canterbury they wend,
> The holy blissful martyr for to seek,
> That them hath holpen when that they were sick.

It was in Chaucer's time that Lanfranc's nave was replaced by the present nave and transepts—excellent examples of the fourteenth century Perpendicular architecture, surpassed only by the "triumphant dominance" of the great central tower erected about a century later. "Such a tower," says Mrs. Schuyler Van Rensselaer, "we can see in England only, and nowhere in England in greater perfection than here."

KNOLE, KENT

PENSHURST

KENT has been called "the garden of England" and is as rich in scenic beauty as in historical memories, so that a large volume would fail to exhaust its varied interests. A pleasant short excursion from London is to Eltham, where there are remains of a very old royal palace, and a little further afield, near Sevenoaks, lies Knole, one of the finest of old English country houses, in a lovely deer-park. Built in the fifteenth century for the Archbishops of Canterbury it passed into the hands of the Crown and was given by Queen Elizabeth to the Sackville family, in whose possession it has remained ever since. Victoria Sackville-West wrote a charming book about it, *Knole and the Sackvilles,* which should be read as a key to Virginia Woolf's *Orlando.* The central theme of the novel is the Sackville family and its connection with Knole, with its 365 rooms (one for every day in the year), seven courts (one for each day of the week), and 52 staircases (one for each week in the year). The leading members of the family throughout the centuries from the Elizabethan poet Thomas Sackville to the novelist's friend, Victoria Sackville-West, are portrayed in the person of the heroine.

Seven or eight miles from Knole is Penshurst, the family seat of Sir Philip Sidney's father, Sir Henry Sidney, and of his brother Sir Robert, who became Baron Sidney of Penshurst and Earl of Leicester. It still retains the beauties ascribed to it in Ben Jonson's lines of more than three centuries ago:

> Thou art not, Penshurst, built to envious show
> Of touch or marble, nor canst boast a row
> Of polished pillars or a roof of gold;
> Thou hast no lantern, whereof tales are told,
> Or stair, or courts, but stand'st an ancient pile,
> And—these grudged at—art reverenced the while.
> Thou joy'st in better marks of soil, of air,
> Of wood, of water; therein art thou fair.
> Then hath thy orchard fruit, thy garden flowers,
> Fresh as the air, and new as are the hours;
> The early cherry, with the later plum,
> Fig, grape, and quince, each in his time doth come;

The blushing apricot and woolly peach
Hang on thy walls that every child may reach—
And though thy walls be of the country stone,
They're reared with no man's ruin, no man's groan;
There's none that dwell about them wish them down,
But all come in, the farmer and the clown,
And no one empty-handed, to salute
Thy lord and lady, though they have no suit.

The English spring, rich in blossoming trees, flowers, and verdure, is at its loveliest in Kent, and in September there is the picturesque migration of thousands of hop-pickers from the London slums to gather the harvest for drying in the "oast" houses which are a characteristic feature of the landscape.

SURREY vies with Kent in natural beauty, and has the further advantage of association with the novels and poems of George Meredith, who lived for the last forty years of his life at Flint Cottage on Box Hill, and was buried in Dorking Cemetery. Between Dorking and Guildford is the Crossways Farm which gave its name to *Diana of the Crossways*. Portsmouth, where Meredith was born, is on the Hampshire coast, and the Bevisham of *Beauchamp's Career* is Southampton, but all the beautiful stretch of country between London and the southern sea is enshrined in Meredith's poetry—the contours of its rolling hills and quiet valleys, its characteristic trees and birds and flowers. The family seats of the county gentry which adorn the landscape are the scenes of his novels. He is as much the poet and novelist of this part of England and the aristocratic society to which it belonged in the nineteenth century as Sir Walter Scott is the novelist of the Scottish Highlands and Wordsworth the poet of the Lake District. The stanzas that follow are from *Love in the Valley:*

Lovely are the curves of the white owl sweeping
    Wavy in the dusk lit by one large star.
Lone on the fir-branch, his rattle-note unvaried,
    Brooding o'er the gloom, spins the brown eve-jar.

CROSSWAYS FARM, SURREY

FLINT COTTAGE, BOX HILL

MEREDITH'S CHALET

Darker grows the valley, more and more forgetting:
   So were it with me if forgetting could be willed.
Tell the grassy hollow that holds the bubbling well-spring,
   Tell it to forget the source that keeps it filled.

Yellow with birdfoot-trefoil are the grass-glades;
   Yellow with cinquefoil of the dew-gray leaf;
Yellow with stonecrop; the moss-mounds are yellow;
   Blue-necked the wheat sways, yellowing to the sheaf.
Green-yellow, bursts from the copse the laughing yaffle,
   Sharp as a sickle is the edge of shade and shine:
Earth in her heart laughs looking at the heavens,
   Thinking of the harvest: I look and think of mine.

MIDDLESEX has been almost completely absorbed by the great metropolis, and ESSEX has been more affected than the counties south of the Thames. Most of the industrial East End of London is in Essex, and one has to get through this before arriving at Epping Forest or the quieter rural parts of the county with great trees and country houses, pleasant fields and gardens. A drive of a little over fifty miles from London to the north east corner of Essex brings us to Colchester, erected as the first Roman colony in Britain after the victory of the Emperor Claudius in 44 A.D. over Kunobelin (Shakespeare's *Cymbeline*), who had made it his capital. The British sacked it in 62 A.D. under Boadicea, and on its recovery the Romans built the city walls, of which there are still considerable remains. Classicianus, the Procurator of the Province of Britain who reëstablished the Roman power after the revolt, was buried near the Roman Wall on Tower Hill, and in 1935 the handsome tomb erected to his memory in A.D. 66 by his faithful and disconsolate wife, Julia, was dug up there in the course of excavations by the London Passenger Transport Board; it was placed in the British Museum, where fragments of the tomb were already preserved, and has served as a basis for the reconstruction of the original. There are interesting Roman relics in the Colchester Museum, and not far away there is a fine Norman castle built in part from Roman materials.

COLCHESTER CASTLE, ESSEX

ROMAN THEATRE, VERULAMIUM

HERTFORDSHIRE, further north, has succeeded in maintaining more of its own individuality, though where it borders Middlesex, its edges are becoming more and more suburban. Lamb's essay "Mackery End in Hertfordshire" gives us a sense of the charm of the old county, "hearty, homely, loving Hertfordshire," before the metropolis, like a gigantic cuttle-fish, spread its tentacles in every direction. One may still take "pretty pastoral walks" about Mackery End in Hertfordshire, but the motor-bus, the char-a-banc, and the automobile have made it much more difficult to get away from the hum and bustle of the traffic going to or coming from the great metropolis.

In Hertfordshire, only twenty miles from London, is the charming old city of St. Albans, near the site of a still older station which was the only town in Roman Britain to be granted the dignity of a self-governing municipality. London, as Tacitus noted, though important commercially, never reached even the lower rank of a *colonia;* the Roman colonies, at which retired legionaries received grants of land, were Colchester, Gloucester, Lincoln, and York. St. Albans was known to the Romans as Verulamium (from the river Ver on which the little city stands), and it was this Latin name that Francis Bacon chose for his title of Lord Verulam. St. Alban was a Roman soldier and the first British martyr, in whose memory a Benedictine abbey was founded in the eighth century, to be enlarged later by a magnificent Norman abbey church. In the middle ages its mitred abbot was the premier abbot of all England. Parts of the present cathedral go back to the eleventh century, and the Norman tower was largely built with bricks and tiles taken from the Roman ruins across the river. These ruins are remarkable and have been recently excavated, consisting of a considerable stretch of wall, villas with heating systems intact, a forum, and a theatre, which has the distinction of being the only Roman theatre in England.

CHAPTER V

CAMBRIDGE

THE UNIVERSITY OF CAMBRIDGE has its own distinguishing characteristics, but its history begins later than that of its great rival, and much that has been said in Chapter III about Oxford holds true of Cambridge. The origin of both universities is lost in medieval mists, but the Oxford claim to earlier organization seems to be established, and it may be that the university at Cambridge was founded by a migration of scholars from Oxford. The college system, which is now a distinguishing feature of both, came first into being by the foundation of Merton College at Oxford in 1264; the first Cambridge college, Peterhouse, was not founded till 1284, and its founder declared his intention to establish a society of "studious scholars living according to the rule of the scholars of Oxford called of Merton." The college communities were, from the beginning, secular (i.e., non-monastic) societies, and for some centuries they constituted the entire body of scholars in residence at the University, as, indeed, they do, in the main, today. The University was in favor with the authorities of Church and State, and used its influence with them to take away from the town of Cambridge all control of local administration. The feeling between "town and gown" provoked the same violent conflicts at Cambridge as at Oxford, and with the same results: after a serious riot in 1381, the town franchises were declared forfeit, and the Chancellor of the University took control of the assize of bread and beer and wine, weights and measures, and all matters concerned with the sale of victuals. About the same date Chaucer was putting into verse in the Canterbury Tales an amusing story of how two Cambridge clerks turned the tables upon a miller at Trumpington, a village two miles from the

141

CAMBRIDGE FROM CASTLE HILL

town. They were of Solar Hall, which has been identified with Clare College, and are described by the poet as two "young poor scholars":

> Lively they were and lusty for to play,
> And, only for their mirth and revelry,
> Upon the warden busily they cry
> To give them leave but for a little stound (time)
> To go to mill and see their corn yground.

They were convinced that the miller stole the college corn he was paid to grind, and they pledged their necks to the warden that under their care the corn would not lose even "half a peck." "And at the last the warden gave them leave"—so they set forth with sword and buckler on the college horse, which they tied up while they watched the corn being ground, one at the millstone where it went in, and the other at the hopper where it came out. But the crafty miller set their horse loose and while they were chasing it over the marsh, stole enough of their corn to have a large cake made of it. They were obliged to stay the night, and by the connivance of the miller's wife and daughter, not only had their revenge on the miller but recovered their cake. These sportive students of The Reeve's Tale differ very little from the Oxford scholar who is the clever schemer of the tale which Chaucer's Miller tells at the expense of the Reeve. In both tales the tradesmen are baffled and outwitted by the frailty of their women folk, who turn a welcoming eye to the admiring glances of the younger men.

IN THE FIFTEENTH CENTURY the pious Henry VI with his own hands laid the foundation stone of King's College, for which he had planned buildings on a magnificent scale, carried out only in part by his more worldly successors, the astute Henry VII, and the exuberant Henry VIII. Begun in 1446, the College Chapel was practically completed in 1534 by the erection of an organ screen in which the initials of Henry VIII and Anne Boleyn are enshrined with numerous true-lovers'

KING'S COLLEGE CHAPEL, INTERIOR

knots—an ironical testimony to the inconstancy of the heart of man—and also of the heart of woman, if the accusations of unchastity which cost Anne her head are to be believed. The Chapel is the chief architectural glory of King's, and perhaps of the whole University. As a noble example of the Perpendicular style, it stands comparison with the Henry VII Chapel at Westminster and the St. George's Chapel at Windsor. Wordsworth was a student at St. John's and not a very happy one; as he himself put it, he "was not for that hour, nor for that place." But he was impressed by the beauty of King's Chapel, and immortalized it in one of his best sonnets:

> Tax not the royal saint with vain expense,
> With ill-matched aims the Architect who planned,
> Albeit laboring for a scanty band
> Of white-robed Scholars only, this immense
> And glorious work of fine intelligence!
> Give all thou canst; high Heaven rejects the lore
> Of nicely-calculated less or more;
> So deemed the man who fashioned for the sense
> These lofty pillars, spread that branching roof,
> Self-poised, and scooped into ten thousand cells,
> Where light and shade repose, where music dwells
> Lingering—and wandering on as loath to die;
> Like thoughts whose very sweetness yieldeth proof
> That they were born for immortality.

Both at Eton and at King's College, which for centuries admitted students only from Eton, the pious Henry provided for seventy scholars—no doubt in memory of the seventy elders ordained by Moses and the seventy disciples sent forth by Jesus with "neither purse, nor scrip, nor shoes"; but this scriptural number had already been consecrated by William of Wyckham in his earlier foundations of Winchester School and New College at Oxford. The Eton scholars were required to be "poor," and not possessed of five marks (about $270 in modern value) annually in their own right. But when Henry VIII made inquiry into the revenues of the Cambridge colleges, King's was

KING'S COLLEGE CHAPEL

KING'S BRIDGE

found to be the wealthiest and was taxed accordingly. When Elizabeth visited the University in 1564 King's was her chief place of entertainment. The College welcomed her with a Latin oration, spoken by the Public Orator, and a song of gladness in English by the choir, after which the Queen went to stay in the Provost's Lodge, thanking God "that had sent her to this University, where she, altogether against her expectation, was so received that she thought she could not be better."

IN THE SIXTEENTH CENTURY, which was a time of increasing national wealth, the Cambridge scholars, like those of Oxford, lost the only virtue which Chaucer had ascribed to them in common, that of poverty. Dr. Thomas Lever, Master of St. John's College in the reign of Edward VI, lamented that the poor divinity students are all gone, and the "small number of poor godly diligent students now remaining only in colleges, be not able to tarry and continue their study in the university for lack of exhibition [scholarships] and help." Harrison, in his *Description of England* written in Elizabeth's reign, makes a similar complaint. He notes, moreover, that such bribery prevails in the allotment of scholarships "that poor men's children are commonly shut out and the richer sort received . . . Yet being placed, most of them study little other than histories [stories], tables [chess or checkers], dice, and trifles, as men that make not living by their study the end of their purposes, which is a lamentable hearing. Beside this, being for the most part either gentlemen or rich men's sons, they oft bring the universities into much slander. For, standing upon their reputation and liberty they ruffle and roist [swagger] it out, exceeding in apparel, and haunting riotous company." J. Bass Mullinger, the learned historian of the University of Cambridge up to 1535, gives an amusing picture of what the Cambridge student was supposed to be in the first half of the sixteenth century and what he really was. "The ideal undergraduate contemplated by university and college codes, was a decorous, modest, soberly attired youth who made his college his habitual home. When-

ST. JOHN'S NEW BRIDGE

ST. JOHN'S OLD BRIDGE

ever he issued forth beyond its gates, it was only with the express permission of his tutor or the dean. Unless it devolved upon him as a sizar or poor scholar to perform some menial errand for a superior, he was always accompanied by a fellow collegian. He wore his academic gown, reaching to his ankles, and, unless a scholar, a round cloth cap. His hair was closely shorn and he eschewed tobacco. He loitered neither in the market-place nor in the streets, and shunned alike the lodging-house and the tavern. He attended no cockfights, no baitings of bears or of bulls, no fencing matches; the popular and apparently innocent diversion of quoits could attract him neither as a player nor even as a spectator. He neither bathed nor boated. At the early morning service at five o'clock and again in the evening, he was regularly to be seen in his place in the college chapel. On Sundays, feast-days, and eves, he wore a shining surplice, and although the garment was then five times more costly than at the present day, no narrowness of means could prevent him from possessing it in due newness and cleanness. Not less assiduous would be his attendance on the public lectures in the schools specially designed to assist him in his undergraduate course of study,—a patient attentive auditor from the commencement of each lecture to its close." Actually, the historian concludes, the average undergraduate was "very much what the statutes expressly forbade him to be." He is described by a contemporary observer as one who "cares naught for wisdom, for acquirements, for the studies which dignify human life, for the Church's weal or for politics. He is all for buffooneries, idleness, loitering, drinking, lechery, boxing, wounding, killing."

It is only fair to add that in this dark picture there were some redeeming bright spots. Thomas Nash, writing in 1589, commends "that most famous and fortunate nurse of all learning, St. John's in Cambridge, that at that time [he matriculated at St. John's in 1582] was as a university within itself, shining so far above all other Houses, Halls, and Hospitals [Hostels, i.e., dormitories] whatsoever that no college in the town was

QUEEN'S COLLEGE

QUEEN'S COLLEGE INNER COURT

able to compare with the tithe of her students, having (as I
have heard grave men of credit report) more candles lit in it
every winter morning before four of the clock than the four
o'clock bell gave strokes." Earlier in the century Queen's College had been honored by the residence of the greatest of living

ERASMUS

scholars, Erasmus of Rotterdam. Queen's cherishes his memory
in an Erasmus Tower and an Erasmus Court and still shows to
visitors the rooms which he occupied and in which he received
students eager to follow the new fashion of learning Greek.

TRINITY COLLEGE,
ENTRANCE GATEWAY

TRINITY COLLEGE
FROM THE CLOISTERS

TRINITY COLLEGE FROM THE RIVER

At Cambridge, as at Oxford, the University was regarded as a closed preserve of the Church of England until the second half of the nineteenth century. The Reformation brought to Cambridge troublesome questions of doctrine and discipline, but enriched the colleges by grants of ancient monastic foundations. Henry VIII, as the founder of Trinity College, still stands in stone effigy, over the great gateway. One of its fellows, the Nonconformist leader Thomas Cartwright, and two of his adherents made three sermons in one day in the College Chapel so vehemently inveighing against the ceremonies of the Church that at evening prayer all the scholars except three and the chaplain "cast off their surplices as an abominable relic of superstition." But the Master, Whitgift (afterwards Archbishop of Canterbury under Elizabeth) was a moderate man and kept the Puritan spirit within bounds; Cartwright, after delivering a course of lectures against episcopacy, was deprived of his fellowship and professorship and expelled from the University. The principal "nurseries of Puritanism," as Archbishop Laud complained to Charles I in 1629, were "Emmanuel and Sidney [Sussex] Colleges in Cambridge."

OLIVER CROMWELL was a student of the latter, and JOHN HARVARD of the former. Emmanuel was founded by Elizabeth's Chancellor of the Exchequer, Sir Walter Mildmay, an able administrator and one of the "chief props of the puritanical party." In the College statutes he not only looked to the abolition of episcopacy, but declared that he had founded the College upon the sole principle of sending forth preachers from it, whose business was to preach the Christian religion to the people; which was as much as to say (comments the Cambridge historian) "that the doctrines of the Church of England were not so, and that the people were still heathens." The first fellow named by the founder was guilty of the still more terrible heresy of speaking against the government of colleges by masters as too much of a monarchic character and of saying that they would be governed as well without heads as with them. Queen

Elizabeth, meeting Mildmay one day soon after the foundation of Emmanuel, saluted him with the remark, "So, Sir Walter, I hear you have erected a Puritan foundation." "No, Madam," he replied, "far be it from me to countenance anything contrary to your established laws; but I have set an acorn which, when it becomes an oak, God alone knows what will be the fruit thereof." The acorn became an oak very quickly, for Fuller, who tells the story, wrote in 1634: "Sure I am at this day it hath overshadowed all the University, more than a moiety of the present masters of colleges being bred therein." Ultimately the fruit of the oak was taken across the sea by John Harvard to Cambridge, Mass., where the Puritan principles and the methods of teaching of Emmanuel set up a model for adoption by scores of colleges in the New World. In the official invitation issued by the President and Fellows of Harvard College for the tercentenary celebration of 1936, they acknowledged their debt to the past, "for in building their House of Learning in the New World our ancestors laid claim to a patrimony in the Old. To Emmanuel, the College of John Harvard, and to his University of Cambridge . . . we are bound by lineage and tradition."

JOHN HARVARD'S SIGNATURE IN THE EMMANUEL COLLEGE
ADMISSION BOOK

SIGNATURE FOR M.A. DEGREE IN UNIVERSITY REGISTER

A RETECTION, OR DISCOVERIE OF A FALSE DETECTION:

Containing a true defence of two bookes, intituled, *Synopsis Papismi*, and *Tetrastylon Papisticum*, together with the author of them, against diuers pretended *vntruths, contradictions, falsifications of authors,* corruptions of *Scripture*, obiected against the said bookes in a certaine Libell lately published. *Liber Johannis haiwardi*

Wherein the vniust accusations of the Libeller, his sophisticall cauils, and vncharitable slaunders are displayed.

by Andrew Willet

IOB. 31. 35.

Though mine aduersarie should write a booke against me, would not I take it vpon my shoulder, and binde it as a crowne vnto me?

Augustine cont. Petilian. lib. 3. 2. Non ago vt efficiar homini conuitiando superior, sed errorem conuincendo salubrior: I go not about to be superior vnto him in railing, but sounder in refuting his error.

AT LONDON

Printed by Felix Kyngston, for Thomas Man. 1603.

EMMANUEL COLLEGE, INNER COURT

EMMANUEL COLLEGE, FRONT

The first Master of Emmanuel was a fellow of Christ's College, at which Sir Thomas Mildmay had been educated, and from the accession of Queen Elizabeth the College had been known to be Puritan in its sympathies. It was therefore not surprising that it was chosen by John Milton's parents as a suitable place of education for their son, who from his modest demeanor and almost feminine beauty of feature soon became known as "our fair lady of Christ's." His name is entered in the College books as having paid 10/- for admission from St. Paul's Grammar School, London, on Feb. 12, 1624; the University records show that he took his B.A. degree in 1628 and the M.A. in 1632. In the College garden is still preserved a mulberry tree which, it is said, Milton planted there when he was an undergraduate.

MILTON'S MULBERRY TREE, CHRIST'S COLLEGE

JOANNES MILTON.
Ætatis LXII 1670.

Τὸν περὶ Μῦς᾽ ἐφίλησε,
δίδυ δ᾽ ἀγαθόνσε κακόνσε·
Ὀφθαλμῶν μὲν ἄμερσε,
δίδυ δ᾽ ἡδῖαν ἀοιδήν.

G. Vertue Sculp.

MILTON was the most distinguished of the long line of Cambridge poets. Chaucer's connection with the University seems apocryphal, but there is no doubt about honest Thomas Tusser, who in his autobiographical poem, written at Trinity College, tells us first of his experience of flogging by Nicholas Udall, headmaster of Eton, and then of finding refuge, later in life, at Cambridge:

> From Paul's I went, to Eton sent,
> To learn straightways the Latin phrase,
> Where fifty-three stripes given to me
>   At once I had,
> For fault but small, or none at all,
> It came to pass, thus beat I was;
> See, Udall, see the mercy of thee
>   To me, poor lad!
>
> When gains were gone, and years grew on,
> And Death did cry "From London fly!"
> In Cambridge then I found again
>   A resting plot,
> In college best of all the rest,
> With thanks to thee, O Trinity!
> Through thee and thine, for me and mine
>   Some stay I got.

Christopher Marlowe was at Corpus Christi College, Robert Greene was at St. John's, Spenser, Crashaw and Gray were at Pembroke, Coleridge was at Jesus, Dryden, Cowley, Herbert, Byron, and Tennyson were at Trinity, and Rupert Brooke was at King's. Wordsworth spent a not altogether happy time at St. John's. A. H. Hallam was at Trinity with Tennyson, whose *In Memoriam* recalls their friendship at college:

> I passed beside the reverend walls
>   In which of old I wore the gown;
>   I roved at random through the town,
> And saw the tumult of the halls;

SPENSER

DRYDEN

COLERIDGE

WORDSWORTH

And heard once more in college fanes
   The storm their high-built organs make,
   And thunder-music, rolling, shake
The prophet blazoned on the panes;

And caught once more the distant shout,
   The measured pulse of racing oars
   Among the willows; paced the shores
And many a bridge, and all about

The same gray flats again, and felt
   The same, but not the same; and last
   Up that long walk of limes I passed
To see the rooms in which he dwelt.

Another name was on the door:
   I lingered; all within was noise
   Of songs, and clapping hands, and boys
That crashed the glass and beat the floor;

Where once we held debate, a band
   Of youthful friends, on mind and art,
   And labor, and the changing mart,
And all the framework of the land.

RUPERT BROOKE'S recollections of Cambridge were of a more sportive kind and he records them in more playful style. When he was elected Fellow of King's, he wrote to a friend: *"Jetzt bin ich Professor.* A gray look of learning has already settled on my face. And I wear spectacles." He gave a mock-heroic account of his formal admission to his fellowship—being "churched," he called it, but this is a jest only for those familiar with the Anglican liturgy. "I dined solemnly with very old white-haired men, at one end of a vast dimly-lit hall, and afterwards drank port somnolently in the Common Room, with the College silver, and 17th Century portraits, and a 16th Century fireplace, and 15th Century ideas. The perfect Don, I." His pleasantest recollections were of Grantchester, a little higher up the river than Cambridge, where he bathed in Byron's

GRAY

BYRON

TENNYSON

RUPERT BROOKE

pool and had tea (with a special brand of honey) in the garden of the old vicarage, in which he lived as a graduate student.

> Oh, is the water sweet and cool,
> Gentle and brown, above the pool?
> And laughs the immortal river still
> Under the mill, under the mill?
> Say, is there Beauty yet to find?
> And Certainty? and Quiet kind?
> Deep meadows yet, for to forget
> The lies, and truths, and pain? . . . oh! yet
> Stands the Church clock at ten to three?
> And is there honey still for tea?

A very different academic type from Rupert Brooke was the eighteenth century poet Gray, who took refuge at Pembroke from the unappreciative society of his fellow-students at Peterhouse. The story is thus told by the staid University chronicler: "Gray was extremely fearful of fire, and he had provided for his personal safety a rope ladder contrived in such a manner that he could easily let himself down with it from his window. This he always kept ready in his bedroom. After exhausting every other mode of tormenting their sensitive companion, the students of Peterhouse one night placed exactly under his bedroom window a large tub of water, and then some who were in the plot raised a cry of 'fire' at his door: Gray, terrified by the report of the calamity he most dreaded, rushed from his bed, threw himself hastily out of the window with his rope ladder, and descended exactly into the tub. This practical joke is said to have decided the poet in his design of leaving the college." In verification of this incident the visitor to Peterhouse is shown the iron bar outside of Gray's rooms to which the rope ladder was attached.

PEPYS'S LIBRARY. Henry Dunster, the first President of Harvard College, was a student of Magdalene (pronounced Maudlen, and said to have been so called by its founder, Lord Audley, because the word contained his own name

The condition of the State was thus viz. The Rump after being disturbed by my Lord Lambert. was lately returned to sit again. The Officers of the Army all forced to yield — Lawson. lies still in the River. & Monk is with his Army in Scotland.

PEPYS FACSIMILE WITH TRANSCRIPTION

THE PEPYS LIBRARY

mAUDLEYn). But the real title of this College to fame is its association with Samuel Pepys, who was a student there and left to the College Library the MS. of his famous diary, consisting of six volumes, and containing upwards of three thousand pages closely written in shorthand, which was not deciphered for more than a hundred years. The Bibliotheca Pepysiana, as it is called by request of Pepys, contains all his books (many of them of unique interest) in the same twelve cases of red oak in which they were kept in his own house. The presses, as he called them, are fitted with glass doors, and the tops of all the books on a shelf are brought to the same level by an ingenious mode of binding, the smaller books being "stilted" so that all the books on one shelf appear to be of the same height. They are in the same places and in the same condition as they were left in by Pepys. There are also many valuable engravings and papers, especially about the British Navy. Apparently they were abstracted by Pepys from the official records when he was Secretary of the Admiralty, and though this conduct cannot be defended, it has had the good effect of preserving treasures which might otherwise have been left to molder in the attics or cellars of government offices. Arthur Bryant's recent three-volume biography of Pepys shows that Pepys was something more than the ingenuous diarist and capable government official with whom the reading public on both sides of the Atlantic have long been familiar. As a personal friend of the Duke of York, before he became James II, Pepys not only shared his patron's zeal for the building up of the British navy but became a victim of the anti-Catholic intrigues which were the most exciting feature of political life in the later years of Charles II. The attack upon James brought in its train a vicious onslaught upon Pepys, who was confined to the Tower under a charge of complicity in a Popish plot brought against him by an unscrupulous political adventurer, Colonel John Scott. Pepys established his innocence and incidentally produced evidence which throws astonishing sidelights upon the crook and gangster life of his day.

BACON AS LORD CHANCELLOR

The antechapel where the statue
   stood
Of Newton with his prism and
   silent face,
The marble index of a mind for
   ever
Voyaging through strange seas
   of Thought, alone.
        Wordsworth's *Prelude*

STATUE OF NEWTON, TRINITY COLLEGE CHAPEL

Brilliant as is the list of Cambridge poets, it is outshone by the roll of honor of the Cambridge scientists. To mention three names only—Francis Bacon, student at Trinity in the sixteenth century, Isaac Newton, fellow of Trinity in the seventeenth century, Charles Darwin, student at Christ's College in the nineteenth century,—is to establish a claim which no other educational institution in the world can equal. Yet this was only a beginning. In more recent times we have Sir Francis Galton (Trinity) the investigator of the influence of heredity on intellectual ability; Lord Kelvin (Peterhouse), whose researches into the transmission of electrical current were of great practical service to navigation, submarine telegraphy, and the whole field of electrical engineering; James Clerk Maxwell (Peterhouse and Trinity), first Professor of Experimental Physics at Cambridge, whose researches laid the foundation of wireless and the radio; Sir J. J. Thomson (Trinity) who began, and Lord Rutherford (Trinity), who continued the "splitting of the atom"; Sir Arthur Stanley Eddington (Trinity) and Sir James Jeans (Trinity), who brought the philosophical effects of these investigations within ordinary comprehension. Also from Trinity come the philosophers Bertrand (Lord) Russell, and Alfred North Whitehead (now at Harvard), joint authors of *Principia Mathematica,* and leading interpreters of the relations between philosophy and modern science.

LORD RUTHERFORD   SIR JAMES JEANS

SIR ARTHUR EDDINGTON

Thomas Hardy

CHAPTER VI

THE WESSEX OF THOMAS HARDY

ANCIENT WESSEX, a kingdom lying between the Thames and the Channel, was established by the West Saxons, who came to South Britain up the Solent early in the sixth century and extended their borders from time to time until, in the ninth century, they held the overlordship of all England. Their capital was Winchester, which shared honors with London as the seat of English government till well into the Norman period. Hardy's Wessex made no pretense of reproducing the boundaries of ancient Wessex at any historical period; it was a romantic region, re-created out of his own imagination, though it has definite topographical limits. In a general way, though not exactly, it consists of half a dozen counties grouped about the great plain of Wiltshire with Stonehenge in the center: Oxfordshire (North Wessex) running up to the Thames at Oxford (Christminster); Hampshire and Berkshire (Upper Wessex) going east as far as Windsor (Castle Royal); Somerset (Outer Wessex) extending north west to the Severn; Devon (Lower Wessex) going west to Exmoor and Exeter (Exonbury), with an extension beyond to Launceston (St. Launce's) and Boscastle (Castle Boterel) on the northwest coast of Cornwall; Dorsetshire (South Wessex), the southern county by the sea. For the convenience of the reader these places will be called by the names under which they may be found on any map of this part of England, the names Hardy gave them in his novels being added in brackets.

DORSETSHIRE was Hardy's native county. He was born in the hamlet of Higher Bockhampton, near Dorchester (Casterbridge), an old Roman town, where Hardy went to school and

HARDY MONUMENT AND BIRTHPLACE

HARDY'S FIRST SCHOOL

MAX GATE

served his apprenticeship in an architect's office; when he had established his reputation as a writer of fiction, he built himself a house on the outskirts of Dorchester, Max Gate, in which he lived for the last forty years of his life. But it was not the chance of Hardy's birth in Dorsetshire that made this region the scene of so many romantic incidents in his novels; it was his deliberate choice. Wessex, more than any other part of England, was in his youth remote from great industrial centres and sparsely provided with railways; it was therefore richer than the commercial and manufacturing districts in "those sequestered spots outside the gates of the world where may usually be found more meditation than action, and more listlessness than meditation; where reasoning proceeds on narrow premises, and results in inferences wildly imaginative; yet where, from time to time, dramas of a grandeur and unity truly Sophoclean are enacted in the real, by virtue of the concentrated passions and closely-knit interdependence of the lives therein."

Passing by the early experiments in fiction by which, as Hardy himself says, "he was feeling his way to a method," we get, in *Under the Greenwood Tree,* the first story with which he caught the ear of the public. It is a simple tale, dealing with the love of the village schoolmistress for the village clergyman, slightly complicated by the supersession of the instrumentalists in the village choir by an organ. "The Mellstock Choir" (as the sub-title of the story runs) was the Stinsford Choir, in which Hardy's father and his uncles and more remote ancestors had played fiddles and a barrel organ for a space of a century and more. It was the church which Hardy (somewhat infrequently) attended when he lived at Max Gate, and in the churchyard his heart (by his own request) lies buried, though his ashes rest in Westminster Abbey.

The Mayor of Casterbridge, a novel of Hardy's maturity, with a somewhat sombre plot, contains the best and fullest descriptions of the town of Dorchester, whose streets Hardy so

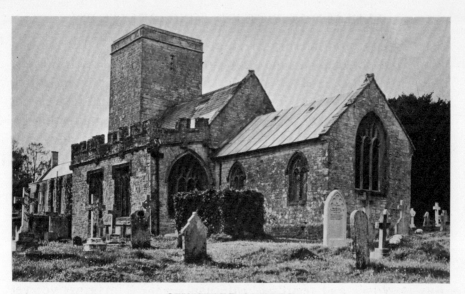

STINSFORD CHURCH

HARDY TOMBS

often trod in the days of his youth. "Casterbridge," he writes, "announced old Rome in every street, alley, and precinct. It looked Roman, bespoke the art of Rome, concealed dead men of Rome. It was impossible to dig more than a foot or two deep about the town fields and gardens without coming upon some tall soldier or other of the Empire, who had lain there in his silent unobtrusive rest for a space of fifteen hundred years. He was mostly found lying on his side, in an oval scoop in the chalk, like a chicken in its shell; his knees drawn up to his chest; sometimes with the remains of his spear against his arm; a fibula or brooch of bronze on his breast or forehead; an urn at his knees, a jar at his throat, a bottle at his mouth; and mystified conjecture pouring down upon him from the eyes of Casterbridge street boys and men, who had turned a moment to gaze at the familiar spectacle as they passed by."

Of the Roman amphitheatre near the town he gives the following account: "The amphitheatre was a huge circular enclosure, with a notch at opposite extremities of its diameter north and south. From its sloping internal form it might have been called the spittoon of the Jötuns. It was to Casterbridge what the ruined Coliseum is to modern Rome, and was nearly of the same magnitude. The dusk of evening was the proper hour at which a true impression of this suggestive place could be received. Standing in the middle of the arena at that time, there by degrees became apparent its real vastness, which a cursory view from the summit at noon-day was apt to obscure. Melancholy, impressive, lonely, yet accessible from every part of the town, the historic circle was the frequent spot for appointments of a furtive kind. Intrigues were arranged there; tentative meetings were there experimented after divisions and feuds. But one kind of appointment—in itself the most common of any—seldom had place in the amphitheatre: that of happy lovers . . . Some old people said that at certain moments in the summer time, in broad daylight, persons sitting with a book, or dozing in the arena, had, on lifting their eyes, beheld the slopes lined with a gazing legion of Hadrian's soldiery as

ROMAN AMPHITHEATRE AS IT WAS 1786

ROMAN AMPHITHEATRE AS IT IS

if watching the gladiatorial combat; and had heard the roar of their excited voices; that the scene would remain but a moment, like a lightning flash, and then disappear. It was related that there still remained under the south entrance arched cells for the reception of the wild animals and athletes who took part in the games. The arena was still smooth and circular, as if used for its original purpose not so very long ago. The sloping pathways by which spectators had ascended to their seats were pathways yet."

Having used the Roman amphitheatre for the secret interview between the Mayor of Casterbridge and his long-lost wife, he uses another ancient monument for Henchard's secret watch of his daughter's meeting with her lover, which brings the story to its tragic close. "A quarter of a mile from the highway was the pre-historic fort called Mai Dun, of huge dimensions and many ramparts, within or upon whose enclosures a human being, as seen from the road, was but an insignificant speck. Hither Henchard often resorted, glass in hand, and scanned the hedgeless *Via*—for it was the original track laid out by the legions of the Empire—to a distance of two or three miles, his object being to read the progress of affairs between Farfrae and his charmer."

The Mayor of Casterbridge is full of touches of local color which it might be interesting to follow upon the spot, but it would be tiresome to detail them here. There are numerous references also to Casterbridge as the county town of South Wessex in the other novels. In *Far from the Madding Crowd* it is to the Casterbridge hiring-fair that Gabriel Oak resorts when he has fallen into poverty. It is there that the lovely Bathsheba comes on market days before she is married, it is through Casterbridge that the betrayed Fanny Robin toils on her dreadful last journey to the poorhouse. But the main action of *Far from the Madding Crowd* takes place at Puddletown (Weatherbury) five miles away. Here we find a fine old church, with a Jacobean choir gallery, in which Gabriel Oak sang, and near the church is a lane leading to Lower Waterston, which has

MAIDEN CASTLE, SOUTH SIDE

MAIDEN CASTLE FROM THE AIR

PUDDLETOWN (WEATHERBURY) CHURCH

THE CHANCEL

been identified with Bathsheba's farmhouse. At any rate it answers to Hardy's description: "By daylight, the bower of Oak's new-found mistress, Bathsheba Everdene, presented itself as a hoary building, of the Jacobean stage of Classic Renaissance as regards its architecture, and of a proportion which told at a glance that, as is so frequently the case, it had once been the manorial hall upon a small estate around it, now altogether effaced as a distinct property, and merged in the vast tract of a non-resident landlord, which comprised several such modest demesnes. Fluted pilasters, worked from the solid stone, decorated its front, and above the roof pairs of chimneys were here and there linked by an arch, some gables and other unmanageable features still retaining traces of their Gothic extraction. Soft brown mosses, like faded velveteen, formed cushions upon the stone tiling, and tufts of the houseleek or sengreen sprouted from the eaves of the low surrounding buildings. A gravel walk leading from the door to the road in front was encrusted at the sides with more moss—here it was a silver-green variety, the nut-brown of the gravel being visible to the width of only a foot or two in the centre."

The pleasant name of Weatherbury, which Hardy gave to the village of Puddletown, really belonged to an old Dorset earthwork, Weatherbury Castle. This was combined with a tower on the Charborough estate (Welland House) near Wimborne (Warborne) to supply the scene of *Two on a Tower*. The Bishop who plays such a curious part in the story has his see at Salisbury (Melchester), but it is safe to say that no such bishop ever existed. The action of *The Trumpet Major* passes almost entirely in or near Weymouth (Budmouth), which also figures in the plot of *The Return of the Native*.

A Pair of Blue Eyes has its scene near the quaint Cornish harbor of Boscastle (Castle Boterel, the old name of the place being Bottreaux Castle). At St. Juliot's (Endelstow) nearby Hardy met, in the sister-in-law of the local clergyman, the young girl who encouraged him to give up ecclesiastical archi-

BOSCASTLE (CASTLE BOTEREL)

tecture for novel-writing, and later became his wife. It is no
wonder that he looked back to it as invested with the glamor
of romance. "The place is preëminently (for one person at least)
the region of dream and mystery. The ghostly birds, the pall-
like sea, the frothy wind, the eternal soliloquy of the waters,
the bloom of dark purple cast, that seems to exhale from the
shoreward precipices, in themselves lend to the scene an atmosphere like the twilight of a night vision."

In each of the three novels last mentioned, there is such a
close tie between the scene and the action that one seems justified
in assuming that the locality suggested the plot. The solitary
tower suggested the young astronomer; the close connection of
George III with Weymouth made the little seaport a suitable
setting for a military novel of the Napoleonic invasion, the
romantic Cornish Coast (and Hardy's successful love adventure
upon it) offered the right atmosphere for the devastation of
masculine hearts wrought by the pretty heroine of *A Pair of
Blue Eyes.*

In *The Return of the Native* the close connection between
place, plot, and characters is even more remarkable. Egdon
Heath is a sort of dark divinity brooding over the action and
involving the actors in inevitable doom. "The untamable, Ish-
maelitish thing that Egdon now was it always had been. Civilization was its enemy; and ever since the beginning of vegetation
its soil had worn the same antique brown dress, the natural and
invariable garment of the particular formation . . . The great
inviolate place had an ancient permanence which the sea cannot
claim. Who can say of a particular sea that it is old? Distilled
by the sun, kneaded by the moon, it is renewed in a year, in a
day, or in an hour. The sea changed, the fields changed, the
rivers, the villages, and the people changed, yet Egdon remained." The attitude of the main characters, Clym Yeobright
and Eustacia Vye, to each other and to their little world, is
determined by their attitude to Egdon Heath. Clym was its
product—permeated with its scenes, with its substance, and with

RAINBARROW

THE QUIET WOMAN

its odors. "His eyes had first opened thereon; with its appearance all the first images of his memory were mingled; his
estimate of life had been colored by it; his toys had been the
flint knives and arrow-heads which he found there, wondering
why stones should 'grow' to such odd shapes; his flowers, the
purple bells and yellow gorse; his animal kingdom, the snakes
and croppers; his society, its human haunters." After he has
seen the world, and known the delights of life in Paris, his heart
turns back to Egdon, and he makes up his mind never to leave
it again. To all this the varying hates felt by Eustacia towards
the heath are the direct opposite. An interloper from the outside world of Weymouth (Budmouth), compelled to constant
contact with Egdon by force of circumstances, her one longing
is to escape from it, and it is yielding to this irrepressible desire of the heart that brings her to destruction.

In editing *The Return of the Native* for the Modern Student's Library (Scribner), I drew attention to Hardy's mastership in controlling the conditions of time and place so as to
concentrate his story and give it the power of a perfect work
of art. His Egdon is not any particular stretch of heath in Wessex, but a combination of various features of the long stretch
of moorland running east from Dorchester almost to Bournemouth (Sandbourne). It is true of all the endeavors of art that
"the best in this kind are but shadows" and must be assisted
by imagination in the mind of the reader as well as of the writer.
Hermann Lea, most diligent of students of Hardy's topography,
comments on the fact that Rainbarrow is not "on the loftiest
ground of the loneliest height that the heath contained . . . the
pole and axis of this heathery world"—it is not in the middle
of the heath by a long way, but nearly on the western edge. To
this the only answer is that, for the purposes of the story, Rainbarrow was where Hardy wanted it. Mr. Lea took quite seriously the novelist's assurance that no one could be said to understand the heath who had not been there from sunset to the
next dawn; he spent a night in the open on Rainbarrow Hill
and says it was a wonderful experience. Any Hardy enthusiast

WOODSFORD FARM

WOODSFORD WEIR

might get a similar impression; or if he were unfortunate in his weather, he might get only a bad cold.

It is certain that Hardy has taken liberties with Nature (as he had a right to do) and has invested Egdon with "the light that never was on sea or land, The consecration and the poet's dream." Of Mistover Knap, where Eustacia Vye lived, no trace can now be found; and if the reader were to walk from where it is supposed to have been to the site of "The Quiet Woman," he would find, not an inn, but a dairyhouse, now known as "The Duck." Blooms-End, the home of the Yeobrights, has been identified with Bhompston Farm, and Alderworth with Affpuddle. More certain is the identification of Shadwater Weir with that over the Frome at Woodsford Meadows, though the latter is further from "The Quiet Woman" in fact than it is in the novel. Still, the agreement between the actual weir and Hardy's description of it is unmistakable: "Shadwater Weir had at its foot a large circular pool, fifty feet in diameter, into which the water flowed through ten huge hatches, raised and lowered by a winch and cogs in the ordinary manner. The sides of the pool were of masonry, to prevent the water from washing away the bank; but the force of the stream in winter was sometimes such as to undermine the retaining wall and precipitate it into the hole. Clym reached the hatches, the framework of which was shaken to its foundations by the velocity of the current. Nothing but the froth of the waves could be discerned in the pool below. He got upon the plank bridge over the race, and holding to the rail, that the wind might not blow him off, crossed to the other side of the river."

Egdon Heath has recently attracted additional attention owing to the tragic death of T. E. Lawrence in a motor-bicycle accident on a moorland road near the cottage he had built on the Heath some years before. He was drawn to the neighborhood by his desire for solitude and the society of Thomas Hardy, whom he liked to consult about his writing, though Hardy protested to his wife that Lawrence was already, in spite of his youth, a master of literary craftsmanship.

T. E. LAWRENCE'S COTTAGE

EGDON HEATH

LAWRENCE'S GRAVE

SHERBORNE ABBEY CHURCH

The Woodlanders is also a novel of environment, but the woodlands do not, like Egdon Heath, dominate the lives of the inhabitants; they merely condition them in a process of mutual reaction. Men made no lasting mark on Egdon Heath; the woodlands are gentler, more submissive, more under human control. The novel conveys in matchless fashion the woodland atmosphere of secluded peace, and the native characters have a resigned acquiescence to fate that goes with their surroundings. Grace Melbury and Giles Winterborne repeat the rôles of Eustacia Vye and Clym Yeobright, but with less violent antagonism. Grace, thanks to her father's wealth, has received the superficial polish of a fashionable education; Giles has stayed in his native village, and his social awkwardness and inexperience lose for him the sweetheart of his childhood; she marries a polite but worthless adventurer who despises and betrays her, while poor Giles dies in miserable frustration. In building up the material surroundings of their story, Hardy did not limit himself to the houses and villages of the particular district which he had chosen as his central scene; his Little Hintock resembles Melbury Osmond more closely than any other village in the neighborhood, but no such grouping of houses as Hardy has created is to be found there, nor is Hintock House nearby, being modeled (as Hardy himself acknowledged) on Turnworth House, near Blandford, a dozen miles away. Great Hintock, where Giles Winterborne was buried, has been identified with Minterne Magna, and Sherton Abbas is undoubtedly Sherborne, whose fine abbey church contains the tombs of two Wessex kings, and was for three centuries the head of a large diocese.

Tess of the D'Urbervilles is not so much a novel of environment as a study in temperament—"a pure woman faithfully presented," as Hardy's sub-title puts it. The surroundings are therefore subordinated to Tess's personal history—the nature she inherited and the circumstances against which she had to contend in a hopeless struggle with fate. The theme was suggested to Hardy by the sight of a handsome country girl driving a broken-down cart, drawn by an even more broken-down horse, and his imagination set to work on what might have been her past and what the future might have in store for her. Like many a humble Wessex peasant she might come of noble lineage, and Hardy chose for her ancestry one of the most distinguished families of Wessex—the Turbervilles, who came over with the Norman Conqueror and by the time of Elizabeth had made themselves masters of the manor of Bere Regis (or as Hardy calls it, Kingsbere) in the valley of the Frome (Froom or Var), the river which flows through Dorchester. They had a house at Wool Bridge (Wellbridge) about ten miles from Dorchester lower down the Frome; in this decayed mansion, now a farmhouse, some of the Turberville portraits are still preserved, but by the beginning of the eighteenth century these and the family tombs in Bere Regis Church seemed all that were left. There were, however, some inhabitants of obscure villages, connections of the family by collateral or illegitimate descent, who preserved the name under such corruptions as Troublefield or Tollafield. Changing these names to D'Urberville and Durbeyfield, Hardy tells much of the history of the Turberville family in Chapter I of his novel and makes frequent reference to it throughout the book. For Tess's birthplace he chose the out-of-the-way village of Marnhull (Marlott) at the head of the vale of Blackmore (Blakemore or Blackmoor), partly, one guesses, because it possessed an old tavern to which he gave the inviting name of The Pure Drop Inn. Of the Vale itself Hardy gives a striking description: "This fertile and sheltered tract of country, in which the fields are never brown and the springs never dry, is bounded on the south by the bold chalk ridge that embraces the prominences of Hambledon Hill, Bulbarrow, Nettlecombe-Tout, Dogbury, High Stoy, and Bubb Down. The traveler from the coast, who, after plodding northward for a score of miles over calcareous downs and corn-lands, suddenly reaches the verge of one of these escarpments, is surprised and delighted to behold, extended like a map beneath him, a coun-

WOOL BRIDGE

ABBOT'S COFFIN

BERE REGIS CHURCH PORCH

try differing absolutely from that which he has passed through. Behind him the hills are open, the sun blazes down upon fields so large as to give an unenclosed character to the landscape, the lanes are white, the hedges low and plashed, the atmosphere colorless. Here, in the valley, the world seems to be constructed upon a smaller and more delicate scale; the fields are mere paddocks, so reduced from this height their hedgerows appear a network of dark green threads overspreading the paler green of the grass. The atmosphere beneath is languorous, and is so tinged with azure that what artists call the middle distance partakes also of that hue, while the horizon beyond is of the deepest ultramarine. Arable lands are few and limited; with but slight exceptions the prospect is a broad rich mass of grass and trees, mantling minor hills and dales within the major." Not far off from Marnhull is the ancient hill town of Shaftesbury (Shaston) and it is to this that Tess makes her way on foot in search of her rich relatives at Pentridge (Trantridge) on the outskirts of Cranborne Chase (The Chase), which is the scene of her first undoing. She returns home to bear an unwished-for child, Sorrow the Undesired, soon laid to rest in the village churchyard, "in that shabby corner of God's allotment where He lets the nettles grow."

So ends the second phase (first "The Maiden," and then "Maiden no More") of Tess's life. The next "The Rally" finds its appropriate setting at a farm Hardy calls Talbothays, situated in the Frome valley not far from Stinsford (Mellstock) Church and Hardy's own birthplace at Upper Bockhampton. The Frome Valley is distant enough from Tess's native village for the fault of her girlhood to be unknown, and she finds encouragement in its broader outlook and more open spaces. "The bird's-eye perspective before her was not so luxuriantly beautiful, perhaps, as that other one which she knew so well; yet it was more cheering. It lacked the intensely blue atmosphere of the rival vale, and its heavy soils and scents; the new air was clear, bracing, ethereal. The river itself, which nourished the grass and cows of these renowned dairies, flowed not like the

CRANBORNE CHASE

streams of Blackmoor. Those were slow, silent, often turbid; flowing over beds of mud into which the incautious wader might sink and vanish unawares. The Var waters were clear as the pure River of Life shown to the Evangelist, rapid as the shadow of a cloud, with pebbly shallows that prattled to the sky all day long. There the water-flower was the lily; the crow-foot here. Either the change in the quality of the air from heavy to light, or the sense of being amid new scenes where there were no invidious eyes upon her, sent up her spirits wonderfully. Her hopes mingled with the sunshine in an ideal photosphere which surrounded her as she bounded along against the soft south wind. She heard a pleasant voice in every breeze, and in every bird's note seemed to lurk a joy."

She meets and marries Angel Clare, and a new chapter of life is opened up. They spend their strange honeymoon in the old Turberville mansion at Wool Bridge, where Hardy places the odd adventure of Angel Clare's walking in his sleep and putting Tess into the Abbot's stone coffin, which is really at Bindon Abbey, some distance away. But one must not bind the wings of a novelist bent on romantic detail, and inclined to weave into his narrative every circumstance that will arouse sympathy for his heroine. Tess's confession of her betrayal by Alec D'Urberville is followed by Angel Clare's flight to Brazil, and Tess's long penance at Bridport (Port Bredy) and Flintcomb Ash Farm, her futile journey as far west as Beaminster (Emminster) to seek help from Angel Clare's parents, the death of her father, the reduction of the family to the bitterest straits of poverty, and her ultimate capitulation to Alec D'Urberville for the second time. Angel Clare, returning to England and his better self, comes in search of her and traces her to Bournemouth (Sandbourne)—evidently chosen by Hardy as a fitting scene for his heroine's final degradation. "This fashionable watering-place, with its eastern and its western stations, its piers, its groves of pines, its promenades, and its covered gardens, was, to Angel Clare, like a fairy place suddenly created by the stroke of a wand, and allowed to get a little dusty.

GREY'S BRIDGE

LOWER BOCKHAMPTON BRIDGE

An outlying eastern tract of the enormous Egdon Waste was close at hand, yet on the very verge of that tawny piece of antiquity such a glittering novelty as this pleasure city had chosen to spring up. Within the space of a mile from its outskirts every irregularity of the soil was prehistoric, every channel an undisturbed British trackway; not a sod having been turned there since the days of the Cæsars. Yet the exotic had grown here, suddenly as the prophet's gourd; and had drawn hither Tess. By the midnight lamps he went up and down the winding ways of this new world in an old one, and could discern between the trees and against the stars the lofty roofs, chimneys, gazebos, and towers of the numerous fanciful residences of which the place was composed. It was a city of detached mansions; a Mediterranean lounging-place on the English Channel; and as seen now by night it seemed even more imposing than it was. The sea was near at hand, but not intrusive, it murmured, and he thought it was the pines; the pines murmured in precisely the same tones, and he thought they were the sea."

Clare finds Tess living under D'Urberville's protection, and when Tess learns that D'Urberville has again beguiled her by falsehoods she stabs her seducer to the heart. She flees with Angel Clare, first through the New Forest to Salisbury (Melchester) and afterwards over Salisbury Plain to Stonehenge, where she is discovered and gives herself up to the police. In the final scene, after the black flag signifying her execution has been hoisted on Winchester gaol, Hardy comments: "'Justice' was done, and the President of the Immortals (in Æschylean phrase) had ended his sport with Tess. And the D'Urberville knights and dames slept on in their tombs unknowing."

Jude the Obscure, the last of Hardy's great novels, is a study in the psychology of sex, but he plans its scenes as carefully as if it were a play. Part I (Jude's childhood and youth) is cast at the village of Fawley Magna (Marygreen) near Wan-

STONEHENGE

WINCHESTER CATHEDRAL

tage (Alfredston), in North Wessex, apparently because it was the ugliest hamlet Hardy could find in the neighborhood of Oxford (Christminster), which is always the spiritual centre of the story. "Many of the thatched and dormered dwelling-houses had been pulled down of late years, and many trees felled on the green. Above all, the original church, hump-backed, wood-turreted, and quaintly hipped, had been taken down, and either cracked into heaps of road-metal in the lane, or utilized as pig-sty walls, garden seats, guard-stones to fences, and rock-eries in the flower-beds of the neighborhood. In place of it a tall new building of German-Gothic design, unfamiliar to English eyes, had been erected on a new piece of ground by a certain obliterator of historic records who had run down from London and back in a day."

In Part II the scene shifts to the university city which is the New Jerusalem of Jude's dreams. In Part III he is working as a stonemason at Salisbury (Melchester) Cathedral. Part IV passes at Shaftesbury (Shaston), "the ancient British Palladour," of whose fallen glories he gives us three pages of description, culminating in the local boast that "Shaston was remarkable for three consolations to man, such as the world afforded not elsewhere. It was a place where the churchyard lay nearer heaven than the church steeple, where beer was more plentiful than water, and where there were more wanton women than honest wives and maids." In Part V Jude has got into such a tangle with the two women who complicate his life that he is constantly on the move, sometimes ashlaring a hotel at Bournemouth (Sandbourne), sometimes a museum at Dorchester, sometimes as far down as Exeter (Exonbury), sometimes at Basingstoke (Stoke-Barehills), later at Newbury (Kennetbridge). In Part VI Jude returns to Oxford, to die alone, deserted by both the women who had shared and ruined his life, and murmuring, "Let the day perish wherein I was born."

Beside the Wessex novels proper, which Hardy lists under the title "Novels of Character and Environment," he wrote

SHAFTESBURY

LULWORTH COVE

"romances and fantasies," including *The Well Beloved* as well as *A Pair of Blue Eyes, The Trumpet Major,* and *Two on a Tower,* and three other novels, *Desperate Remedies, The Hand of Ethelberta,* and *A Laodicean,* which he classes as "Novels of Ingenuity." In *The Well Beloved* the scene shifts between London and Portland (The Isle of Slingers), *The Hand of Ethelberta* has its action at Wareham (Anglebury), Corfe (Corvesgate) Castle, Swanage (Knollsea) and Bournemouth (Sandbourne). *A Laodicean* is placed at Dunster (Markton), a quaint old town with an interesting inn, the Luttrell (Lord Quantock) Arms, Dunster (Stancy) Castle, and the neighboring town of Taunton (Toneborough). In *Desperate Remedies,* Hardy's first published novel, the scene is divided between Weymouth (Budmouth), Lulworth (Lulstead) Cove, and Ringstead (Ringsworth), on the Coast, and further inland, Tolpuddle (Tolchurch), and other places in the Frome valley, some of them not far from Upper Bockhampton, where Hardy was born.

If one had time and patience, it would not be difficult to trace many other references to actual places in Hardy's novels, and also in the poems and short stories. His knowledge of the whole district was amazing, even when we take into consideration that he was born in it and spent within its borders the greater part of his life; and if one wishes to see the England of the romantic past, one cannot do better than follow in his footsteps.

SALISBURY CATHEDRAL

EXETER CATHEDRAL CHAPTER HOUSE

CHAPTER VII

KING ARTHUR AND THE WEST

IN DORSETSHIRE there are few literary and historical interests that Hardy does not present in his novels, short stories or poems, but in the neighboring counties there are naturally many places or associations with places which did not serve his immediate purpose. He was quite aware that in making Stonehenge the scene of Tess's capture and Winchester the scene of her execution, he was dealing only with one aspect of these ancient fanes. He writes at the end of the novel of the view of Winchester from the great West Hill when Angel Clare and 'Liza-Lu climbed it on that fateful morning:—"The prospect from this summit was almost unlimited. In the valley beneath lay the city they had just left, its more prominent buildings showing as in an isometric drawing—among them the broad cathedral tower, with its Norman windows and immense length of aisle and nave, the spires of St. Thomas's, the pinnacled tower of the College, and, more to the right, the tower and gables of the ancient hospice, where to this day the pilgrim may receive his dole of bread and ale. Behind the city swept the rotund upland of St. Catherine's Hill; further off, landscape beyond landscape, till the horizon was lost in the radiance of the sun hanging above it. Against these far stretches of country rose, in front of the other city edifices, a large red-brick building, with level gray roofs, and rows of short barred windows bespeaking captivity, the whole contrasting greatly by its formalism with the quaint irregularities of the Gothic erections. It was somewhat disguised from the road in passing it by yews and evergreen oaks, but it was visible enough up here. The wicket from which the pair had lately emerged was in the wall of this structure. From the middle of the building an ugly

THE EAST PROSPECT OF THE CITY OF WINCHESTER.

flat-topped octagonal tower ascended against the east horizon, and viewed from this spot, on its shady side and against the light, it seemed the one blot on the city's beauty. Yet it was with this blot, and not with the beauty, that the two gazers were concerned."

The modern visitor who climbs the hill to view the city as Angel Clare and 'Liza-Lu saw it might be disappointed, for the ugly tower from which the black flag was hoisted to announce the death of Tess is now embowered with trees so that it can hardly be seen, but the cathedral, the church spires, the pinnacled tower of the College which William of Wyckham founded, and the ancient hospice, "where to this day the pilgrim may receive his dole of bread and ale" are still as Hardy saw them. William of Wyckham's school and its association with New College have already been discussed in our chapter on Oxford. The "ancient hospice" is the Hospital of St. Cross, where the "Wayfarer's Dole" of bread and ale is still served to everyone who asks for it; it was the original of the foundation in *The Warden* by Anthony Trollope, who was at Winchester School, though the Barchester Series (of which *The Warden* forms a part) was conceived by the novelist in Salisbury Close. The Cathedral goes back to the seventh century, and is interesting not only for its history and architectural magnificence, but as the burial place of Jane Austen, to whose memory a tablet and a window are dedicated; she died in a modest house on College Street which may still be seen. She was born at the neighboring village of Steventon, of which her father was rector, and spent the first four years of the nineteenth century at Bath, which often appears in her novels. *Pride and Prejudice* and *Sense and Sensibility* were begun at Steventon and recast at another village not far from Winchester, Chawton, where she wrote *Mansfield Park, Emma,* and *Persuasion.* The Lyme of *Persuasion* is Lyme Regis near Axminster. *Northanger Abbey* was written at Steventon and sold to a Bath bookseller in 1803, but did not appear till after her death.

TINTAGEL

WINCHESTER boasts among its lesser glories the Round Table of King Arthur's Knights, which is said to have been there since the thirteenth century; but that is not far back for Winchester, which was a British settlement and a Roman town before it became the capital of Wessex in 519. King Arthur (if he existed at all) also goes back to the sixth century, and in the fifteenth century Caxton adduced "the Round Table at Winchester" as one of the proofs in contradiction of the opinion, held even then, "that there was no such Arthur, and that all such books as [have] been made of him be feigned and fabled." Modern opinion inclines rather to the latter view, for the first historical mention of Arthur (if such it can be called) is in the History of the Britons compiled in the ninth century by the Welsh Nennius, who states that Arthur fought twelve great battles against the Saxons and in the twelfth, at Mount Badon, slew 960 men with his own hand. Where Mount Badon lies, the experts are not agreed—perhaps at Badbury Rings in Dorsetshire—some point where, after the Roman withdrawal, the Saxons were slowly pushing the Britons back to the southwest peninsula of Devon and Cornwall.

KING ARTHUR may have been a historical leader of the Britons or merely a traditional hero of romance,—it really does not greatly matter: it is in tradition and romance that he lives. According to tradition enshrined for English speaking readers in Malory and Tennyson, he was born at Tintagel Castle in Cornwall, the son of King Uther, and held his court at Camelot, which has been variously identified with Camelford (six miles from Tintagel), Glastonbury, Winchester, and Cadbury Castle (in Somersetshire), which anciently was called Camalat or Camellek, and did not lose that name till the eighteenth century. Drayton describes the river Ivel which flows not far away as

The nearest neighboring flood to Arthur's ancient seat,
Which made the Briton's name through all the world so great.
Like Camelot what place was ever yet renowned?
Where, as at Caerleon, oft he kept the Table Round,

> Most famous for the sports at Pentecost so long,
> From whence all knightly deeds and brave achievements sprung.

Cadbury certainly provides a British hill-fort, thirty acres in extent, and one finds a river Camel there as well as at Camelford in Cornwall. The Somersetshire Camel has a bridge over it called Arthur's Bridge, but the bridge at Camelford is called Slaughter Bridge; there was a battle between the Britons and the Saxons there in 823—but that was long after King Arthur's time. At Cadbury Castle, says Sir Edward Strachey, "Arthur's Well still springs from the hillside, and if Arthur's Hunting Causeway in the field below, Arthur's Round Table and Arthur's Palace within the camp, cannot still, as of old, be pointed out to the visitor, the peasant girl will still tell him that within the charmed circle they who look may see through golden gates a king sitting in the midst of his court."

There is less agreement about the place of Arthur's death than about that of his birth. The Cornish say it is at Dozmare Pool on Bodmin Moor, but the Somerset folk hold by the neighborhood of Glastonbury. Tennyson, with characteristic vagueness and characteristic beauty of phrase, speaks of

> the sunset bound of Lyonnesse
> A land of old upheaven from the abyss
> By fire, to sink into the abyss again;
> Where fragments of forgotten peoples dwelt,
> And the long mountains ended in a coast
> Of ever-shifting sand, and far away
> The phantom circle of a moaning sea.

So far, it sounds like Cornwall; but then the scene shifts

> to a chapel nigh the field,
> A broken chancel with a broken cross,
> That stood on a dark strait of barren land.
> On one side lay the Ocean, and on one
> Lay a great water, and the moon was full.

Finally, Arthur says he is going

GLASTONBURY VILLAGE

GLASTONBURY ABBEY

To the island-valley of Avilion,
Where falls not hail, or rain, or any snow,
Nor ever wind blows loudly; but it lies
Deep-meadowed, happy, fair with orchard lawns
And bowery hollows crowned with summer sea.

To many this seems to point to the Western Isles of Celtic and Classical mythology; but again the Somerset advocates cry out "Glastonbury." Caxton's first proof of Arthur's historicity was that "ye may see his sepulchre in the monastery of Glastonbury." So one might, in the fifteenth century, but it was a tomb built in 1276 by Edward I, who, it is said, took the skulls of Arthur and Guinevere for himself and his Queen, Eleanor of Castile. But when the bodies were sought in Edward III's reign, they could not be found. They were said to have been discovered, after the great fire which swept the abbey in the twelfth century, by Henry II, who marveled at Guinevere's yellow hair; but then Almesbury, in Wiltshire, puts in a claim, for tradition has it (is it not written in Caxton's Malory?) that after her disgrace she became a nun at Almesbury and died there. So, as Tennyson puts it, "all the mind is clouded with a doubt."

GLASTONBURY has a legend of its own, of greater antiquity than the Arthurian legend, and, in its origin, independent of it. According to this, Joseph of Arimathea in A.D. 31, brought to Britain the dish in which the paschal lamb had been served at the Last Supper and in which at the Crucifixion the precious blood of Christ had been gathered. He had been warned of God in a dream that he should erect a shrine wherever, when he put his staff into the earth, it broke forth into buds; this happened at Glastonbury, and up to the time of the Commonwealth the tree was shown in the abbey grounds, but the ruthless Puritans hacked it down; two offshoots are, however, still to be seen (*Cratægus Præcox*), which still bloom yearly when "the time draws near the birth of Christ." At the Reformation the abbot was executed on the tor nearby, and the abbey fell into ruins, which were used by the neighborhood as a stoneyard till, in the present century, they were bought for the Church of England and put in the hands of trustees, who admit visitors on payment of a small fee. The Abbey represents the oldest Christian foundation in Britain, if not in the world, dating from the first church built by Joseph and his companions of "wood and wattle-work."

It was in the twelfth century that the story of Joseph of Arimathea was combined with the Arthurian legend in "The Holy Grail," which we now know best in Tennyson's version:

> The cup, the cup itself, from which our Lord
> Drank at the last sad supper with his own.
> This, from the blessed land of Aromat—
> After the day of darkness, when the dead
> Went wandering o'er Moriah—the good saint
> Arimathæan Joseph, journeying brought
> To Glastonbury, where the winter thorn
> Blossoms at Christmas, mindful of our Lord.
> And there awhile it bode; and if a man
> Could touch or see it, he was healed at once,
> By faith, of all his ills. But then the times
> Grew to such evil that the holy cup
> Was caught away to heaven, and disappeared.

With this legend was united the figure of the virgin knight, Sir Galahad, who sang, "My strength is as the strength of ten, Because my heart is pure":

> So pass I hostel, hall, and grange;
> By bridge and ford, by park and pale
> All-armed I ride, whate'er betide,
> Until I find the Holy Grail.

A skeptical Oxford don asked, "What would he do with the Holy Grail, if he found it?", but it is useless to visit Glaston-

AVEBURY CIRCLE

bury without faith. If the visitor is possessed by the modern
spirit of scientific criticism, he would spend his time to better
advantage in Wiltshire at Stonehenge or Avebury. Of these
ancient British, or (rather) prehistoric monuments, Stonehenge
is the most spectacular, on account of the size and number of
the monoliths left in position. Some of the stones are of a kind
of granite not found in the neighborhood, and were apparently
brought by land or across the Severn estuary from the Prescelly
Hills in Wales. A further distinction is that several of the upright stones have "imposts" or lintels morticed to them, and
in the middle of the concentric rings and horseshoes lies the
altar stone. The altar, the entrance, the opening of the inner
horseshoe, and a stone outside the circles all face the sunrise at
the summer solstice, with a slight deviation which has enabled
astronomers to conjecture a date of about 1700 B.C. It was
probably a temple of the sun, though the numerous barrows in
the neighborhood indicate that it was also a burial place. The
barrows are outside the circular earthwork surrounding the
stone circles.

THE AVEBURY CIRCLE is another prehistoric monument of
a religious character; according to old Aubrey, it surpasses
Stonehenge "as much as a cathedral doth a parish church."
It is a massive circular earthwork enclosing the village of Avebury, about three quarters of a mile in circumference and about
fifteen feet high, fringed on its inner side with a large circle
of great stones and two smaller circles nearer the centre. There
are fewer stones standing than at Stonehenge, but some of them
are very large, one weighing about 60 tons. Originally there
were 100 huge stones in the largest circle, as well as many of
great size in the two smaller circles, but many of them have been
broken up in the last three or four centuries for building purposes in the village. Avebury as it stands, with its neighboring
barrows, is regarded as unique, not only in Britain but in
Europe, and is now undergoing careful and prolonged investigation.

STONEHENGE FROM THE EAST

STONEHENGE FROM THE WEST

PREHISTORIC MONUMENTS abound in this western country, especially on Dartmoor. Some of them are by the roadside, like the hut circles and stone avenues at Merrivale Bridge, near Princetown (where the great convict prison is, the scene of Galsworthy's *Escape*). Oftener they are away in the moorlands, and need to be approached on foot; but all one needs is an ordnance map, stout boots, strong legs, and a good heart—perhaps a pocket compass too, in case a mist should come on and make the stone avenues and circles look even more eerie than they do in the sunshine. It is well to know beforehand a bit about the terms the antiquarians use and the different chronological periods to which the monuments are (somewhat conjecturally) assigned. Furthest back we have the Old Stone Age, a matter of some 25,000 or even 100,000 years ago, for in these remote periods, about which little can be known, the scientists are generous with time. Most of us would be content to start with the New Stone Age, which began about 5,000 years ago and ended about 2000 B.C. In this age man had begun to make dwellings for himself instead of living in caves, he had greatly improved the clumsy flint tools and weapons used by his ancestors, he practised agriculture and kept domestic animals, and had learnt how to make pottery and baskets and to weave cloth. Next comes the Bronze Age, when the use of metal had been acquired, and finally the Iron Age, which begins about 500 or 600 B.C. After that we get into the period of Roman history, and Cæsar tells us that the Belgæ, a Celtic race who used iron, crossed from the Continent into Britain about 250 B.C.

From the Neolithic or Bronze Age come the pit dwellings and hut circles, round holes in the ground, surrounded by a bank of earth with a gap serving as an entrance to a dugout for which boughs and skins might serve as roof; sometimes, as at Grim's Pound on Dartmoor near Chagford, these may be gathered into a village within an enclosure of earth. Other earthworks more obviously meant for defense against human enemies, are found at the tops or on the sides of hills; a good example is Maiden Castle, near Dorchester, "a great oval, 900 yards long and 400 yards wide, surrounded by three and in places four lines of terrific ramparts, with immensely complicated entrances."

Beside the earthworks for habitation or defense, there are burial mounds, or barrows, of two main types, the long and the round. The long barrows are older—before the Bronze Age—and usually contain no metal except perhaps gold. G. M. Boumphrey recommends the long barrow to those who desire a permanent abode for their last resting place. He says of two long barrows he came across on Gossage Down: "They have already lasted anything from 5,000 to 10,000 years and will still be there perhaps, when churches and cathedrals and even pyramids are far more likely to have been despoiled or crumbled away." It may be a good idea, but it would be well to choose a site for one's long barrow sufficiently removed from the big commercial centers; a building contractor with a steam-devil at his disposal would make short work of a long barrow.

The characteristics of the long barrows are described by Canon Greenwell, who spent many years of his life in examining them, both in the north and the west of England, thus: (1) they are very long in comparison with their breadth; (2) they are almost always placed with their long diameter running east and west; (3) the east end is both broader and higher than the west; (4) the interments are generally at the east end; (5) the bones are frequently disjointed and sometimes lie apart from each other, as if the bodies had been dismembered, and the flesh removed from the bones before they were placed in the mound; nor, in many cases, are all the bones of the body present; (6) the skulls are eminently and invariably long-headed; (7) weapons and implements are of rare occurrence; (8) pottery of any kind is infrequent, and when it does occur is fragmentary and plain in pattern. The slaughtering of slaves, captives, and even wives, and the practice of cannibalism at the funeral feast have been suggested as explanations of some of these characteristics, but this is unproven; it is certain that the builders of the long barrows were long-headed people, that they lived a long time ago, and that their civilization was of a primitive character.

The round barrows are of the Bronze Age and are classified as of three shapes: "bowl" (inverted), "bell," and "disc" barrows; these usually contain ashes, the bodies having been cremated. The round-headed people who built them had pottery of a more advanced and ornamental type, and had arrived at a higher stage of civilization. Dr. Rolleston, after examining the numerous skulls Canon Greenwell had collected, called the long-headed people Silurians and associated them with the black-haired type, short of stature, still found living in the west of England; the round-headed people he called Cimbric, and thought they migrated from Denmark in the pre-historic period; but more recent scholars are inclined to call them simply "beaker-folk," in allusion to the prevalent form of their pottery, which is found in many parts of western Europe and is widely distributed in prehistoric Britain. It is a cause of confusion to the ordinary visitor that the same site, to say nothing of museums, often contains samples of pottery from various ages, piled one upon the other in successive layers. At Avebury, for instance, the "beaker-folk" put up the stone circles and the great rampart of earth, using the antlers of the wild red deer for picks and the shoulder blades for shovels; for stone work they used flints and stone axes imported from North Wales or even from the Rhine valley. But below their pottery are found bowls of a characteristic shape and ornamentation known as "Neolithic B," and below that again, is found "Neolithic A, a type of fine, smooth, unornamented, round-bottomed pottery, apparently imitating the forms of leather vessels."

Of the stone monuments, the simplest form is the solitary pillar or menhir. When these are set in a straight line or parallel lines, it is called an alignment or avenue. If the line is curved, and the stones form a circle, it is a cromlech. Two upright stones joined by a flat stone or stones at the top form a dolmen. When the long barrow of the Neolithic period is combined with roofed upright stones forming a chamber surrounded by earth, it is said to be "chambered." If the rain and wind remove the earth, they leave a small dolmen.

SIR FRANCIS DRAKE

DARTMOOR has antiquities of more recent interest than these rather grim reminders of life and death in a remote past. There are the open channels of clear water known as "leets," which Sir Francis Drake constructed for the water supply of Plymouth some three centuries and a half ago. Drake was born on the moor near Tavistock, and lived for some years at Buckland Abbey, now the estate of Lord Seaton, where there is still preserved Drake's drum, of which Sir Henry Newbolt wrote:

Drake he was a Devon man, an' ruled the Devon seas,
  (Capten, art tha sleepin' there below?)
Rovin' tho' his death fell, he went wi' heart at ease,
  An' dreamin' arl the time o' Plymouth Hoe.
"Take my drum to England, hang et by the shore,
  Strike et when your powder's runnin' low;
If the Dons sight Devon, I'll quit the port o' Heaven,
  And drum them up the Channel as we drummed them long ago."

Perhaps the best memorial of Drake is Plymouth Hoe (one of the finest of sea promenades), where he was playing at bowls with the other Elizabethan admirals when news was brought of the sighting of the Spanish Armada off the coast, and he declared that there was time to finish the game and whip the Spaniards afterwards. Others of the Elizabethan seadogs are connected with this western country. Sir Walter Raleigh was born at Hayes Barton near East Budleigh and smoked his pipe at two or three other places in Devon, at one of which his fire is said to have been extinguished by an over zealous maidservant with a tankard of ale. His half-brother, Sir Humphrey Gilbert, who planted the British flag in Newfoundland, was born at Greenway on the Dart. Of less savory memory is Sir John Hawkins, the founder of the Bristol slavetrade, and not at all ashamed of it himself, for he took a negro bound with a cord as his coat of arms. The greatest fire-eater of them all was Sir Richard Grenville, whose "last fight of the Revenge at sea" is commemorated in Tennyson's stirring ballad founded upon the no less stirring prose accounts of Raleigh and Linschoten:

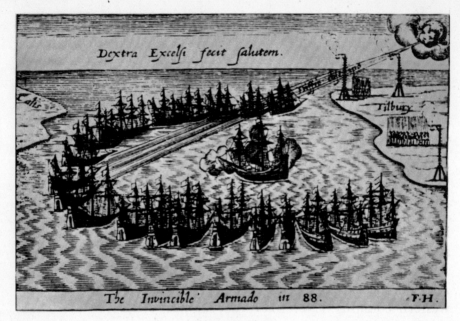

THE ARMADA

THE ARK ROYAL

So Lord Howard passed away with five ships of war that day,
Till he melted like a cloud in the silent summer heaven;
But Sir Richard bore in hand all his sick men from the land
Very carefully and slow,
Men of Bideford in Devon
And we laid them on the ballast down below:
For we brought them all aboard,
And they blest him in their pain, that they were not left to Spain,
To the thumb-screw and the stake, for the glory of the Lord.

This militant Protestantism, now somewhat out of fashion, is well represented in Kingsley's *Westward Ho,* but for sheer adventure and enterprise it is better to read the *Voyages* of Richard Hakluyt, who was a clergyman at Bristol before he was Archdeacon of Westminster. But the greatest attraction of these western counties is the natural charm of their scenery. For a good walker, there is no more delightful experience than to track down to its source a little stream like the Meavy, with a climb here and there to a neighboring Dartmoor tor to get a wider view. Of the greater rivers—and they are not so very large—the Dart, the Tamar, and further west the Fal afford scenes of quiet beauty among the best that England has to offer.

One of these secluded spots, the Doone Valley on Exmoor, has been immortalized by Richard Blackmore in *Lorna Doone,* and Sir Arthur Quiller-Couch has made the little Cornish port of Fowey his own by *Troy Town* and other novels. Hugh Walpole's father was a tutor at the Chancellor's School at Truro, and Cornwall was the scene of the three "studies in place" with which the novelist began his literary career, beside giving hints for *The Cathedral.* Compton Mackenzie also lived in Cornwall and used his knowledge of its romantic coast in *Carnival.* It was to a Cornish cottage at Zennor, near St. Ives, that D. H. Lawrence retired during the Great War with his German wife and sang German songs with her to the accompaniment of a cracked old piano, bringing down upon their heads the suspicions of their neighbors and the unwelcome attentions of the police.

NETHER STOWEY in Somerset offers, however, the classic instance of the clash between literary interests and military stupidity. S. T. Coleridge took a cottage there in the summer of 1797 and was joined by the Wordsworths at Alfoxden Manor near by. The story is best told in Coleridge's own words: "The dark guesses of some zealous *Quidnunc* met with so congenial a soil in the grave alarm of a titled Dogberry of our neighborhood, that a spy was actually sent down from the government *pour surveillance* of myself and friend. There must have been not only abundance, but variety of those 'honorable men' at the disposal of Ministers; for this proved a very honest fellow. After three weeks' truly Indian perseverance in tracking us, (for we were commonly together), during all which time seldom were we out of doors but he contrived to be within hearing,—and all the while utterly unsuspected; how indeed *could* such a suspicion enter our fancies?—he not only rejected Sir Dogberry's request that he would try yet a little longer, but declared to him his belief, that both my friend and myself were as good subjects, for aught he could discover to the contrary, as any in His Majesty's dominions. He had repeatedly hid himself, he said, for hours together behind a bank at the sea-side, (our favorite seat), and overheard our conversation. At first he fancied, that we were aware of our danger; for he often heard me talk of one *Spy Nozy* [Spinoza—then pronounced Spī-noza] which he was inclined to interpret of himself, and of a remarkable feature belonging to him; but he was speedily convinced that it was the name of a man who had made a book and lived long ago. Our talk ran most upon books, and we were perpetually desiring each other to look at *this,* and to listen to *that*; but he could not catch a word about politics. Once he had joined me on the road; (this occurred as I was returning home alone from my friend's house, which was about three miles from my own cottage) and, passing himself off as a traveler, he had entered into conversation with me, and talked of purpose in a democrat way in order to draw me out. The result convinced him that I was no friend of Jacobism."

BATH, rather than Nether Stowey or Glastonbury, is, however, the main centre of literary and historical interest in the County of Somerset. No ancient monument in England is in a better state of preservation than the Great Bath (82 feet by 40) which was built in the first century of the Christian Era by the Romans at *Aquæ Solis* (the Waters of the Sun) and excavated only about half a century ago. The hot springs themselves are of timeless antiquity, unaffected by weather or other conditions on the earth's surface, for they come up from sources probably volcanic, about a mile below; to such waters the scientists give the name "juvenile," for they are ever young, being derived not from superficial drainage, but from the union of elements in the depths of the earth. They contain a large amount of radio-active material, and their curative properties have been recognized for two thousand years or more. The bottom of the Great Bath consists of about sixty tons of lead plate, obtained by the Romans from mines in the Mendip Hills, and the baths themselves are built of stone hewn in the neighborhood about the same date. One may lounge in the recesses where the Romans rested or chatted while they were cooling off (the lead pipe from the cold spring is still in place), the Roman central heating system may be inspected, and the waste waters are discharged through the Roman culvert, its masonry still sound and firm.

The Saxons captured *Aquæ Solis* in 577 and gave the city its present name. In the Middle Ages it was famous for its cloth, as Chaucer's Wife of Bath reminds us, for she surpassed even the weavers of Ypres and of Ghent, then the great centres of the manufacture of cloth in the Low Countries, from which the Flemings came to develop the English textile industries. Its fame as a social and literary centre was established in the eighteenth century by the enterprise of the merchant-philanthropist Ralph Allen (the original of Fielding's Squire Allworthy), the architectural genius of John Wood and his son, and the organizing ability of Beau Nash, who founded the Royal Mineral Water Hospital and the Pump Room Orchestra, both of them still active in providing medical care and musical enter-

ROMAN BATH

tainment. To mention the celebrities who visited the Spa or made their homes in Bath would be to make an index of the great historical and literary names of the eighteenth and the early nineteenth century. To take only one of the architectural triumphs of John Wood senior—the Circus, photographed on the following page—at No. 7-8 lived the Earl of Chatham, who when he was still William Pitt was Bath's member of Parliament; at 13 dwelt David Livingstone, the African explorer and missionary; at 14, Lord Clive, who won India for the British Empire; at 22, Major André, of unhappy renown; at 24, Thomas Gainsborough, the artist; at 27, Sir Edward Parry, the Arctic explorer. It was at Bath that Sheridan wooed and won the beautiful Elizabeth Linley, who lies buried with her no less beautiful sister in Wells Cathedral; and Mrs. Siddons made her first triumphs on the stage at the Bath Theatre. Fanny Burney the novelist lived in Guy Street, and lovers of Jane Austen, who lived for some years at Bath, will recall how often she makes the city, its streets and places of entertainment, the scenes of her story, especially in *Persuasion*. Dickens also wrote at Bath and made some of the most amusing incidents of *Pickwick* happen there. Goldsmith was there, Johnson and Burke, Wordsworth and Southey, Landor and Scott. Henry Fielding, the father of the modern English novel, was a Somerset man, born at Sharpham near Glastonbury. He was very often a guest at Ralph Allen's magnificent estate, Prior Park, on the outskirts of Bath, and Ralph Allen, beside suggesting one of the principal characters of *Tom Jones,* gave Fielding financial help so that he might have leisure for the composition of his masterpiece. *Tom Jones* was largely written in the little room with an oval window (*œil de bœuf*) in the upper front of Widcombe Manor, shown on the following page by the courtesy of the present owner, the well-known English novelist, Horace Annesley Vachell. It has been handed down as a credible tradition that the owner in Fielding's time of this fine estate and his lovely daughter gave the novelist hints for Squire and Sophia Western.

THE CIRCUS, BATH

WIDCOMBE MANOR

WELLS CATHEDRAL, WEST FRONT

Bath was for a time the head of a diocese and its Abbey Church, whose tower overlooks the Roman Bath, is a noble edifice; but it had long ago to yield ecclesiastical precedence to its more secluded and stately neighbor, Wells Cathedral, which overwhelms by its magnificence the secular interests and frivolous amusements of mankind. Its western front has long been admired as the finest existing example of Early English architecture, and the 300 figures with which it is adorned (half of them life-size) afford some of the best examples of medieval sculpture, illustrating Scripture history from Genesis and general history up to the reign of Henry III. The Vicars' Close has since 1348 been the residence of the vicars choral and is unique in its unbroken history since that date, with its two rows of fourteenth century "chambers," its chapel and dining hall, with their ancient furniture and stained glass windows. The Bishop's Palace has all the features that one would expect the stronghold of a medieval prelate to possess—a massive iron-bound gate, a drawbridge with wheel and chains still in working order, and a real moat with swans in it. They know, it is said, how to ring the bridge bell when they think the hour for supper has arrived, and what more than that could be expected even of episcopal swans?

CHAPTER VIII

SEVERN AND WYE

THE SEVERN and the Trent form a natural division of Britain, as the Romans found when they first seriously attempted the conquest of the island at the end of the first half of the first century of the Christian era. As the English schoolboy's rhyme puts it:

> B.C. 55 and B.C. 54
> Julius Cæsar arrived and did nothing much more.
> Next, Claudius coming, A.D. 48,
> First made of Britannia a real Roman state.

Filling up these bald outlines in his recent book, *Along the Roman Roads,* G. M. Boumphrey tells us that in A.D. 43 the Emperor Claudius sent four legions, the Second, Ninth, Fourteenth, and Twentieth, who landed near Dover, concentrated at Canterbury, forced the Thames and the Medway and made Colchester the Roman headquarters. From Colchester followed a combined drive with the Twentieth and Fourteenth legions working northwest in the centre, the Second on the left flank, working west, and the Ninth on the right working north. In about three years they had reached the line of the Severn and the Trent, and just within it they built the Fosse Way. "It is an amazing road in itself—over 200 miles long and practically dead straight from end to end. It runs from Axminster in Devonshire to Lincoln and never gets more than six miles off a straight line drawn between the two." Along this line the Roman general, Osorius Scapula, built a string of forts and, proceeded to consolidate his gains. It was not the limit of Roman occupation, the line of which was advanced away up to the north in later

CHEPSTOW CASTLE

RAGLAN CASTLE

years, but it was the limit of assimilation. Northwest of the line of the Severn and the Trent, "Britain was never completely Romanized in all the 365 years of Roman occupation that followed. Below this line, the richer Britons no doubt came to consider themselves—and to be considered—Romans." Below this line hundreds of Roman villas have been dug out of the soil; very few beyond it.

In the thousand years that followed the Roman withdrawal, successive waves of invasion—Saxon, Danish, Norman—broke upon Britain, but served only to drive the Britons back beyond the line of the Severn, where they remained irredeemably Welsh—"foreigners." At the beginning of the fifteenth century, Shakespeare's Owen Glendower could boast:

> Three times hath Henry Bolingbroke made head
> Against my power; thrice from the banks of Wye
> And sandy-bottomed Severn have I sent him
> Bootless home and weather-beaten back.

When Glendower and his fellows in rebellion proceed to divide Britain among themselves, it is along the lines of the ancient river boundaries. Mortimer says:

> The archdeacon hath divided it
> Into three limits very equally:
> England, from Trent and Severn hitherto,
> By south and east is to my part assigned:
> All westward, Wales beyond the Severn shore,
> And all the fertile land within that bound,
> To Owen Glendower: and, dear coz, to you
> The remnant northward, lying off from Trent.

It is along the valleys of Severn and Wye—the "marches" of the Welsh border—that we find the strongest castles, and that mixture of populations which happens in all borderlands. Monmouth is an English county for civil purposes, but ecclesiastically it is Welsh, and in the fifteenth century it was accounted

TINTERN ABBEY

MONNOW BRIDGE

and Briton and Briton and Saxon. Shrewsbury is finely situated
in a bend of the Severn which makes it almost an island; first
as a Saxon and then as a Norman outpost, it saw much violent
conflict. Not far to the southeast is Wroxeter, with its Roman
remains of the city of Uriconium, from which a Roman road
(Watling Street) formerly ran north to Chester and south to
Church Stretton and Leintwardine (Bravonium) on the Welsh
border. It was Uriconium and its burning by the West Saxons
in 584 that suggested to Housman the thought of the permanence
of Nature and the evanescence of all the works of man. The
Wrekin, which dominates the valley of the Severn, remains, but
Uricon, once the capital of Britannia Secunda, has left hardly
a trace:

> Then, 'twas before my time, the Roman
>   At yonder heaving hill would stare:
> The blood that warms an English yeoman,
>   The thoughts that hurt him, they were there. . . .
>
> The gale, it plies the saplings double,
>   It blows so hard, 'twill soon be gone:
> Today the Roman and his trouble
>   Are ashes under Uricon.

Shrewsbury still has two bridges across the Severn—one
called the English bridge, leading almost due east, and the other
the Welsh bridge, northwest into Wales. This simple fact is
used by Housman to suggest the psychological division which
must often have arisen in the minds of the offspring of a mingling of the two races:

> High the vanes of Shrewsbury gleam
> Islanded in Severn stream;
> The bridges from the steepled crest
> Cross the water east and west.
>
> The flag of morn in conqueror's state
> Enters at the English gate:

ENGLISH BRIDGE, SHREWSBURY

WELSH BRIDGE, SHREWSBURY

The vanquished eve, as night prevails,
Bleeds upon the road to Wales.

It was at Shrewsbury early in the fifteenth century, when
Henry IV was contending with his rebellious nobility, that
Harry Hotspur was killed on the battlefield—but not by Fal-
staff, who claims, in Shakespeare's play, to have fought with
him "a long hour by Shrewsbury clock"—the jest lying in the
fact that the battle was fought some four miles outside the town.
There was more fighting in the Civil War, when Charles I
made Shrewsbury his headquarters; and after the Restoration
Farquahar made Shrewsbury the scene of his comedy *The Re-
cruiting Officer,* which he wrote in the Raven Hotel and dedicated to "all friends round the Wrekin," which is still a popular
Shropshire toast.

MARY WEBB is as completely the Shropshire novelist as
Sheila Kaye-Smith is the novelist of Sussex. She was born at
Cressage, a few miles down the Severn from Shrewsbury, and
when she and her husband, a Cambridge graduate who did
not like teaching, took to their garden for a living, they sold
their produce at Shrewsbury market. "All the novels except
Precious Bane," says Stanley Baldwin, "are set in the hill country of southwest Shropshire, between the Clee Hills and the
Breiddens, and between Shrewsbury and Ludlow. The scene
of *Precious Bane* is the country of north Shropshire meres—
the Ellesmere district, but the dialect is that of south Shropshire." Her description of a hiring fair at Lullingford market
is a companion piece to Hardy's description of a similar scene
at Dorchester (Casterbridge), when Gabriel Oak, having lost
his flock of sheep, offers himself, shepherd's crook in hand,
for employment, and finds no man to hire him. "At one end of
the street stood from two to three hundred blithe and hearty
laborers waiting upon Chance—all men of the stamp to whom
labor suggests nothing worse than a wrestle with gravitation,
and pleasure nothing better than a renunciation of the same.

Among these, carters and waggoners were distinguished by having a piece of whip-cord twisted round their hats; thatchers wore a fragment of woven straw; shepherds held their sheep-crooks in their hands; and thus the situation required was known to the hirers at a glance." Mary Webb's description came later but it will stand comparison with the work of the master. "The long row of young folks, and some not so young, who were there to be hired, began near our stall. Each one carried the sign of his trade or hers. A cook had a big wooden spoon, and if the young fellows were too gallus she'd smack them over the head with the flat of it. Men that went with the teams had whips, hedgers a brummock, gardeners a spade. Cowmen carried a bright tin milk pail, thatchers a bundle of straw. A blacksmith wore a horseshoe in his hat, and there were a tuthree of them, for a few big farms would club together and hire a blacksmith by the year. Shepherds had a crook and bailiffs a lanthorn, to show how late they'd be out and about after robbers." Mary Webb's picture is at once more detailed and more varied, and her characteristic use of dialectical expressions in the narrative gives it an added charm.

IN THE CITY OF WORCESTER (pronounced Wooster), lower down the Severn Valley, the visitor will find much to engage his attention. Near the Cathedral is the Diocesan Registrar's Office in which is preserved the contract of marriage between William Shakespeare and Anne Hathaway (1582). True to its motto of "loyal in peace and war," the city has statues of Charles I and Charles II at the entrance to its old Guildhall, while over the doorway is the carved head, nailed by the ears, of Cromwell, who defeated the Royalists in their last stand nearby in 1651. A more modern interest (though it goes back to 1750) is Royal Worcester porcelain, noted for its exquisite finish and color. Worcester shares with Hereford and Gloucester (pronounced Gloster) the glory of the Triennial Musical Festival, in which the choirs of the three cathedrals combine.

WORCESTER

WORCESTER BRIDGE AND CATHEDRAL

BERNARD SHAW

THE MALVERN HILLS in the distance round out the picturesque situation of Worcester in the Severn Valley. They can be
more easily climbed from Great Malvern, famous as a watering
place and as the scene of the Malvern Dramatic Festival, at
which some of Shaw's and Drinkwater's latest plays had their
first production. Of the Malvern Hills the highest is the Wor-
cestershire Beacon (1396 ft.), which may be climbed in half an
hour from Great Malvern and commands a magnificent view.
Slightly lower is the summit of the Herefordshire Beacon, but
it has the additional attraction of being the site of a British
camp, in which Caractacus was defeated and captured by the
Romans in A.D. 71. It is doubtless to this tradition that John
Masefield, the poet laureate, refers in his verses entitled "On
Malvern Hill":

> Spearman and charioteer and bowman
>   Charged and were scattered into spray,
> Savage and taciturn the Roman
>   Hewed upwards in the Roman way.
>
> There—in the twilight—where the cattle
>   Are lowing home across the fields,
> The beaten warriors left the battle
>   Dead on the clansmen's wicker shields.
>
> The leaves whirl in the wind's riot
>   Beneath the Beacon's jutting spur,
> Quiet are clan and chief, and quiet
>   Centurion and signifer.

Masefield was born in the neighboring town of Ledbury,
midway between the Severn and the Wye, and he has repeatedly
acknowledged that much of his poetry is founded on Herefordshire material. The best of his stories in verse, *The Everlasting
Mercy* and *The Widow in the By Street,* were both based upon
memories of his early life in Ledbury, the first on a quarrel
between two poachers, and the second on the building of a railway line on the site of an old canal. The country on the Glouces-

JOHN MASEFIELD   JOHN DRINKWATER

MALVERN

tershire side of Ledbury gave him the setting of *Reynard the Fox*. "On Eastnor Knoll" and "Tewkesbury Road" are again recollections of the scenes of his boyhood, and "London Town" tells us how his heart still lies "In the comely land of Teme and Lugg, and Clent and Clee, and Wyre . . . In the hearty land, where I was bred, my land of heart's desire."

The Tragedy of Nan is founded on a story told to Masefield "as something that had occurred in Kent about a century ago." "As I am ignorant of Kentish country people," Masefield adds, "I placed the action among a people and in a place well known to me . . . at an imaginary farmhouse in the hamlet of Broad Oak, on the brink of the Severn near Newnham-on-Severn in Gloucestershire." On a peculiarity of the Severn tide, Masefield contributes an explanatory Note:—"The Severn is a tidal river in which a Bore or Eager forms at high water, owing to the channel being too narrow for the volume of water rushing in. The tide, being constricted or pent in, is heaped up, so that it advances much as I describe it, in a wall of water across the river, two or three feet higher than the level of the stream up which it comes. As it advances, it roars like an express train. The certainty and fatality of its march make it a very noble and very terrible sight."

It was at Newnham-on-Severn that Henry II and Strongbow embarked for the conquest of Ireland in 1171; and Berkeley Castle, on the other side of the river and a little lower down, was the scene of the murder of Edward II in 1327, which gave Marlowe the subject of his great tragedy—"the summit of his art." It preceded Shakespeare's *Richard II*, and, many have thought, surpasses it. "The death-scene of Marlowe's King," wrote Charles Lamb, "moves pity and terror beyond any scene, ancient or modern, with which I am acquainted." Berkeley is still one of the best preserved examples of a feudal castle, with moat and bridge, keep and gateway, all complete as they stood six centuries ago.

BERKELEY CASTLE

GLOUCESTER FROM THE DOCKS

GLOUCESTER CATHEDRAL, NORTH AISLE OF THE NAVE

GLOUCESTER is architecturally the finest of this Wye-Severn group of cathedrals, and its history is of interest. It was founded as a nunnery by King Osric in the seventh century, became a college for secular priests in the ninth, was converted into a Benedictine monastery in the eleventh, made a cathedral church by Henry VIII, and saved by the intervention of Cromwell from the destruction which most of the cathedrals underwent at the hands of Puritan troopers. The fortunes of the ecclesiastical structure were made by the burial there of Edward II, murdered at Berkeley Castle, and the erection in the church of a magnificent tomb to his memory by his son, Edward III. This became a famous shrine and out of the pockets of innumerable pilgrims came the contributions which in the fourteenth and fifteenth centuries provided the funds for the building of the Cloisters, with their wonderful fan vaulting, the West front and South porch, the stately central tower, and the beautiful Lady Chapel.

The city has memories going back to British and Roman times, perpetuated in the plan of its four principal streets, Northgate, Southgate, Eastgate, and Westgate, branching at right angles from the ancient central cross; opposite the West Gate the Protestant martyr, Bishop Hooper, was burnt in 1555. Gloucester has more recent religious associations with George Whitefield, the eighteenth century reformer, who was born here and died at Newburyport, Massachusetts, and with Robert Raikes, who opened the first Sunday School here in 1780. The New Inn vies with The Feathers at Ledbury in antique charm.

TEWKESBURY lies east of the Severn on Shakespeare's Avon, which joins the greater river after passing through the beautiful Vale of Evesham. Tewkesbury is a quiet little town, the Nortonbury of Mrs. Craik's Victorian novel, *John Halifax Gentleman*. In 1471 it was the scene of a decisive battle in the Wars of the Roses and of the cold-blooded slaughter of the young Lancastrian Prince of Wales, Edward, son of Henry VI, by the fierce Yorkist brothers. The Abbey Church has a brass, marking his last resting place. His assassination was a favorite theme with Shakespeare, who not only dramatizes the incident in *3 Henry VI* but twice recalls it in *Richard III*. The first is in the dream of Clarence, in which he imagines himself as already transported to "the kingdom of perpetual night:"

> Then came wandering by
> A shadow like an angel, with bright hair
> Dabbled in blood; and he shrieked out aloud,
> "Clarence is come: false, fleeting, perjured Clarence,
> That stabbed me in the field by Tewkesbury.
> Seize on him, Furies, take him unto torment!"

The second is at the end of the play, when, on the eve of the battle of Bosworth Field, the Ghost of Prince Edward appears to Richard and says to him:

> Let me sit heavy on thy soul tomorrow!
> Think how thou stabb'dst me in my prime of youth
> At Tewkesbury. Despair, therefore, and die!

TEWKESBURY ABBEY CHURCH

STRATFORD-ON-AVON

CHAPTER IX

THE SHAKESPEARE COUNTRY

STRATFORD has undergone few changes since the time of Shakespeare. The principal change is that it has become the centre of attraction for pilgrims who come from all over the world to worship at the shrine of the poet whose name is the symbol of unity for all English-speaking people, and whose genius gave to dramatic literature its highest and most abiding expression. Stratford still gives us the best attainable idea of the conditions under which Shakespeare was born and grew to manhood. It is still a small town (population 11,616 at the census of 1931) and it has not encroached to any great extent upon the country from which Shakespeare's parents came to live in the small house now dignified with the name of "The Birthplace". Shakespeare must have been from the beginning a country boy and in constant touch with country life, for his father, the son of a farmer, was himself a dealer in agricultural produce. Yet Shakespeare was born in a town and familiar with the conditions and vagaries of municipal government as it was conducted in the days of Elizabeth. In 1552 his father was fined a shilling for keeping a dunghill before his door. But John Shakespeare none the less held the honorable office of ale-taster for the town and became in due course an alderman and "high bailiff", though his career was not one of uninterrupted success, for in 1592 he was reported to be absenting himself from church because he was afraid of being arrested for debt.

When Shakespeare was passing through the second phase of his childhood:

> First the infant,
> Mewling and puking in the nurse's arms,

THE BIRTHPLACE

THE BIRTHPLACE RESTORED

And then the whining school-boy, with his satchel
And shining morning face, creeping like snail
Unwillingly to school,

it was undoubtedly to Stratford Grammar School that he went.
The knowledge of classical literature that he shows in his poems
and plays is such as would be gained from a grammar school
education of that period—Latin grammar (*Merry Wives of
Windsor* IV. i. and *Love's Labour's Lost* IV. ii. and V. i.) and
a first-hand acquaintance with the easier Latin authors—the
poems of Ovid and the tragedies of Seneca and the comedies of
Plautus; but the W.S. carved on a desk in the Grammar School
and still shown to admiring tourists is as likely to have been
the work of an unknown William Smith as of William Shakespeare. The tradition that Shakespeare became a country schoolmaster is more probable than the other tradition that he was
forced to leave Stratford through being concerned in a poaching
expedition to the neighboring deer park of Sir Thomas Lucy;
but it is likely enough that he was more interested in outdoor
life in the country than in his work at school.

The river Avon, which flows through Stratford on its way
to Severn and the sea, must have afforded to the boy Shakespeare
many forms of sport—swimming, fishing, fowling and boating.
He gives us a lifelike picture of such an English stream in *Two
Gentlemen of Verona,* though the scene of the play is in Italy:

The current that with gentle murmur glides,
Thou know'st, being stopped, impatiently doth rage;
But when his fair course is not hinderèd,
He makes sweet music with the enamelled stones,
Giving a gentle kiss to every sedge
He overtaketh in his pilgrimage;
And so by many winding nooks he strays,
With willing sport, to the wild ocean.

Venus and Adonis, though written years after Shakespeare
left Stratford, shows that in manhood his memory was still full

of the country sights and sounds of his youth. He writes of country sports—hawking, the hunting of the boar, the deer, the fox, the hare "poor Wat", the hot "scent-snuffing hounds", the spirited horse:

> Round-hoofed, short-jointed, fetlocks shag and long,
> Broad breast, full eye, small head, and nostril wide,
> High crest, short ears, straight legs and passing strong,
> Thin mane, thick tail, broad buttock, tender hide—

things seen and noted by the poet's eye. He knew the kind of talk that went on when country people met together, talk of kinsfolk and neighbors, the price of bullocks and ewes (*2 Henry IV* III. ii). But he knew the townspeople too, for a little higher up the Avon were Warwick, Kenilworth, and Coventry—not too far for an enterprising youth, on horseback or even on foot. Coventry was famous for its plays, especially for the Miracle Plays acted at Whitsuntide by the local Guilds. It is something more than a coincidence that made Shakespeare place the amateur theatricals mentioned in *Two Gentlemen of Verona* IV. iv. at Whitsuntide, or, as he calls it, Pentecost:

> At Pentecost,
> When all our pageants of delight were played,
> Our youth got me to play the woman's part
> And I was trimmed in Madame Julia's gown
> Which servèd me as fit, by all men's judgments,
> As if the garments had been made for me.

The subject of the play, thus recalled, was "Ariadne passioning for Theseus' perjury and unjust flight", and in *A Midsummer Night's Dream* (in which Theseus is a character) the play presented has as its theme the misfortunes of another pair of classical lovers, Pyramus and Thisbe. The actors are "hardhanded men" who work at a craft for a living—Quince, a carpenter; Snug, a joiner; Bottom, a weaver; Flute, a bellowsmender; Snout, a tinker; and Starveling, a tailor. They are grotesquely comic characters, as are the village curate and the village schoolmaster who with the aid of a country bumpkin, a fantastical Spaniard and his page, present a pageant of the Nine Worthies and other rustic impersonations to the courtiers of *Love's Labour's Lost.* At such ambitious but unskilled amateurs Shakespeare could afford to poke fun as curiosities of the current craze for theatrical performances; when he deals with the professionals, as in "the play within the play" in *Hamlet,* he is more respectful, and even sympathetic.

At Kenilworth Castle, the seat of the royal favorite Robert Dudley, Earl of Leicester, there were in 1575 memorable entertainments, including fireworks and dramatic performances, at which Queen Elizabeth herself was present and had to repress the too ardent solicitations of Leicester to accept the offer of his hand in marriage. Shakespeare may have heard of the festivities as a boy or even been present at them in person, but it seems most likely that he read of them in a contemporary pamphlet written by George Gascoigne. In any case the reference to them in *A Midsummer Night's Dream* II. i. seems unmistakable:

> *Oberon.* My gentle Puck, come hither. Thou remember'st
> Since once I sat upon a promontory,
> And heard a mermaid on a dolphin's back
> Uttering such dulcet and harmonious breath,
> That the rude sea grew civil at her song,
> And certain stars shot madly from their spheres
> To hear the sea-maid's music.
> *Puck.*   I remember.
> *Oberon.* That very time I saw, but thou couldst not,
> Flying between the cold moon and the earth,
> Cupid all armed: a certain aim he took
> At a fair vestal throned by the west,
> And loosed his love-shaft smartly from his bow,
> As it should pierce a hundred thousand hearts;
> But I might see young Cupid's fiery shaft
> Quenched in the chaste beams of the watery moon,
> And the imperial votaress passed on,
> In maiden meditation, fancy free.

KENILWORTH

Noblemen such as Leicester and his brother Ambrose Dudley, Earl of Warwick, kept in their retinue professional actors, musicians, and other entertainers, who occupied the minstrels' gallery or a stage set up in the great hall for banquets or similar festivities. When not thus engaged, they were allowed to travel about for their own profit, and became known as "Lord So-and-so's Servants". When complaint was made of the conduct of these wandering companies of players, a statute was passed (1583) that to escape from being treated as "rogues and vaga-bonds", all such should be registered as in the service of some nobleman, who should hold himself responsible for their good behavior. In some cases the noble patron took an active interest in the welfare of his "servants", in other cases the connection seems to have been merely nominal. During Shakspeare's youth dramatic performances were given by such traveling companies at Stratford, probably in the Guildhall, and it may have been with one of them that he made his way to London.

Shakespeare's name is entered on the baptismal register of the Collegiate Church of the Holy Trinity at Stratford under date April 26, 1564. This is the only recorded date in his biography up to the granting in 1582 at Worcester (see p. 254) of a special license for his marriage to Anne Hathaway. The rest of his youth is a matter for inference and conjecture. The date of his birth, like the date of his marriage, is not precisely known; children were usually baptized soon after birth (in fear of eternal damnation), and a special license was as a rule speedily followed by marriage. In Shakespeare's case the baptismal date of his firstborn child, Susanna, in 1583 affords a natural explanation for his hasty marriage at eighteen to a woman some years older than himself. The actual place of his marriage is as unknown as the actual date; it was not at Stratford, and the popular choice is for Luddington Church, about two miles from Anne Hathaway's cottage at Shottery. The connection of this cottage with Anne Hathaway rests entirely on tradition, but it belongs to that period, has a pretty garden, and makes a charming walk from Stratford through fields where

TRINITY CHURCH, STRATFORD

ANNE HATHAWAY'S COTTAGE

the romantically inclined may imagine themselves as tread-
ing in the footsteps of the lovelorn poet. The next fact
to be recorded is the birth of twins (Hamnet and Judith) in
1585. Hamnet died in 1596; the two daughters (Susanna and
Judith) married and survived Shakespeare but their children
left no inheritor to his fame.

Shakespeare had no other children and various circumstances lead us to suppose that he left Stratford for London in
1584-5. When we next hear of him in 1595 he is an established
actor and dramatic author, with an excellent professional reputation and an acknowledged standing in London society. He was
a member of the Lord Chamberlain's Company when it played
before the Queen in 1594, and his plays began to be published,
first anonymously and afterwards with his name on the title
page, probably without his consent. He published his erotic
poem *Venus and Adonis,* with a dedication to Lord Southampton, a dashing young nobleman of the time, in 1593, and a more
assured and intimate dedication accompanied the publication of
Lucrece in 1594. Southampton may not have been the admired
young friend of Shakespeare's *Sonnets,* but there is no improba-
bility in the tradition that Southampton gave him a thousand
pounds for a purchase he had a mind to—the purchase being
New Place, which Shakespeare bought in 1597. It was the
finest house in Stratford, built about a century before by Sir
Hugh Clopton, who also built the stone bridge across the Avon
called by his name, rebuilt the nave of the Guild Chapel, and
adorned with his family tombs the Lady Chapel (now called the
Clopton Chapel) of Holy Trinity Church. Shakespeare, soon
after acquiring New Place, formally established his standing as
a gentleman by having a coat of arms assigned to his father, and
further secured his social position by buying the local tithes and
other property.

On the accession of James I he became one of the King's
Players with the rank of groom of the Chamber and walked in
the coronation procession in scarlet cloth provided by the royal
bounty. In 1611, at the height of his dramatic achievement, he

NEW PLACE

CLOPTON BRIDGE

TRINITY CHURCH CHANCEL

SHAKESPEARE'S TOMB

retired to New Place and died there five years later, of a fever contracted (the gossips said) through drinking too hard at a merry meeting with his fellow poets and dramatists Ben Jonson and Michael Drayton. He was buried on the north side of the chancel of Holy Trinity Church, with a monument in the adjacent wall, consisting of an arch with two black marble columns supporting a cornice and entablature. The arch contains a contemporary bust of colored wood, done by a London artist Jansen or Johnson, presumably at the request of the family. Though not much can be said for its artistic merit, the bust is the only authenticated portrait of Shakespeare except the engraving prefixed to the collected edition of his plays published seven years after his death (the First Folio).

SHAKESPEARE'S BUST

Mr. WILLIAM
SHAKESPEARES

COMEDIES,
HISTORIES, &
TRAGEDIES.

Published according to the True Originall Copies.

Martin Droeshout sculpsit London.

LONDON
Printed by Isaac Iaggard, and Ed. Blount. 1623.

CHAPTER X

THE NORTHEAST COAST

THE NORTHEAST COUNTIES from the Tweed to the Thames are less known than those of the South and the West because of their natural situation. They face the inhospitable North Sea and the less developed communities behind it; the southern counties look toward the older centres of civilization on the European Continent, and the western shires look out to the New World across the Atlantic. The eastern shores are as a rule less interesting from a scenic point of view, so that they are less visited. Yet they have many places of great natural beauty and have been the scene of important historical events, with notable literary associations.

It is an open question whether England was Christianized from the North or the South. After the Roman conquest had been consolidated by the building of the Roman Wall from the Solway Firth to the Tyne, the capital of the Roman province was not Colchester in the South or Lincoln in the Midlands, but York, which was visited by the Emperor Hadrian in 120 A.D. Two Roman emperors in the next two centuries died at York, and it was there that Constantine the Great was proclaimed emperor in 306.

YORK was the capital of the Anglian kingdom of Deira, stretching from the Humber to the Tyne, and it was captives from Deira, offered for sale as slaves in the market-place at Rome, who about 586 A.D. attracted the attention and stirred the missionary zeal of Gregory, Abbot of the monastery of St. Andrew, and later Pope. We know this from his famous series of puns, recorded in Bede's *Ecclesiastical History*. Passing one day through the Forum and noticing these fairhaired youths, he

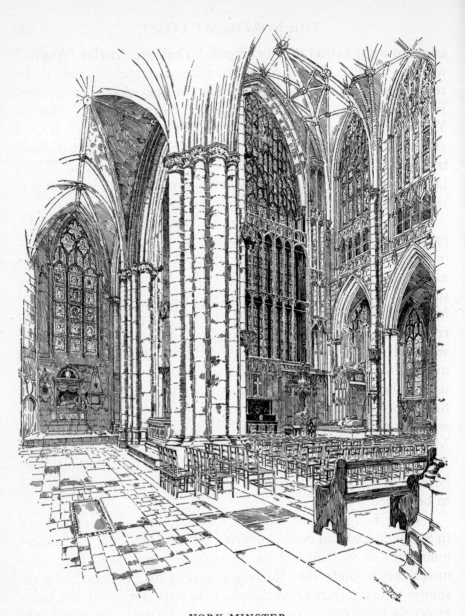

YORK MINSTER

asked to what nation they belonged. "They are Angles (Angli)" was the answer. "They have the faces of angels (angeli)" he responded "and should be co-heirs of the angels in heaven. From what province do they come?" "From Deira." "Deira. Yea, verily, they shall be saved from the wrath (*de ira*) of God and called to the mercy of Christ. How is the king of that country named?" "Ælla." "Then must Alleluia be sung in Ælla's land." He actually set out to Christianize the English, but was recalled to Rome for duties regarded as more important.

When Gregory became Pope, he bethought him of the fair-haired youths, and Augustine was sent to convert the heathen of Kent, as already noted. Augustine in his turn sent Paulinus as a missionary to the northern heathen. At first the mission was successful. Bede tells us that Edwin, King of Northumbria, listened doubtfully to the ministrations of Paulinus till an aged councillor said, "Our life, O King, is like that of the sparrow which flies for a moment from the night into the firelight and out again into the darkness. If these men have anything to tell us of a better life to come, let us give heed to what they say." So Edwin was baptized at York on Easter Day 627 by Paulinus, who set up a wooden church on the site of the now famous Minster. But when Edwin was defeated and slain by the heathen Penda, King of Mercia, Paulinus fled back to the South, and became Bishop of Rochester; his work in the North seemed to be wiped out.

A new King of Northumbria, Oswald, who had been an exile in Scotland and had been converted to Christianity at the famous monastery of St. Columba on the island of Iona, sent there for a missionary to undertake the conversion of his new realm. In response to his appeal came Aidan, who built a church and monastery on Lindisfarne (later called Holy Island), separated only at high tide from Bamborough, Oswald's capital. As Sir Walter Scott puts it in *Marmion,* improving upon a local rime:

> Over the sands twice every day,
> The Pilgrims to the Shrine find way;

WHITBY ABBEY

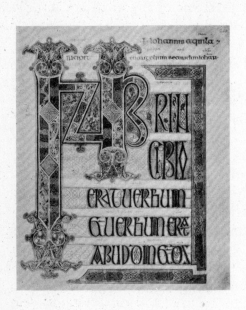

LINDISFARNE GOSPEL MS.

> Twice every day the waves efface
> Of staves and sandalled feet the trace.

There in July, 1935, the Archbishop of York and other bishops and minor clergy (some of whom crossed barefoot over the sands) held a service to commemorate the landing of Aidan thirteen centuries ago. The Archbishop of York preached the commemoration sermon and re-asserted the claim of the great English church historian Lightfoot that, "Iona succeeded where Rome had failed. Not Augustine but Aidan was the true Apostle of England. Augustine was the apostle of Kent, but Aidan was the Apostle of England."

We may leave these questions of credit to the ecclesiastical authorities concerned. If the Celtic Church for the time being scored a signal success, its influence did not long prevail. An issue soon arose about the right date of celebrating Easter, as to which the usage of the Celtic Church differed from that of Rome. The matter was settled by a great Synod, held at Whitby in 664, over which Oswy, then King of Northumbria, presided. He decided the argument in his own way. "Is not St. Peter the keeper of the keys of heaven?" he asked the Celtic representatives, and they assented. "Was he not the chief of the Apostles?" They could not deny it. "Then I will decide for St. Peter, lest haply when I come to the gates of heaven, they should be closed against me, if he is my adversary who is the keeper of the keys."

More was implied in this decision than appears on the surface. It was a contest between the Continental influence of Rome, represented by the see of Canterbury, and the influence of Ireland and Scotland, represented by the see of York. The latter indeed continued to claim certain rights which the Archbishop of Canterbury did not allow. But when, centuries later, the issue was finally settled, the Archbishop of York (to whom jurisdiction was assigned over the ten counties constituting the Northern Province) was indeed allowed to call himself "Primate of England," but the Archbishop of Canterbury was confirmed in the title of "Primate of all England," and so it is unto this day.

DURHAM CATHEDRAL

The Celtic Church in Northumbria, however, in these early centuries conferred great benefits upon religion and civilization. The first Bishop of Lindisfarne, the missionary Aidan, was succeeded by an even greater saint, Cuthbert, whose body was preserved on Holy Island until, during a Danish foray, the monks fled with it, first to Chester-le-Street, and afterwards to Durham Cathedral, where fragments of his coffin are still to be seen in the Chapter Library. His tomb was destroyed in a burst of iconoclastic fury, but in the ages of faith it won fame by the many miracles wrought at it.

The saint of the Northern Church best known to the modern world is the Venerable Bede, who was not only the first historian of the English Church, but the first English historian whose record can be trusted. He had not only some sense of the value of evidence, but possessed real literary gifts and enriched his narrative with much picturesque and vivid detail. To him we owe the account of the beginnings of old English sacred poetry at Whitby Abbey under Abbess Hilda, when the pious but humble Cædmon was inspired by a heavenly vision to write in Anglo-Saxon verse the story of Creation and other passages of Scripture. It is a tale often retold and may be found in our *Pictured Story of English Literature*. But nothing in the *Ecclesiastical History* is so moving as the account of Bede's death in 735 at the Saxon monastery of Jarrow, where he was engaged in translating the Gospel of St. John. The twelve-hundredth anniversary of Bede's death was observed in 1935 with many spoken and written tributes to the beauty and simplicity of his character.

In his own time the most renowned scholar of the Northern Church was Alcuin, who was born in the year of Bede's death. During his lifetime he not only made York a famous school of monastic learning, but was invited by the emperor Charlemagne to his court at Aachen (Aix-la-Chapelle) to organize the educational system of the Frank Empire. He spent ten years in the task before returning to York and was soon recalled to become head of the Abbey School of St. Martin at Tours, which until his death was an important centre of European culture.

BEVERLEY ABBEY

BOLTON PRIORY

THE YORKSHIRE COAST, from its natural situation, felt the full force of the Viking invasions, and the fisher folk from Whitby to Scarborough bear strong marks, both in speech and character, of their Scandinavian origin. The coast scenery is ruggedly romantic, in accord with the adventurous disposition of its inhabitants. Further inland there is the gentler landscape about Knaresborough, and the woods and moors of the Yorkshire dales. Ripon Cathedral, the Abbeys of Fountains, Kirkstall, Rievaulx (pronounced Rivers) and Beverley, and Bolton Priory are magnificent survivals of the architectural glories of the past. Bolton Abbey (as it is commonly called) has the additional charm of an ancient legend enshrined in Wordsworth's *The White Doe of Rylstone,* and if we pursue the beautiful valley of the Wharfe into its bleaker heights over Barden Moor, we get into the wilder country of Emily and Charlotte Brontë, about the rather grim manufacturing town of Haworth, where their father was perpetual curate of the church near which they are buried. The neighboring moorland is the scene of Emily's masterpiece, *Wuthering Heights,* and of Charlotte's *Shirley.* Some scenes of *Jane Eyre* are also suggested by the Yorkshire moorlands, and Ferndean Manor in that novel has been identified with Wycollar Hall, just across the Lancashire border from Haworth, on the way to Colne. It is the ancient home of the Cunliffe family, but except for a fine old fireplace nothing of it is now left standing.

THE FEN COUNTRY is a term loosely applied to the group of counties south and east of Yorkshire, but by no means all of it is fen. Strictly speaking, the fens are drained swamps, and are very fertile; the coastal marshland, recaptured from the sea, is only good for grazing. Lincolnshire, the county immediately south of Yorkshire, is largely made up of chalk-downs, woods, heath, and marshland; only the southeast "riding", known as "Holland", is wholly fen. But both fen and marshland have the characteristic flatness which throws into bold relief the cathedral towers of Lincoln, Ely, and Peterborough.

LINCOLN CATHEDRAL

PETERBOROUGH CATHEDRAL

Peterborough, which is in the adjoining county of North-amptonshire, is directly south of the Wash, in which King John's army, in the thirteenth century, was overtaken by the advancing tide and lost all its baggage, including the royal treasure. It is to this incident that Faulconbridge refers in Shakespeare's *King John* V. v.:

> Withhold thine indignation, mighty heaven,
> And tempt us not to bear above our power!
> I'll tell thee, Hubert, half my power this night,
> Passing these flats are taken by the tide,
> These Lincoln washes have devourèd them;
> Myself, well mounted, hardly have escaped.
> Away, before! conduct me to the king;
> I doubt he will be dead, or e'er I come.

SOMERSBY RECTORY in Lincolnshire was the birthplace of Alfred Tennyson, who went to school at Louth nearby and published his first poems with a Louth bookseller. Lincolnshire supplied the scenery for many of his poems—for instance, "Locksley Hall that in the distance overlooks the sandy tracts," though the metre and some of the thought of the poem were suggested by Tennyson's journey in the first train from Liverpool to Manchester in 1830. "It was a black night and there was such a vast crowd round the train at the station that we could not see the wheels." He supposed that the wheels ran in a groove and on the spur of the moment he made the line:

Let the great world spin for ever down the ringing grooves of change.

It is in the dialect poems that we get most of the Lincolnshire spirit as Tennyson knew and interpreted it. He knew the rustic speech of Lincolnshire well and was fond of telling stories in it. When the dialect poems were first read in Lincolnshire, a farmer's daughter exclaimed: "That's Lincoln laborers' talk, and I thought Mr. Tennyson was a gentleman."

The Northern Farmer (both Old and New Style) was taken by the poet from life. The earlier poem was founded on the

SOMERSBY CHURCH

SOMERSBY RECTORY

TENNYSON IN OLD AGE

dying words of a farm-bailiff, reported to Tennyson by his great-uncle: "God A'mighty little knows what He's about, a-taking me. An' Squire will be so mad an' all." In the poem this becomes:

Do godamoighty knaw what a's doing a-taäkin' o' meä?
I beänt wonn as saws 'ere a beän an' yonder a peä;
An' Squoire 'ull be sa mad an' all—a' dear a' dear!
And I 'a managed for Squoire coom Michaelmass thutty year.

The later poem, *Northern Farmer* (*New Style*) was likewise founded on an actual farmer of the neighborhood, who was fond of saying, "When I canters my 'erse [horse] along the ramper [highway] I 'ears proputty, proputty, proputty." This becomes:

Dosn't thou 'ear my 'erse's legs, as they canters awaäy?
Proputty, proputty, proputty, that's what I 'ears 'em saäy.

This part of the country appeals especially to New Englanders because it was a stronghold of seventeenth century Puritanism. Such place-names as Bedford, Boston and Northampton, and such family names as Bradford and Brewster are significant. Oliver Cromwell was a Huntingdon squire and represented Cambridge in Parliament before the outbreak of the Civil War. John Bunyan wrote *Pilgrim's Progress* in Bedford Gaol; he was born at the neighboring village of Elstow, and its church bells had for him a fascination he regarded as diabolical; "Now you must know that before this [my conversion] I had taken much delight in ringing, but my conscience beginning to be tender, I thought such practice was but vain, and therefore forced myself to leave it; yet my mind hankered. Wherefore I should go to the steeple house, and look on it though I durst not ring. But I thought this did not become religion neither, yet I forced myself, and would look on still. But quickly after I began to think *How if one of the bells should fall?* Then I chose to stand under a main beam that lay overthwart the steeple, from side to side, thinking there I might stand sure. But then I should think again,

we pray you in the bowels of christ.

Jo: Bunyan 1682

BUNYAN'S BIRTHPLACE

ELSTOW CHURCH AND BELFRY

Should the bell fall with a swing, it might first hit the wall, and then rebounding on me might kill me for all this beam. This made me stand in the steeple-door; and now, thought I, I am safe enough; for if a bell should then fall, I can slip out behind these thick walls and so be preserved notwithstanding. So after this I would yet go to see them ring, but would not go further than the steeple-door; but then it came into my head, How if the steeple itself should fall? And this thought, It may fall for ought I know, when I stood and looked on did continually so shake my mind that I durst not stand at the steeple-door any longer, but was forced to flee, for fear the steeple should fall upon my head."

OLNEY, halfway between Bedford and Northampton, has close associations with the poet Cowper, who in the latter part of the eighteenth century passed many peaceful years here in the sympathetic society of Mary Unwin and her children. The influence of the "perpetual curate" of the parish, the Reverend John Newton, was perhaps less cheerfully beneficent, but it is only fair to remember that Cowper's fits of insanity began before his acquaintance with this somewhat overzealous evangelist: they wrote together the "Olney Hymns," a still valued collection of sacred lyrics, in which Cowper's contributions were marked by a "C." The poet was more fortunate in his later acquaintance with Lady Austen, who established herself at Olney to be near him, and suggested the composition of some of his best-known poems—*John Gilpin, The Royal George,* and *The Task.* Cowper's two Egerias, alas!, did not get on any too well together, and through Mrs. Unwin's jealousy his friendship with Lady Austen came to an end, but her place as an intellectual stimulus was taken by Cowper's cousin, Lady Hesketh, who complained of Mrs. Unwin but managed to put up with her. For ten years Cowper made his home with Mrs. Unwin at Weston Underwood, two miles from Olney, and when they were too old and infirm to look after each other they were cared for by devoted friends in Norfolk until their death.

COWPER

COWPER'S HOUSE AT WESTON

NORWICH

NORFOLK, separated from Lincolnshire by the Wash, shares with Suffolk (easternmost of the English shires) the right to be called "East Anglia." Norfolk and its "Broads" have their champion and apostle in George Borrow, who wrote most of his books in his house on Oulton Broad, the home of his manhood and old age. He was born at Dumpling Green near East Dereham and passed his youth at Norwich, of which he has given us an admirable description in *Lavengro:* "A fine old city, truly, is that, view it from whatever side you will; but it shows best from the east, where the ground, bold and elevated, overlooks the fair and fertile valley in which it stands. Gazing from these heights, the eye beholds a scene which cannot fail to awaken, even in the least sensitive bosom, feelings of pleasure and admiration. At the foot of the heights flows a narrow and deep river, with an antique bridge communicating with a long and narrow suburb flanked on either side by rich meadows of the brightest green, beyond which spreads the city, the fine old city, perhaps the most curious specimen at present extant of the genuine old English town. Yes, there it spreads from north to south, with its venerable houses, its numerous gardens, its thrice twelve churches, its mighty mound, which if tradition speaks true, was raised by human hands to serve as the grave heap of an old heathen king, who sits deep within it, with his sword in his hand and his gold and silver treasures about him. There is a grey old castle upon the top of that mighty mound; and yonder, rising three hundred feet above the soil, from among those noble forest trees, behold that old Norman master-work, that cloud-encircled cathedral spire, around which a garrulous army of rooks and choughs continually wheel their flight."

NEWMARKET in Suffolk is the most important centre of that almost universal English interest, horse-racing. Until very recently Parliament adjourned in order to allow its members to attend the chief horserace of the year, the Derby, which is run on Epsom Downs. But the real headquarters of the turf as an organized sport are at Newmarket, which is perhaps the most

NEWMARKET

enduring contribution to English life of Charles II, if we except the children of his mistresses who established some of the great ducal families. Charles liked nothing better than to run away from political responsibilities and perplexities to the Newmarket stables, for he enjoyed the society of trainers and jockeys more than that of the statesmen at Westminster or of the philosophers of the Royal Society he gets the credit for founding, though its scientific work was really begun under the Commonwealth.

Not far from Newmarket is Bury St. Edmunds, so called in commemoration of St. Edmund, the last king of East Anglia, who was killed on the battlefield by the Danes in 870. Among the town's many claims to antiquarian interest, it has the ruins of the abbey (made famous by Edmund's shrine) which Carlyle took as the scene for his story and the text of his sermon in *Past and Present*. He described Bury St. Edmunds in 1843 as "still a prosperous, brisk town, beautifully diversifying, with its clear brick houses, ancient clean streets, and twenty or fifteen thousand busy souls, the general grassy face of Suffolk; looking out right pleasantly, from its hill-slope, towards the rising sun: and on the eastern edge of it still runs, long, black and massive, a range of monastic ruins; into the wide internal spaces of which the stranger is admitted on payment of one shilling. Internal spaces laid out, at present, as a botanic garden. Here stranger or townsman, sauntering at his leisure amid these vast grim venerable ruins, may persuade himself that an Abbey of St. Edmundsbury did once exist; nay, there is no doubt of it: see here the ancient massive gateway, of architecture interesting to the eye of Dilettantism: and farther on, that other ancient gateway, now about to tumble, unless Dilettantism, in these very months can subscribe money to cramp it and prop it!" Not only has posterity preserved the Abbey, but in 1903 the Tomb of Abbot Samson, Carlyle's hero, was uncovered by excavation and identified.

The mitred abbot of St. Edmund's could cross swords with his powerful ecclesiastical neighbor, the Lord Bishop of Ely

ELY CATHEDRAL FROM THE NORTHEAST

ACROSS THE FENS

ELY CATHEDRAL FROM THE SOUTHEAST

THE OUSE

(in the incident Carlyle relates, it is axes), and come off better in the encounter. Even after the Reformation the Bishop of Ely was a great dignitary. Queen Elizabeth found it necessary to write to him: "Proud prelate, you know what you were before I made you what you are; if you do not immediately comply with my request, by God I will unfrock you." Oliver Cromwell in his day found the cathedral authorities somewhat recalcitrant and dealt with them in a fashion equally uncompromising. He wrote requiring them to "forbear altogether your choir-service, so unedifying and offensive, lest the soldiers should in any tumultuary or disorderly way attempt the reformation of the cathedral church." When his order was not complied with, Cromwell attended a service held under the central octagon, one of the greatest triumphs of English ecclesiastical architecture, "with a rabble at his heels and his hat on," and commanded the officiating clergyman to "leave off your fooling and come down, sir," in a voice which (as Carlyle says) the clergyman "did now instantaneously give ear to." The greatest admirer of Puritan zeal may regret the damage done to the cathedral by fanatical imagebreakers (also, it must be added, by modern restorers), but they have not robbed Ely of the peculiar charm of its situation and the constructive skill of Alan of Walsingham, sacrist of the monastery in the first half of the fourteenth century and now recognized as probably the most original of English architects.

CHAPTER XI

THE INDUSTRIAL MIDLANDS AND NORTH

INDUSTRIAL CENTRES are avoided as far as possible by visitors to England, and the home-staying English in search of rest and quiet instinctively seek out country places. The encroachment upon rural areas resulting from the steady extension of the manufacturing districts has been intensified by improved means of communication and transportation. The telegraph and telephone, the radio, automobiles, motor buses, and charabancs have urbanized almost the whole of England to a greater or less extent. Even in a remote Devon village, with the cry of the plover over Dartmoor or the cooing doves in ancestral woods on the one hand, the passerby may hear on the other hand the mechanical music of radio or phonograph from the open doors of a score of charming thatched cottages. The increased wages of the workers, both industrial and agricultural, and the decreased incomes of the country gentry have made it difficult (though not yet impossible) for the seeker after quiet to satisfy his heart's desire. As Professor G. M. Trevelyan points out in a recent article, up to the end of the last century "the system of great estates and country houses acted, in the rural parts, as a strong preservative of natural beauty. Today the estates, parks, and country houses are being broken up for economic and politico-social reasons, and the motor-car has made every 'beauty spot' in the island a desirable building-site available for development by villas or bungalows. Remoteness from towns no longer affords protection to natural beauty . . . Under modern conditions it generally pays someone to destroy beauty, and it generally costs something to save or to replace it . . . The State, by its system of taxation, particularly death-duties, forces landowners to sell their parks and roadside beauty spots to the jerry-builder. The action of the

305

MONTACUTE HOUSE, SOMERSET

RIEVAULX ABBEY, YORKSHIRE

State greatly speeds up the destruction of beauty going on in the ordinary economic processes of the day." Montacute House, Somerset, "perhaps the most beautiful of all Elizabethan private palaces," was in 1935 seeking in vain for a tenant in spite of the fact that the expense of its upkeep would be partially met by rental from the land about it, and we need only glance at the advertising columns of the London *Times* or *Observer* to realize that it is one of many country houses in a similar predicament. "A few more rounds of death-duties," (writes Professor Trevelyan) "and they will be gone; their lovely walls and gables a habitation for owls; the parks in which they stand treeless, and cut up with bungalows and villas."

In order to limit a process of devastation which has become increasingly obvious, Parliament in 1907 established a National Trust for Places of National Beauty or Historic Interest, and more recent legislation authorized the remission of death-duties on lands bequeathed to the permanent protection of the Trust, which now owns 237 properties covering 57,000 acres, mostly in the Lake District and in the Home Counties. The Trust has also acquired powers to protect the neighborhood of beauty spots from the predatory exploitation of the speculative builder; and the Town and Country Planning Act (1932) made further efforts in the same direction. The Act against "Ribbon Development" passed in 1935 aims at preventing the erection of flimsy bungalows and ugly rows of cheap houses along the borders of the newly-constructed trunk roads. Under the Ancient Monuments Act of 1913 a great many medieval castles and abbeys, fast falling into decay, have been preserved from destruction by the Crown Commissioners of Works. An example (Rievaulx Abbey in Yorkshire) of their success in saving a place of distinguished beauty and historic interest is shown on the opposite page.

All this goes to show that although in modern England industrial interests are heavily predominant, the nation has not of late years been altogether unmindful of the heritage bequeathed to it by antiquity. The Housing Act of 1935 provides for the re-

TOLPUDDLE, MARTYRS' TREE

MARTYRS' MEMORIAL

STANDFIELD COTTAGE

conditioning of old dwellings so that they may be made comfortable and sanitary without losing their ancient charm. The problem of the rural slums is, however, a comparatively simple one where space is available and government subsidies ease the financial difficulties. Before the Housing Act was passed there were many instances of successful enterprise on the part of farsighted landlords and private corporations. A notable example, which commanded universal approval, was the erection by the Trades Union Congress, at the charming Dorset village of Tolpuddle, of a terraced row of cottages as a centenary tribute to "the faithful and brave men of this village who in 1834 so nobly suffered transportation in the cause of liberty, justice, and righteousness, and as a stimulus to our own and future generations." The Tolpuddle Martyrs (as they are commonly called) were agricultural laborers who formed a trade union to better their condition, and being convicted of taking an unlawful oath, were transported to New South Wales. Great indignation was aroused by the severity of the sentence and within a year a reprieve was offered to those who could be found and brought back. Some had disappeared or died, but among those who were pardoned was the leader, George Loveless, who declared at the trial: "We have injured no man's reputation, character, person, or property; we were uniting together to preserve ourselves, our wives and our children from utter degradation and starvation." These words are inscribed on a tablet to the memory of the martyrs, unveiled by Arthur Henderson, M.P., in 1912. The room in which the men met, and the tree under which they took the oath of mutual help—the only crime alleged against them—are still to be seen. The Trades Congress has been fortunate in securing a descendant of George Loveless to enjoy the privilege of living, rent free, in one of the cottages.

IN TOWNS AND CITIES the housing of the poor tenants evicted from overcrowded or insanitary areas offers a more difficult problem. On the whole, the boroughs endowed with the right of self-government under the Municipal Corporations Act of a

TOLPUDDLE, MODEL COTTAGES

TOLPUDDLE, VILLAGE STREET

century ago have not done badly, but they have not done enough. In 1835 the City of Liverpool was dependent for its water supply on a few communal pumps and on hawkers' carts, but today its people have 16,314,000,000 gallons a year brought into their homes. A hundred years ago rubbish of every kind was thrown into open sewers. Now Leeds disposes of a billion gallons of sewage annually without danger to public health, and Birmingham even contrives to make an income from its citizens' garbage. In housing, the standards of the past was "not more than two persons to a room," but the standard of the Housing Act of 1935 goes beyond that in its requirements. London alone has been building from 50,000 to 80,000 houses a year since 1932, but the rate will now have to be increased to 100,000. Mr. Herbert Morrison, leader of the London County Council, which has been very energetic and successful in its building campaigns, said in 1935: "There is a great army of people living under insanitary and overcrowded conditions in the East End of London. A large proportion are children. The only open space for most of them is the street. If they are left in their present housing conditions, the health of these children in after-life is going to suffer." To provide suitable accommodation for these families, not too far away from their former homes, if such they could be called, the Council proposed a scheme to take over for building sites 30 of the 340 acres of Hackney Marsh, hitherto accessible to the public for purposes of recreation. Immediately a great outcry was raised by the defenders of open spaces and the issue had to be referred to the Minister of Health for solution. Fortunately the Minister of Health was able to make a satisfactory compromise by reducing the 30 acres to 20 and allowing a grant of £10,000 to improve the neighboring marsh. The Act forbids overcrowding and requires the municipalities to take immediate steps to prevent it: but what are they to do? If the slum dwellers are dispossessed, houses have to be provided for them somewhere, and in many cases this cannot be done without encroaching upon the rural areas on the outskirts of the town.

MODEL COTTAGES AT WYTHENSHAWE

THE WYTHENSHAWE MAIN STREET

MODEL FLATS FOR AGEING PERSONS AT LEEDS

LEEDS WORKMEN'S DWELLINGS AS THEY USED TO BE

MANCHESTER is planning a model suburban community of 100,000 population with its own industries, playing fields, parkways and other amenities. Some such provision is urgently required. Sir E. D. Simon and J. Inman in their book *The Rebuilding of Manchester* (1935) point out that out of a total of 180,000 houses the city has a slum belt of 80,000. "Most of the houses in the slum belt are now dilapidated, verminous, damp, and worn out . . . The chief failure of the post-war housing campaign is that the overcrowded children in the slums who need help most have so far got no relief whatever." It is hoped that Wythenshawe, the new suburb in which houses are never more than twelve to the acre and sometimes less, may be the first of a string of satellite garden towns in the neighborhood.

LEEDS has recently embarked on a scheme to transfer slum families to satellite towns on the outskirts of the city with new roads, schools, baths, and libraries, likely to cost nearly a hundred million dollars. With a population of less than half a million, the municipality has built 20,000 dwellings to accommodate 80,000 people and is planning to build 20,000 more by 1939, when it is expected that low rental houses will be provided for more than one-third of the population. A New York architect, Albert Mayer, in a recent article gave an interesting account of the scheme of "preferential rentals" in force: "The large family with its breadwinner earning the same low wages as the head of a small family is called on to pay less rent. The unemployed in many cases pay no rent at all, though all tenants pay their rates or local taxes, which amount to about a dollar a week per dwelling. Out of 11,500 families, 4,500 have never required rent relief and the remaining 7,000 are now in receipt of rent relief ranging from a few pence a week to complete relief. There are 1,050 families paying no rent at all." Beds and bedding for the more commodious quarters to be occupied under the new scheme will be provided at the expense of the municipality for families who are too poor to buy them for themselves, subject to repayment under a loan system.

KIRKSTALL ABBEY IN 1769

KIRKSTALL ABBEY

The poet Gray spent a night at Leeds on his return from the Lake District to Cambridge in 1769, for the sake of seeing Kirkstall Abbey, which he describes in his Journal as follows: "Kirkstall is a noble ruin in the Semi-Saxon style of building, as old as King Stephen, toward the end of his reign, 1152. The whole church is still standing (the roof excepted) seated in a delicious quiet valley on the banks of the River Aire, and preserved with religious reverence by the Duke of Montagu. Adjoining to the church between that and the river are variety of chapels and remnants of the abbey, shattered by the encroachments of the ivy, and surmounted by many a sturdy tree, whose twisted roots break through the fret of the vaulting, and hang streaming from the roofs. The gloom of these ancient cells, the shade and verdure of the landscape, the glittering and murmur of the stream, the lofty towers and long perspectives of the church, in the midst of a clear bright day, detained me for many hours and were the truest subjects for my glass I have yet met with anywhere."

Kirkstall Abbey is now swallowed up by "that smoky ugly busy town of Leeds," as Gray calls it, but it is still in an excellent state of preservation, surpassed in this respect by no other Cistercian abbey in Yorkshire except Fountains. This may serve to remind us that while the manufacturing towns of the North have inevitably spoiled the surroundings of many of the old abbeys by the factories and crowded dwellings of the industrial revolution, they have in many cases proved better guardians of the fabric than the great landed proprietors into whose hands the abbeys fell at the dissolution of the monasteries of Henry VIII, often to be looted for building purposes or to be allowed by neglect to fall into irremediable decay.

In some cases it is not the urbanization of country districts that is in question, but the sacrifice of town buildings of ancient beauty or historic interest. Visitors to Coventry will doubtless regard with disapprobation the plan to transform the ancient city of Coventry into a modern town. The foundations of the Benedictine monastery founded by Lady Godiva in the eleventh

COVENTRY

BABLAKE HOSPITAL

century are to be uncovered, not from any curiosity as to her gallant ride in the nude through the city streets but to clear the way for a new thoroughfare, on which is to be erected a department store to employ 200 people and to cost nearly half a million dollars. The old Butcher Row with its quaint half-timbered buildings and low-browed shops, some of which have been in existence for three or four centuries, will disappear, and in its place will be a new market, a shopping centre, and "a much needed traffic artery." Some of the older citizens remember Coventry as it looked when George Eliot immortalized its commercial and municipal life in *Middlemarch,* and its political and industrial life in *Felix Holt.* They regret the change, but nevertheless accept it as an inevitable step in the march of progress.

THE ABBOTSBURY SWANS are concerned in a still more questionable modern "improvement"—the establishment of an air bombing practice range on the Chesil Bank, a pebbly ridge which extends for some miles along the southwestern coast. This ridge affords shelter for inland waters on which from time immemorial the wild swans of Abbotsbury—now over 1000 in number—have fed and bred. The air experts contend that swans and other wild fowl are more disturbed by the presence of human beings than by the swooping of airplanes and the noise of gunfire; but this remains to be proved. The swans (as may be seen from the photographs on the following page, taken from a few feet distance) have not been restrained by visitors from making their nests and bringing up their young. If the machine guns drive them away, it will not be easy to persuade them to come back again.

In all these cases the problem has been to balance material advantages (real or supposed) against the claims of natural beauty or architectural antiquity; and it is not surprising that the material advantages have prevailed, for they are obvious and ponderable; the advantages of preserving an old castle or a pretty village or protecting a charming landscape or saving the Abbotsbury swans are ideal and imponderable. Yet the interest

SWANS AT ABBOTSBURY

in natural beauty and ancient architecture has never been greater·
in England than it is at the present time. We must not therefore
be too hasty in blaming the industrial cities and towns which
developed at such an astonishing rate during the nineteenth
century if in their building operations they showed less respect
for antiquity and less regard for beauty than their posterity
would now desire. They were not always or altogether oblivious
of such considerations; and while we may justly regret much
that they destroyed or allowed to fall into decay, we should be
grateful to them for some things that they have preserved.

Bishop Welldon, writing from Sevenoaks, Kent, deplores the
increasing tendency to transfer industry from the North to the
South of England, for two reasons. In the first place, he believes
that "the migration of industry from the North to the South,
if it continues, will, in the end, impair, and perhaps destroy,
the peculiar charm of the southern counties, and not least of that
county, the Garden of England, from which I write." He is also
afraid that the depletion of the northern industrial population
will impoverish that part of the country intellectually and spiritually. He points out that the North has developed a type of
character "strong, energetic, and decisive, and fully prepared
for enterprises of high moment and value," and that "the great
political movements of the nineteenth century may be said
to have generally originated in the North." Naturally the
people of the North are more concerned about the demorali-
zation and diminution of their population through lack of employment than about the injury done to the scenery of Kent;
they have always been prouder of the men they raised and the
movements they started than of the scenery of Dovedale and the
Lake District, which are nearer home than Kent, or the buildings they have erected, or the ancient monuments they have
spared. It is an old saying (and in part, at least, a true one)
that what Lancashire says today, England will say tomorrow.
When the landed gentry, about the middle of the nineteenth
century, began to lose social predominance and political control,
it was to the North that the country looked for the leaders of

RICHARD COBDEN   JOHN BRIGHT

FREE TRADE HALL, MANCHESTER

the new policies. Sir Robert Peel, the prime minister who put an end to the duties on wheat under pressure from the manufacturing interests, was born at Bury in Lancashire, the grandson of a less celebrated namesake who introduced calico-printing there. Gladstone, Peel's distinguished follower, who developed still further the application of the principles of free trade, came of a family of Liverpool merchants. Both graduates of Oxford (Christ Church), they were by education and association partially assimilated to the rural aristocracy and were essentially conservative in spirit. The true apostles of the Manchester School of Liberalism in politics and economics were Richard Cobden, long a Manchester citizen and the donor of its Free Trade Hall, in which the greatest political meetings of the nineteenth century were held, and John Bright, a Rochdale cotton manufacturer, whose simple eloquence and profound conviction impressed the House of Commons almost as much as it thrilled the many thousands of his hearers in Lancashire and the Midlands.

THE INDUSTRIAL REVOLUTION. The real begetters of the industrial revolution were, however, not the political leaders but the inventors, the organizers of the factory system, the "captains of industry." The foundations of the mechanical civilization which was to spread from England all over the world were laid deep and far back in history. The archeologists engaged in exploring the prehistoric lake village at Meare reported in 1935: "Judging from the range of specimens found it is obvious that the huts in this part of the village were used not only for habitation but as weaving establishments." In support of this view they report the discovery in this one place of "four weaving combs, a number of bobbins, a few bone needles, and no less than 24 spindle whorls." But without going so far back, it is safe to say that the factory system, at any rate in embryo, had existed in England for centuries before the date usually accepted for the beginning of the industrial revolution. Thomas Fuller in his *Church History of Britain* gives a long account of the introduction of Flemish weavers into England by Edward III, and the "heightening of the manufacture to a higher perfection" by the Dutch who came over under Elizabeth. He makes a list of sixteen centres of the industry in various parts of the country, including, in the North, Kendal in Westmoreland, Manchester (cotton) in Lancashire, and Halifax in Yorkshire. Elizabethan legal documents describe a Salford (Lancashire) merchant as holding "a moiety of a water mill and fulling mill," and the Elizabethan silk-weaver and ballad-journalist, Thomas Deloney, gives an elaborate account of a cloth factory carried on by his hero, Jack of Newbury, in Berkshire:

> Within one room being large and long,
> There stood two hundred looms full strong:
> Two hundred men—the truth is so,—
> Wrought in these looms all in a row.
> By every one a pretty boy,
> Sat making quills with mickle joy;
> And in another place hard by,
> An hundred women merrily,
> Were carding hard with joyful cheer,
> Who singing sate with voices clear.
> And in a chamber close beside,
> Two hundred maidens did abide,
> In petticoats of Stammell red,
> And milk-white kerchers on their head:
> Their smock-sleeves like to winter snow,
> That on the western mountains flow,
> And each sleeve with a silken band,
> Was featly tied at the hand.
> These pretty maids did never lin,
> But in that place all day did spin:
> And spinning so with voices meet,
> Like nightingales they sung full sweet.

But at the beginning of the eighteenth century the spinning wheel was still a simple device, operated by hand, and the hand-loom, with some slight improvements, remained in principle the same as that in use for centuries until 1733, when John Kay, of

Bury, Lancashire, invented the flying shuttle. This invention materially increased the speed of weaving, and the spinning wheels were unable to meet the demands made upon them for yarn. The need for a mechanical spinning device which would produce more yarn was obvious, and in 1764 James Hargreaves, a weaver living near Blackburn, Lancashire, with the help of a neighboring mechanic, invented a machine which would spin eight threads at the same time. This was the famous "spinning Jenny," so named in honor of Hargreaves' wife. The story is that Hargreaves, entering the house suddenly one day, startled his wife, who jumped to her feet and upset the wheel at which she was spinning. The fact that the wheel continued to whirl while in a horizontal position, with the spindle in a vertical position, struck Hargreaves with an idea which revolutionized the cotton industry. He used one wheel to cause a number of spindles to revolve by means of a continuous band, and substituted for the human hand a pair of bars which could be successively separated and closed, and which by means of wheels could be brought nearer to or further from the spindles. In 1768 the Lancashire barber, Richard Arkwright, perfected a spinning machine which made possible the spinning of a number of threads at the same time very much more rapidly than the spinning-jenny.

NOTTINGHAM established its position as an early centre of organized industry by the adoption of the stocking frame invented by the Reverend William Lee, of Calverton, in 1589. About half a century later, when Charles I was excluded from London because of its adherence to the Parliamentary cause, he chose Nottingham Castle to raise the royal standard, partly no doubt because of its position in the Midlands, but also because it was a leading provincial town. When Hargreaves and Arkwright made their inventions, though they were both Lancashire men, it was to Nottingham that they made their way, and there the first cotton-spinning mill was set up in 1771. Finding the use of horse-power too costly, Arkwright removed his cotton

EDMUND CARTWRIGHT

SAMUEL CROMPTON

RICHARD ARKWRIGHT

factory to Cromford in Derbyshire, where he had the advantage
of water-power; at the same time he associated himself with
Strutt and Need, a well-established Nottingham hosiery firm,
who gave him financial assistance in developing his enterprise.

ARKWRIGHT made a success of his first cotton factories and
was knighted in 1786; Hargreaves was less fortunate in securing
recognition. The inventors of the new mechanical appliances
were by no means universally regarded as rendering a service to
mankind. Hargreaves left Blackburn because a mob of his fel-
low-townsmen destroyed not only his machine but even his house,
and at Bolton, in 1779, Samuel Crompton had to conceal his
spinning-mule from the rioters for fear of similar treatment.

Unlike Arkwright, Crompton made no effort to protect his
invention by acquiring patent rights. His father was a farmer
who lived in the old manor house on the outskirts of Bolton
still known as Hall i' th' (in the) Wood, and took to weaving
as a domestic industry to eke out a not too prosperous farm. The
son was brought up to the same craft and being of an inventive
turn devised a machine for the spinning of yarn for the fine
fabrics known as muslins, up to that time imported from India.
His "mule" was not, as is sometimes supposed, a hybrid combining the "Jenny" of Hargreaves with Arkwright's water-
frame, but was an independent invention different in principle
from either. The Hargreaves machine had fixed spindles and
moving frames for the "roving" (cotton prepared for spinning).
In Crompton's mule the spindles, mounted in a carriage, moved
to and fro so that the movements for thinning, spinning, stretching and winding corresponded as nearly as possible to the movements of the spinster at her wheel and placed the least possible
strain on the thread, so as to avoid breakages. Crompton was for
some years content with the moderate profits arising from his
own weaving of the fine yarn produced by his new process and
the sale of this yarn to other weavers; but in the early years of
the nineteenth century, when the prevailing distress reduced
him to poverty, he obtained a parliamentary grant of £5000 in

CROMPTON'S MULE

HALL I' TH' WOOD, BOLTON

recognition of the facts that (as his petition set forth) his invention was used for four-fifths of the cotton spun in Lancashire, and that the industry had in 1811 a capitalization of nearly four millions sterling and gave employment to 700,000 people. About 1808 Crompton set up in Bolton a small spinning mill, for which he used steam-power (first applied in 1785 to a cotton factory in Nottinghamshire), but he ended his life in comparative poverty.

The inventions of Hargreaves, Arkwright and Crompton put spinning ahead of weaving, and it was evidently necessary to improve the weaving machines to maintain production. The story runs that Dr. Edmund Cartwright in 1784 paid a holiday visit to Matlock, in Derbyshire, and went over to Cromford to see the spinning mills. Soon after his return home Cartwright constructed and patented a power-loom—a clumsy machine inadequate as an effective substitute for the hand-loom, but capable of development in the next fifteen years so as to be a commercial and practical success. At the beginning of the nineteenth century hand-loom weavers were still sitting at their looms in their own homes. It is in that period that George Eliot places her story of *Silas Marner,* from her own recollection of having seen an old hand-loom weaver almost bent double with a load of cloth on his back. In the opening of the story she goes back to the previous century: "In the days when the spinning-wheels hummed busily in the farmhouses—and even great ladies, clothed in silk and threadlace, had their toy spinning-wheels of polished oak— there might be seen in districts far away among the lanes, or deep in the bosom of the hills, certain pallid undersized men, who, by the side of the brawny country-folk, looked like the remnants of a disinherited race. The shepherd's dog barked fiercely when one of these alien-looking men appeared on the upland, dark against the early winter sunset; for what dog likes a figure bent under a heavy bag?—and these pale men rarely stirred abroad without that mysterious burden. The shepherd himself, though he had good reason to believe that the bag held nothing but flaxen thread, or else the long rolls of strong linen

NEWSTEAD ABBEY

spun from that thread, was not quite sure that this trade of weaving, indispensable though it was, could be carried on entirely without the help of the Evil One." But when, at the end of the story, Silas goes back to his native town to seek again the small house where he had sat at his loom, he finds in its place "a large factory, from which men and women were streaming for their midday meal." The transition from a domestic industry to mass production in a factory had been accomplished.

It was not accomplished without a great deal of suffering and a good deal of disturbance. The hand-loom weavers saw their domestic industries on the verge of destruction (as indeed they were) by the competition of mechanical mass-production in factories, and the Napoleonic wars at the end of the eighteenth century intensified the prevailing distress. Early in the nineteenth century Nottingham, which was then the leading centre of the textile industry, was the principal scene of the Luddite riots; bands of starving work people went about to break the machines which they regarded as the cause of unemployment. The nearness of Newstead Abbey to Nottingham led Lord Byron, who had succeeded to the estate and taken his seat in the House of Lords, to make the labor troubles of the time the subject of his maiden speech and he delivered to the astonished Peers an impassioned address on the wrongs of the Nottingham stockingers, in which he pointed out that the real cause of the distress and the resulting disturbances was the War. "When we are told that these men are leagued together, not only for the destruction of their own comfort, but of their very means of subsistence, can we forget that it is the bitter policy, the destructive warfare, of the last eighteen years, which has destroyed their comfort, your comfort, all men's comfort."

Byron's interest in the Nottingham stockingers was short-lived, and probably not very deep-seated. On attaining his majority he gave a ball to his tenants at Newstead, but he did not trouble to attend in person. He spent the following summer on the estate, but the main interest he showed was in the pretty girls of the neighborhood—not always to their advantage.

CHARLOTTE BRONTË   MRS. GASKELL

HAWORTH VILLAGE STREET

THE LUDDITE RIOTS which began in Nottingham in 1811 extended in the next half dozen years to the neighboring counties of Derbyshire, Leicestershire, Cheshire, Lancashire and Yorkshire. In this period lies the action of Charlotte Brontë's *Shirley,* which has as its background the manufacturing village of Haworth in the Yorkshire moors, where she spent her girlhood. The opening scene of the story is the destruction of some newly-imported machinery by bands of infuriated workmen, who leave behind the message: "Your hellish machinery is shivered to smash on Stilbro' Moor, and your men are lying bound hand and foot in a ditch by the roadside. Take this as a warning from men that are starving and have starving wives and children to go home to." Dorothy Wordsworth, who visited the manufacturing town of Halifax in the same region in 1817, strikes a more modern note; there is no hint of disorder, merely the recognition of wide-spread distress: "Cotton and worsted mills and steam-engines are no better than encumbrances on the ground, trade being so bad. The wealthy keep their mills going, chiefly for the sake of employing workmen, and few get more than half work—great numbers none at all, so that really a great part of the population is reduced to pauperism, a dreadful evil. Things cannot go on in this way. For a time whole streets—men, women and children—may be kept alive by public charity, but the consequences will be awful, if nothing can be manufactured in these places where such numbers of people have been gathered together."

Disraeli in *Sybil* and Dickens in *Hard Times* showed sympathy for the northern workpeople, but their best-informed advocate in Victorian fiction was Mrs. Gaskell, who, as the wife of a Manchester Unitarian minister, came into frequent contact with them and was able to plead their cause with direct knowledge of the actual facts. No novel drew greater attention to the wrongs of the cotton operatives than her *Mary Barton;* indeed, she showed so much sympathy with the workers that the employers protested, and she offered some solatium to their wounded feelings in a later novel—*North and South.*

JAMES WATT

The application of steam power was the decisive blow to both spinning and weaving as domestic industries. The possibility of using the expansive power of water under heat had suggested itself as early as the middle of the seventeenth century, but it was not until the last quarter of the eighteenth century that Boulton and Watt in the famous Soho Works at Birmingham demonstrated that it was practicable to apply steam power to industry. The industries of Birmingham are various, chiefly in the metal trades, and its modern business has been largely in small arms, but Birmingham had a manor and a market before the Norman Conquest, and as early as the sixteenth century Leland remarked that "a great part of the town is maintained by smiths, who have their iron out of Staffordshire and Warwickshire, and their seacoal out of Staffordshire." The central situation of the city and the mineral resources lying nearby gave it great natural advantages, but it has also had the services of distinguished citizens, in science and politics, as well as in business. Joseph Priestly, the discoverer of oxygen, was a Birmingham Unitarian until a riotous mob burnt down his house and drove him for refuge to Philadelphia. A distinguished family of Unitarians during the later nineteenth century was that of Joseph Chamberlain, the promoter of trade within the Empire, and his no less distinguished sons, Austen and Neville.

There are other industries in the Midlands worthy of the visitor's attention. One of the first and most attractive of model villages is Bournville, about four miles south of Birmingham, built in 1879 to house the chocolate works and workers. Burton-on-Trent is renowned for its ales. Most famous (or most notorious) of all is the pottery district, of which some southern rimester wrote:

Up towards the North of England hangs a horrid pall of smoke,
And its horrid name is Hanley, Burslem, Longton, Tunstall, Stoke.

This unhappy notoriety was confirmed to "the Potteries" when they were made the scene of masterpieces of modern fiction.

ARNOLD BENNETT   D. H. LAWRENCE

When George Moore was on the lookout for a typically dismal
manufacturing town as the scene of his projected realistic study
A Mummer's Wife, Hanley was recommended to him as too
prosaic to be romanticized even by a George Borrow; he went
to see it and found it just what he wanted. Arnold Bennett, who
was born in Hanley, read the novel three or four times and was
entranced by it; he saw in it "squalor and sordidness turned into
poetry"; he proceeded to apply the same method to half a dozen
novels about the Five Towns and made thereby the largest fortune credited to any English writer up to the date of his death.
He thought the Potteries "the most English piece of England
that I ever came across," and wrote of Burslem, not for publication but in his private diary, with genuine enthusiasm: "It
thrills and reverberates with the romance of machinery and
manufacture, the romance of our fight against nature, of the
gradual taming of the earth's secret forces. And surrounding the
town on every side are the long straight smoke and steam

CHETHAM HOSPITAL

wreaths, the dull red flames, and all the visible evidences of the immense secular struggle for existence, the continual striving towards a higher standard of comfort." D. H. Lawrence in *Sons and Lovers* and other novels of the Nottinghamshire border saw equal beauty in the rather drab mining district in which he was born.

Even to those who have not the eye for beauty of a George Moore, a Bennett or a Lawrence, there are many interesting and beautiful places in and about the manufacturing centres of the Midlands and the North of England. In a Birmingham suburb there is Aston Hall, a fine old English mansion, the original of Washington Irving's *Bracebridge Hall*. In the very centre of Manchester is the Chetham Hospital, a baronial hall dating from the fifteenth century when the lord of the manor, who was also rector of the collegiate church (now the cathedral), gave it as a residence for the warden and fellows. Dr. Dee, the astrologer of Queen Elizabeth, lived there as warden, and the next century Humphrey Chetham made it into a free

HADDON HALL

CHESTER

school for poor boys. They may still be seen running about the playground in their picturesque seventeenth century costume or heard singing in their fifteenth century refectory the Latin grace which has been heard within those walls for hundreds of years. There is also a lovely wainscoted reading room (the first free library in England) where the studious visitor may sit on ancient chairs to read old books or look out of oriel windows on the sooty air overhanging the busiest of Manchester streets and the noisiest of railway stations.

SHEFFIELD, on the Yorkshire and Derbyshire border, has been famous for its cutlery since the time of Chaucer, whose Miller bore "a Sheffield thwitel" [knife] in his hose. Horace Walpole described eighteenth century Sheffield as "one of the foulest towns in England in the most charming situation" and the charm of the moors and hills that surround it has been retained, while the smoke nuisance has been abated. The Derbyshire Peak is close at hand and not far away are the lovely Derbyshire Dales of the Derwent and the Dove. Bakewell, on the Derbyshire Wye, is a charming old town and in its church is the monument of Dorothy Vernon, whose romantic elopement from Haddon Hall in the sixteenth century is now held to be founded on fact. In any case the Hall is a picturesque and well preserved old house, beautifully situated on the bank of the Wye. Most visitors prefer its ancient charm to the palladian magnificence of the neighboring Chatsworth House, one of the palaces of the Duke of Devonshire begun at the end of the seventeenth century and finished in the first half of the nineteenth.

CHESTER, though it is not actually in a manufacturing district, is within easy reach from either Manchester or Liverpool. With its Roman remains, the Norman tower of its Castle, its fourteenth century walls, its Tudor timbered houses and "rows" (arcaded shops), its Phœnix Tower, from which Charles I saw the defeat of the Royalist army on Rowton Moor, Chester offers a sort of panorama in little of English history. In the tenth century the Anglo-Saxon king Edgar was rowed in a barge on the Dee by eight British chiefs; in the fourteenth, fifteenth and sixteenth centuries, the guilds of Chester presented on movable platforms or "pageants" their famous cycle of mystery plays at Whitsuntide, nine on Monday, nine on Tuesday, and seven on Wednesday. "The places where they played them was in every street. They began first at the Abbey gates, and when the pageant was played, it was wheeled to the High Cross, before the Mayor; and so to every street, and so every street had a pageant playing before them till all the pageants for the day appointed were played. And when one pageant was near ended, word was brought from street to street, that so the [next] might come in place thereof, exceeding orderly. And all the streets had their pageant before them, all at one time playing together." One may pass down Watergate Street and imagine "the Waterleaders and Drawers of Dee" enacting the famous scene in which Noah's wife refused to go into the Ark without her gossips. She says to her husband:

> Yea, sir, set up your sail,
> And row forth with evil hail!
> For without any fail
>   I will not from this town.
>
> Unless I have my gossips every one
> One foot further I will not gone;
> They shall not drown here, by St. John!
>   If I may save their life!
> They loved me full well, by Christ!
> Unless thou'lt let them in thy chest,
> Row forth, Noah, whither thou list,
>   And get thee a new wife.

Eventually her eldest son Shem forces her into the Ark, "whether she will or no," but as she passes Noah, she gives him a hearty slap for his pains.

CHAPTER XII

THE LAKE DISTRICT

IT may have been the accident of Wordsworth's birth at Cockermouth that made him the poet of the English Lake District, but it was no accident that made him the leader of the movement in English literature known as the Romantic Revival, unless we regard as an accident the conjunction of genius with favorable conditions of time and place. No more suitable setting could be found under English skies for the revival of nature-worship than the combination of romantic natural beauty to be found in the mountains and lakes, moorland fells and secluded valleys among which Wordsworth was born, educated, and passed almost the whole of his adult life. Born at Cockermouth in Cumberland, he went to school at Hawkshead in the Esthwaite Valley between Windermere and Coniston Water; after graduating at Cambridge and wandering for a while in France, Germany, and the West of England, before he was thirty he settled down to live, first at Dove Cottage near Grasmere, and then at Rydal Mount, where he continued to reside for the next half century. He was himself fully conscious of the influence of these surroundings upon the development of his attitude to Nature and to life. In *The Prelude,* in which he analyzed the unfolding of his own mind, he writes:

> Fair seed-time had my soul, and I grew up
> Fostered alike by beauty, and by fear:
> Much favored in my birthplace, and no less
> In that belovèd Vale to which erelong
> We were transplanted.

He gave thanks therefore to the Divine Wisdom that

WINDERMERE AND ESTHWAITE WATER

> from my first dawn
> Of childhood thou didst intertwine for me
> The passions that build up our human soul
> Not with the mean and vulgar works of man,
> But with high objects, with enduring things—
> With life and Nature.

In his attitude to Nature during his childhood and youth Wordsworth distinguished three periods: (1) that of his early boyhood with its "glad animal movements" and "coarser pleasures," when he was given up to sports and games, such as bird-nesting, boating, and skating on Esthwaite Water. Then there was a period when the sensuous enjoyment of Nature was everything to him:

> The sounding cataract
> Haunted me like a passion: the tall rock,
> The mountain, and the deep and gloomy wood,
> Their colors and their forms, were then to me
> An appetite; a feeling and a love
> That had no need of a remoter charm,
> By thought supplied, nor any interest
> Unborrowed from the eye.

This was his state of mind in his earlier twenties; but before he was thirty he had passed into another phase, of thought rather than feeling:

> For I have learned
> To look on Nature, not as in the hour
> Of thoughtless youth; but hearing oftentimes
> The still, sad music of humanity,
> Nor harsh nor grating, though of ample power
> To chasten and subdue. And I have felt
> A presence that disturbs me with the joy
> Of elevated thoughts; a sense sublime
> Of something far more deeply interfused,
> Whose dwelling is the light of setting suns,
> And the round ocean and the living air,
> And the blue sky, and in the mind of man.

He had passed into this phase before he made his home in the Lake District and settled down to the deliberate exercise of his poetic vocation.

Those who formed their first impressions of the Lake District from the Lake poets may feel a bit disappointed when they first come into sight of the "mountains" and the "sounding cataracts"—the mountains may seem mere hills and the cataracts just small cascades to those whose eyes are accustomed to Nature on a grander scale. Not one of the lakes is over a dozen miles long, not one of the mountains over 3500 feet high. The ground of Ruskin's objection to railways in the Lake District was that the scenery is in miniature, easily spoiled by embankments and station buildings, and the beauty of the landscape can only be felt in quiet walks or drives through it. Ruskin knew the Lake District from his childhood: he paid his first visit to it when he was four, and at the age of ten was not merely regarding Wordsworth with awed curiosity in his pew at Grasmere Church but was writing poems on the beauties of the Lake District in the Wordsworth manner. What is more important is that he owed to Wordsworth the central thought of his artistic and literary criticism and of his philosophy of life—that we must "go to Nature in all singleness of heart, and walk with her laboriously and trustingly, having no other thoughts but how best to penetrate her meaning and remember her instruction, rejecting nothing, selecting nothing, and scorning nothing, and rejoicing always in the truth." When the passionate conflicts of his stormy manhood were over, Ruskin retired to his country place at Brantwood overlooking Coniston Water—"five acres of rock and moor and streamlet; and I think the finest view I know in Cumberland or Lancashire." Now that automobiles and charabancs crowd the roads, Ruskin's renewed campaigns to save the Lake District from the intrusion of railways seem almost a waste of effort; but the visitor who prefers a quiet approach to it may seek it by way of Coniston or by Wordsworth's birthplace at Cockermouth. Even if he takes the more convenient route to Windermere, he may find seclusion between Ruskin's Brant-

JOHN RUSKIN

GRASMERE

wood and the Esthwaite Valley, where Wordsworth spent his enchanted boyhood.

By whatever route the visitor reaches the Lake District from the South, he is pretty sure to find himself speedily at Grasmere where Wordsworth spent his young manhood and old age. Grasmere and Rydal, on whose banks he dwelt, are surely two of the smallest bodies of water anywhere to be dignified by the name of lakes: Grasmere is barely a mile long and about half a mile wide; Rydal Water is still smaller. But Wordsworth was intent on beauty, not on size, and in that respect he considered his tiny streams superior to the gigantic torrents of the Alps. "The principal charm," he writes in his *Guide to the Lakes,* "of the smaller waterfalls or cascades consists in certain proportions of form and affinities of color, among the component parts of the scene; and in the contrast maintained between the falling water and that which is apparently at rest, or rather settling gradually into quiet in the pool below. The beauty of such a scene, where there is naturally so much agitation, is also heightened, in a peculiar manner, by the *glimmering,* and towards the verge of the pool, by the *steady,* reflection of the surrounding images. Now, all those delicate distinctions are destroyed by heavy floods, and the whole stream rushes along in foam and tumultuous confusion. A happy proportion of component parts is indeed noticeable among the landscapes of the North of England; and in this characteristic essential to a perfect picture, they surpass the scenes of Scotland, and, in a still greater degree, those of Switzerland."

DOVE COTTAGE, where Wordsworth first set up house at Grasmere with his sister Dorothy, was, as she said, "truly and literally a cottage, not an advertisement cottage with coach house and even stable, but a little low-roofed building with the entrance through the kitchen." The cottage had been a village inn, and the kitchen was a low room, five yards by four, wainscoted with dark oak and with diamond-paned windows overlooking the lake; adjoining it was a bedroom, which had another room above it, reserved for guests; above the kitchen was the main

DOVE COTTAGE, GRASMERE

WORDSWORTH'S SCHOOL AT HAWKSHEAD

living room and in an outjutting extension at the back were the laundry, pantry, and a small bedroom for Dorothy. In these modest quarters the poet and his sister lived for nearly ten years, doing their own work with only occasional help and entertaining, among others, Coleridge and De Quincey. De Quincey was enthusiastic about the peerless little vale of Grasmere, "the very Eden of English beauty, peace, and pastoral solitude," and greatly admired the cottage—not so much picturesque as lovely: "one gable-end was, indeed, most gorgeously appareled in ivy, and so far picturesque; but the principal side, or what might be called the front, as it presented itself to the road and was most illuminated by windows, was embowered—nay, it may be said, smothered—in roses of different species, amongst which the moss and the damask prevailed."

DE QUINCEY was so enchanted by it that when the Wordsworths moved out into a larger house, he moved into the cottage, married the daughter of a neighboring farmer, and lived there for twenty-seven years. It was there that occurred the incident he relates in *The Confessions of an English Opium Eater* as having happened about the time he had succeeded in cutting down his allowance of laudanum to 1000 drops per day. "One day a Malay knocked at my door. What business a Malay could have to transact amongst English mountains, I cannot conjecture; but possibly he was on his road to a seaport about forty miles distant. The servant girl who opened the door to him was a young girl born and bred amongst the mountains, who had never seen an Asiatic dress of any sort; his turban, therefore, confounded her not a little; and, as it turned out that his attainments in English were exactly of the same extent as hers in the Malay, there seemed to be an impassable gulf fixed between all communication of ideas, if either party had happened to possess any. In the dilemma, the girl, recollecting the reputed learning of her master (and, doubtless, giving me credit for a knowledge of all the languages of the earth, besides, perhaps, a few of the lunar ones), came and gave me to understand that there was a sort of demon below, whom she clearly imagined that my art could exorcise from the house. I did not immediately go down; but, when I did, the group which presented itself, arranged as it was by accident, though not very elaborate, took hold of my fancy and my eye in a way that none of the statuesque attitudes exhibited in the ballets of the opera house, though so ostentatiously complex, had ever done. In a cottage kitchen, but paneled on the wall with dark wood that from age and rubbing resembled oak, and looking more like a rustic hall entrance than a kitchen, stood the Malay—his turban and loose trousers of dingy white relieved upon the dark paneling; he had placed himself nearer to the girl than she seemed to relish; though her native spirit of mountain intrepidity contended with the feeling of simple awe which her countenance expressed as she gazed upon the tiger-cat before her. And a more striking picture there could not be imagined, than the beautiful English face of the girl, and its exquisite fairness, together with the erect and independent attitude, contrasted with the sallow and bilious skin of the Malay, enameled or veneered with mahogany by marine air, his small, fierce, restless eyes, thin lips, slavish gestures and adorations. Half-hidden by the ferocious-looking Malay, was a little child from a neighboring cottage who had crept in after him, and was now in the act of reverting its head, and gazing upwards at the turban and the fiery eyes beneath it, whilst with one hand he caught at the dress of the young woman for protection. My knowledge of the Oriental tongue is not remarkably extensive, being indeed confined in two words—the Arabic word for barley, and the Turkish for opium (madjoon), which I have learned from Anastasius. And, as I had neither a Malay dictionary, nor even Adelung's *Mithridates,* which might have helped me to a few words, I addressed him in some lines from the Iliad; considering that, of such languages as I possessed, Greek, in point of longitude, came geographically nearest to an Oriental one. He worshiped me in a most devout manner, and replied in what I suppose was Malay. In this way I saved my reputation with my neighbors; for the Malay had no means

THOMAS DE QUINCEY

of betraying the secret. He lay down upon the floor for about an hour, and then pursued his journey. On his departure I presented him with a piece of opium. To him, as an Orientalist, I concluded that opium must be familiar; and the expression on his face convinced me that it was. Nevertheless, I was struck with some little consternation when I saw him suddenly raise his hand to his mouth, and (in the school-boy phrase) bolt the whole, divided into three pieces, at one mouthful. The quantity was enough to kill three dragoons and their horses; and I felt some alarm for the poor creature; but what could be done? I had given him the opium in compassion for his solitary life, on recollecting that if he had traveled on foot from London, it must be nearly three weeks since he could have exchanged a thought with any human being. I could not think of violating the laws of hospitality, by having him seized and drenched with an emetic, and thus frightening him into a notion that we were going to sacrifice him to some English idol. No: there was clearly no help for it;—he took his leave, and for some days I felt anxious; but as I never heard of any Malay being found dead, I became convinced that he was used to opium: and that I must have done him the service I designed, by giving him one night of respite from the pains of wandering."

The young girl De Quincey mentions was the one celebrated by Wordsworth as "little Barbara Lewthwaite, a child of beauty rare," said by De Quincey to have unconsciously suggested to Wordsworth what is regarded by many as his finest poem, *Intimations of Immortality from Recollections of Early Childhood*. The Lewthwaites and the Sympsons, whose daughter De Quincey married, were excellent representatives of the farming families Wordsworth esteemed so highly: "Every family spun from its own flock the wool with which it was clothed; a weaver was here and there found among them; and the rest of their wants was supplied by the produce of the yarn, which they carded and spun in their own houses, and carried to market, either under their arms, or more frequently on pack-horses, a small train taking their way weekly down the valley or over the mountains to the most commodious town. They had, as I have said, their rural chapel, and of course their minister, in clothing or in manner of life in no respect differing from themselves, except on the Sabbath-day; this was the sole distinguished individual among them; everything else, person and possession, exhibited a perfect equality, a community of shepherds and agriculturists, proprietors, for the most part, of the lands which they occupied and cultivated."

De Quincey gives an amusing description of a trip he made with Mrs. Coleridge, her three children, Wordsworth, his wife and sister, in a common farmer's cart. "Such a vehicle I had never seen used for such a purpose, but what was good enough for the Wordsworths was good enough for me: and, accordingly, we were all carted to the little town, or large village of Ambleside—three and a half miles distant. Our style of traveling occasioned no astonishment; on the contrary, we met a smiling salutation wherever we appeared—Miss Wordsworth being, as I observed, the person most familiarly known of our party, and the one who took upon herself the whole expenses of the flying colloquies exchanged with stragglers on the road." They went over Kirkstone Pass by Brothers Water to Ullswater, where Wordsworth and De Quincey left the "carriage" to the ladies and the children and made their way on foot to Penrith; in the evening Wordsworth read his new poem *The White Doe of Rylstone* to De Quincey, who remarks it as "an incident ever memorable to me." The next day De Quincey went on alone to Greta Hall, whither Mrs. Coleridge and her children had preceded him.

GRETA HALL had caught Coleridge's fancy during his first visits to the Lake District where he stayed with the Wordsworths soon after they had established themselves at Dove Cottage. The Hall was too large for him and for his income, so he arranged to divide it with the owner. Next to Wordsworth, his greatest friend was Robert Southey, with whom in their enthusiastic youth he had planned an ideal community, the Pantisoc-

GRETA HALL AND KESWICK BRIDGE

racy, on the banks of the Susquehanna. They had taken to wife two sisters, the Misses Fricker, of Bristol, to share with them this Arcadian bliss, and when the emigration scheme fell through for lack of funds, they settled down to the realities of family life. Coleridge took possession of Greta Hall in midsummer, 1800, and wrote to Southey the following spring: "Our house stands on a low hill, the whole front of which is one field and an enormous garden, nine-tenths of which is a nursery garden. Behind the house is an orchard and a small wood on a steep slope, at the foot of which is the river Greta, which winds round and catches the evening's light in the front of the house. In front we have a giant camp—an encamped army of tent-like mountains which, by an inverted arch, gives a view of another vale. On our right the lovely vale and the wedge-shaped lake of Bassenthwaite; and on our left Derwentwater and Lodore full in view, and the fantastic mountains of Borrowdale. Behind is the massy Skiddaw, smooth, green, high, with two chasms and a tent-like ridge in the larger. A fairer scene you have not seen in all your wanderings."

The upshot was that Southey, who was not a genius, but a hard-working man of letters with a good deal of common sense and some business ability, became responsible not only for all of Greta Hall, where he came to live in 1803, but for Coleridge's wife and family into the bargain. Coleridge was only thirty, but his health and his morale had already begun the process of disintegration which he hastened by the use of narcotics. Also he found Mrs. Coleridge impossible—and she found him difficult —"he would walk up and down composing poetry when he ought to have been in bed"—and she was quite reconciled to his staying away from home if he did not make a scandal by an avowed separation. So Coleridge sent De Quincey to escort his family to the Lake District and lodge them under Southey's hospitable roof. He himself paid only one more visit to Greta Hall and left it for ever to live abroad or in London under medical care, for his addiction to drugs had got beyond his self-control.

S. T. Coleridge

HUGH WALPOLE in *Judith Paris,* perhaps the best of his Lake District series of novels, makes an entertaining page or two setting forth the patronizing airs of the Fricker sisters as they served tea at Greta Hall and the amiable condescension of the hospitable Southey to his less literary guests. He has also an excellent description of a walk in the neighborhood taken by his hero, Francis Herries: "He had reached now the spot where Watendlath Beck tumbled into Lodore, and as always when he was here he must stop and breathe in deeply that perfect beauty. This was surely one of the loveliest places in all England— English, too, in its qualities of old imperturbable age, a kind of wistful tranquillity, a cosiness of beauty mingled with an almost fierce suggestion of force. Here Vikings had stood, here two hundred years later his descendants would stand, and at every time the cataract (when the rains had fallen) would fling clouds of mist above the turning flower-like whiteness of the water that leapt and fell and leapt again between the thin brown stones. The dark bare stems of the larch and oak stood sentinel on either side, and exactly framed the delicate pattern of Derwentwater lay, in color now snow upon steel, a thin shadow of stainless white hovering over the silver gray. Skiddaw and Blencathra seemed to sway under the changing passing cloud. Every color— white and gray and brown—although so delicate, seemed to hint at the coming Spring; there was the promise of saffron and primrose in the stems of the trees, in the leaping water of the fall."

THE POET GRAY in his *Journal,* written in 1769, began the difficult task of describing the beauties of the Lake District, and it is interesting to compare his description of Lodore with that quoted above, written nearly two centuries later. On a heavenly October day, Gray walked from Keswick under the conduct of his landlord to Borrowdale. "The crags named Lodore banks now begin to impend terribly over your way; and more terribly, when you hear that three years since an immense mass of rock tumbled at once from the Brow, and barred all access to the dale

(for this is the only road) till they could work their way through it. Luckily no one was passing at the time of this fall; but down the side of the mountain, and far into the lake lie dispersed the huge fragments of this ruin in all shapes and in all directions. Something farther we turned aside into a coppice, ascending a little in front of Lodore waterfall; the height appears to be about 200 feet, the quantity of water not great, though (these three days excepted) it had rained daily in the hills for near two months before: but then the stream was nobly broken, leaping from rock to rock, and foaming with fury. On one side a towering crag, that spired up to equal, if not overtop, the neighboring cliffs (this lay all in shade and darkness) on the other hand a rounder broader projecting hill shagged with wood and illumined by the sun, which glanced sideways on the upper part of the cataract. The force of the water wearing a deep channel in the ground hurries away to join the lake."

Wordsworth, in one of his earliest poems *The Evening Walk* wrote of the

> bare grey dell, highwood, and pastoral cove
> Where Derwent rests, and listens to the roar
> That stuns the tremulous cliffs of high Lodore.

Southey in a poem once very popular told "how the water came down at Lodore"—"And dashing and flashing and splashing and crashing." In the minds of many American visitors Southey's phrases aroused expectations which were sorely disappointed if their visit happened in a dry season when the waterfall had been reduced to not much more than a trickle.

Southey's fame has undergone a similar reduction by the mere lapse of time. In his own day he was apparently thought superior to Wordsworth, whom he preceded as laureate; he was offered a baronetcy and a seat in Parliament, honors which he wisely declined, as well as a doctor's degree from Cambridge, which was not his, but Wordsworth's university. Wordsworth was content with the modest government sinecure of a distributor of stamps, of which the duties were discharged by a deputy.

RYDAL MOUNT

RYDAL LAKE

This enabled him to retire in 1814 to a larger house, Rydal Mount, still within the limits of his beloved Vale of Grasmere, of which he had written in his teens:

> Where peace to Grasmere's lonely island leads,
> To willowy hedgerows, and to emerald meads;
> Leads to her bridge, rude church, and cottaged grounds,
> Her rocky sheepwalks, and her woodland bounds.

After his death at Rydal Mount, which is still occupied by his descendants, he was buried in Grasmere Churchyard where his constant companions, his sister Dorothy and his wife, Mary Hutchinson, rest by his side.

DOROTHY WORDSWORTH. There are few scenes of beauty in the Lake District which cannot be associated with some passage in Wordsworth's poems, but his sister Dorothy, who had no gift of poetical expression, had, in prose description, a surer as well as a lighter and more delicate touch. As her latest biographer, Ernest de Selincourt, says, "she had the same vibrant artistic sensibility, with an even quicker response than his to the sights and sounds of the world about her, and a still happier gift for the inevitable words to communicate what she saw and heard and felt." Take for instance the charming poem about the daffodils they came across at Gowbarrow Park, on the banks of Ullswater; the first stanza reads:

> I wandered lonely as a cloud
>   That floats on high o'er vales and hills,
> When all at once I saw a crowd,
>   A host of golden daffodils;
> Beside the lake, beneath the trees,
> Fluttering and dancing in the breeze.

Wordsworth's prose comment is in his usual pedestrian style: "The daffodils grew and still grow on the margin of Ullswater, and probably may be seen to this day as beautiful in the month of March, nodding their golden heads beside the dancing and

DOROTHY WORDSWORTH

foaming waves." By contrast with this, read the entry in Dorothy Wordsworth's diary under date April 15, 1802: "When we were in the woods beyond Gowbarrow Park we saw a few daffodils close to the water-side. We fancied that the sea had floated the seeds ashore, and that the little colony had so sprung up. But as we went along there were more and yet more; and at last, under the boughs of the trees, we saw that there was a long belt of them along the shore, about the breadth of a country turnpike road. I never saw daffodils so beautiful. They grew among the mossy stones about and above them; some rested their heads upon these stones, as on a pillow, for weariness; and the rest tossed and reeled and danced, and seemed as if they verily laughed with the wind, that blew upon them over the lake; they looked so gay, ever glancing, ever changing." But if we go back to the poem, the last stanza reaches the height of Wordsworth's contemplative philosophic vein:

> For oft when on my couch I lie
>   In vacant or in pensive mood,
> They flash upon that inward eye
>   Which is the bliss of solitude,
> And then my heart with pleasure fills,
> And dances with the daffodils.

Yet the central two lines of the stanza, apparently so characteristically Wordsworthian, were supplied by his wife, Mary Hutchinson. It was of her he wrote the poem "She was a Phantom of Delight." To Dorothy he was, intellectually and spiritually, more deeply indebted. He pays an eloquent tribute to her influence in the "Lines composed a few miles above Tintern Abbey," and there is a shorter, simpler reference in "The Sparrow's Nest":

> She gave me eyes, she gave me ears;
> And humble cares, and delicate fears;
> A heart, the fountain of sweet tears;
>   And love, and thought, and joy.

HEAD OF ULLSWATER

THE DUDDON VALLEY offers to the devoted Wordsworthian
the most appropriate way to leave the Lake District, for the
poet has celebrated it in his best sonnet series, consisting of
thirty-five poems. The valley should be traversed on foot with
the text of the poems in head or hand or at least in pocket, if the
quiet beauty of the vale is to be duly appreciated. Wordsworth
begins by saluting the infant stream while it is still in the clouds
which too often envelop Wrynose Pass, and follows its curves
as the "Nurseling of the Mountain":

> Thridding with sinuous lapse the rushes, through
> Dwarf willows gliding and by ferny brake,
> Starts from a dizzy steep the undaunted Rill
> Robed instantly in garb of snow-white foam.

He pursues its course through the woods and fells to the open
fields and the quiet pools where the shepherds do their sheep-
washing, and arrives at last where the

> Majestic Duddon, over smooth flat sands
> Gliding in silence with unfettered sweep

pours into the sea, where he bids it a moving farewell:

> I thought of Thee, my partner and my guide,
> As being past away. Vain sympathies!
> For, backward, Duddon! as I cast my eyes,
> I see what was, and is, and will abide;
> Still glides the Stream, and shall for ever glide;
> The Form remains, the Function never dies;
> While we, the brave, the mighty, and the wise,
> We Men, who in our morn of youth defied
> The elements, must vanish;—be it so!
> Enough, if something from our hands have power
> To live, and act, and serve the future hour;
> And if, as towards the silent tomb we go,
> Through love, through hope, and faith's transcendent dower,
> We feel that we are greater than we know.

The last levels of the Duddon as it makes its way through
the marshes to the sea are the tamest part of its course, and at

FURNESS ABBEY

Duddon Bridge the pedestrian may be inclined to turn aside to Broughton, where he may take rail or car to Furness Abbey. This magnificent ruin shares with Fountains Abbey, near Ripon in Yorkshire, the fame of being in the later middle ages among the greatest achievements of Cistercian architecture.

The return to the South may also be made by Ambleside to Kendal and Lancaster—the route chosen by Gray on his way back from the Lake District to Cambridge in 1769. At Lancaster he stayed a day or two, although it was fair time and the inn was crowded, "a great old gloomy house full of people," because he was interested in Shakespeare's "Old John of Gaunt, time-honored Lancaster," the patron of Wyclif and Chaucer and the progenitor of a long line of English kings. The Castle interested him particularly and his account of it is worth quoting: "Ascended the castle-hill in a fine afternoon; it takes up the higher top of the eminence on which it stands, and is irregularly round, encompassed with a deep moat. In front towards the town is a magnificent Gothic gateway, lofty and huge; the overhanging battlements are supported by a triple range of corbels, the intervals pierced through and showing the day from above; on its top rise light watch-towers of small height, it opens below with a grand pointed arch; over this is a wrought tabernacle, doubtless once containing the founder's figure, on one side a shield of France semi-quartered with England, on the other the same with a label ermine for John of Gaunt, Duke of Lancaster. This opens to a court within, which I did not much care to enter, being the county gaol and full of prisoners, both criminals and debtors. From this gate-way the walls continue and join it to a vast square tower of great height, the lower part at least of remote antiquity; for it has small round-headed lights with plain short pillars on each side of them; there is a third tower also square and of less dimensions, this is all the castle; near it and but little lower stands the church, a large and plain Gothic fabric; the high square tower at the west end had been rebuilt of late years, but nearly in the same style. There are no ornaments of arms, etc., anywhere to be seen; within it is light-

LANCASTER CASTLE, GATEWAY

LANCASTER CHURCH AND CASTLE

some and spacious, but not one monument of antiquity, or piece of painted glass is left: from the church-yard there is an extensive sea-view (for now the tide had almost covered the sands, and filled the river), and besides greatest part of Furness, I could distinguish Peele Castle on the Isle of Fowdrey, which lies off its southern extremity." The Peele Castle is the one which Wordsworth invested with

> the gleam,
> The light that never was on sea or land,
> The consecration and the poet's dream.

From Lancaster Gray "set out for Settle by a fine turnpike road, 29 miles." His purpose was not to see the great natural curiosity of the quaint old Yorkshire town, the Ebbing and Flowing Well (celebrated by the Elizabethan poet Drayton in his *Polyolbion*), but to visit what he regarded as the still greater curiosity of that limestone region, Gordale Scar, of which his *Journal* gives us a lively description. "Oct. 13, to visit Gordale Scar. Wind N.E.: day gloomy and cold. It lay but six miles from Settle, but that way was directly over a fell, and it might rain, so I went round in a chaise, the only way one could get near it in a carriage, which made it full thirteen miles; and half of it such a road! But I got safe over it, so there's an end; and came to Mallham (pronounce it Maum) a village in the bosom of the mountains seated in a wild and dreary valley; from thence I was to walk a mile over very rough ground. A torrent rattling along on the left hand. On the cliffs above hung a few goats; one of them danced and scratched an ear with its hind foot in a place where I would not have stood stock-still for all beneath the moon. As I advanced the crags seemed to close in, but discovered a narrow entrance turning to the left between them. I followed my guide a few paces, and lo, the hills opened again into no large space, and then all further way is barred by a stream, that at the height of above 50 feet gushes from a hole in the rock, and spreading in large sheets over its broken front, dashes from steep to steep, and then rattles away in a torrent down the valley.

MALHAM COVE

GORDALE SCAR

The rock on the left rises perpendicular with stubbed yew-trees
and shrubs, staring from its side to the height of at least 300 feet;
but those are not the things: it is that to the right under which
you stand to see the fall, that forms the principal horror of the
place. From its very base it begins to slope forwards over you
in one block and solid mass without any crevice in its surface
and overshadows half the area below with its dreadful canopy.
When I stood at (I believe) full four yards distance from its
foot, the drops which perpetually distil from its brow, fell on
my head, and in one part of the top more exposed to the weather
there are loose stones that hang in the air; and threaten visibly
some idle spectator with instant destruction. It is safer to shelter
yourself close to its bottom, and trust the mercy of that enormous
mass, which nothing but an earthquake can stir. The gloomy
uncomfortable day well suited the savage aspect of the place
and made it still more formidable. I stayed there (not without
shuddering) a quarter of an hour, and thought my trouble richly
paid, for the impression will last for life."

CHAPTER XIII

THE NORTHERN BORDER

THE NORTHERN BORDER, like the Welsh marches, is rich in castles, ballads, and tales of derring-do. It was the part of England dearest to the heart of Walter Scott, who wedded Charlotte Mary Charpentier, in Carlisle Cathedral, after wooing her at Gilsland Spa, not many miles away. Scott used his memories of the Spa for the setting of some of the characters of *St. Ronan's Well,* one of the last of his novels and the least successful, for in it he deserted the romantic manner, of which he was the supreme master, for the social satire of Jane Austen and other lady novelists who easily surpassed him in that line. He was more fortunate in using his recollections of the neighborhood for the description in *Guy Mannering* of the "little inn called Mump's Hall, that is, being interpreted, Beggar's Hotel, near to Gilsland, which had not then attained its present fame as a Spa. It was a hedge alehouse, where the Border farmers of either country often stopped to refresh themselves and their nags, in their way to and from the fairs and trysts in Cumberland, and especially those who came from or went to Scotland, through a barren and lonely district, without either road or pathway, emphatically called the Waste of Bewcastle. At the period when the adventures described in the novel are supposed to have taken place, there were many instances of attacks by freebooters on those who traveled through this wild district, and Mump's Ha' had a bad reputation for harboring the banditti who committed such depredations." So far, Scott himself explains in a note to his own novel. In the novel itself he says: "The alehouse, for it was no better, was situated in the bottom of a little dell, through which trilled a small rivulet. It was shaded by a large ash tree, against which the clay-built shed,

SIR WALTER SCOTT

that served the purpose of a stable, was erected, and upon which it seemed partly to recline. In this shed stood a saddled horse, employed in eating his corn. The cottages in this part of Cumberland partake of the rudeness which characterizes those of Scotland." Humble as the hostelry is, it serves as the scene for the introduction of the hero to two of Scott's best known characters, Dandie Dinmont and Meg Merrilies, and it also gives occasion for a description of the wild borderland which still holds true of the country-side, though, in the century that has passed since Scott wrote, its inhabitants have become more civilized. "In truth, nature, as if she had designed this tract of country to be the barrier between two hostile nations, has stamped upon it a character of wildness and desolation. The hills are neither high nor rocky, but the land is all heath and morass; the huts poor and mean, and at a great distance from each other. Immediately around them there is generally some little attempt at cultivation; but a half-bred foal or two, straggling about with shackles on their hind legs, to save the trouble of enclosures, intimate the farmer's chief resource to be the breeding of horses. The people, too, are of a ruder and more inhospitable class than elsewhere to be found in Cumberland, arising partly from their own habits, partly from their intermixture with vagrants and criminals, who make this wild country a refuge from justice."

In his poems Scott makes fuller use of the English Border than in the novels. They were written before the novels, and the period in which the action is cast is generally of earlier date, when the English Border was as much given to lawlessness and disorder as the Scottish and therefore lent the poet full scope for the romantic incidents which were the favorite subjects of his Muse. In the first of his metrical romances, *The Lay of the Last Minstrel,* the scene is laid in Scotland, but the subject is an English foray in which the minstrel does full justice to the chivalry of both sides. In the next poem, *Marmion,* the scene opens on the English side of the Border at Norham Castle:

> Day set on Norham's castled steep,
> And Tweed's fair river, broad and deep,

NORHAM CASTLE

BAMBOROUGH CASTLE

And Cheviot's mountains lone:
The battled towers, the donjon keep,
The loophole grates, where captives weep,
The flanking walls that round it sweep,
    In yellow lustre shone.
The warriors on the turrets high,
Moving athwart the evening sky,
    Seemed forms of giant height:
Their armor, as it caught the rays,
Flashed back again the western blaze,
    In lines of dazzling light.

Saint George's banner, broad and gay,
Now faded, as the fading ray
    Less bright, and less, was flung;
The evening gale had scarce the power
To wave it on the Donjon Tower,
    So heavily it hung.
The scouts had parted on their search,
    The Castle gates were barred;
Above the gloomy portal arch,
Timing his footsteps to a march,
    The Warder kept his guard;
Low humming, as he paced along,
Some ancient Border gathering song.

The second canto is mainly a description of the voyage of
the Abbess of St. Hilda's monastery at Whitby in Yorkshire to
"St. Cuthbert's Holy Isle" (Lindisfarne in Northumberland)
and of the castles they passed on their way along the coast:

Thy tower, proud Bamborough, marked they there,
King Ida's castle, huge and square,
From its tall rock look grimly down,
And on the swelling ocean frown;
Then from the coast they bore away,
And reached the Holy Island's bay.

After this the action crosses and re-crosses the Border to arrive
at its main theme, the defeat of the Scots and the death of their

BAMBOROUGH CASTLE FROM THE NORTHWEST

king, James IV, at Flodden Field in Northumberland. A monument "To the Brave of Both Nations" now marks the spot where the king fell, and the scene of Marmion's death, Sybil Grey's Well, is still to be seen on Flodden Hill, with its inscription:

> Drink, weary pilgrim, drink and pray
> For the kind soul of Sybil Grey
> Who built this cross and well.

The Scottish Border is only three miles away, and on the Border is Coldstream, once almost as famous as Gretna Green for runaway marriages, but now more familiar as the name of a famous regiment of English Guards, first raised here by General Monk in 1650.

In *The Lady of the Lake* Scott took his admirers to the most congenial scene of his romantic genius, the Highlands of Scotland, but in his next metrical romance he returned to the English side of the Border. *Rokeby* takes its title from the old Yorkshire mansion of his friend Morritt, whose family still live there. It is near the quaint old town of Barnard Castle, which is picturesquely situated on the bank of the Tees. The Castle itself is magnificently placed and commands a fine view, which Scott has described in both prose and verse. "Immediately adjacent to the river, the banks are very thickly wooded; at a little distance they are more open and cultivated; but, being interspersed with hedge-rows, and with isolated trees of great size and age, they still retain the richness of woodland scenery. The river itself flows in a deep trench of solid rock, chiefly limestone and marble." Poetically rendered, this becomes:

> What prospects, from his watch-tower high,
> Gleam gradual on the warder's eye!—
> Far sweeping to the east, he sees
> Down his deep woods the course of Tees,
> And tracks his wanderings by the steam

DAIRY BRIDGE AND ABBEY BRIDGE, TEESDALE

Of summer vapors from the stream;
And ere he paced his destined hour
By Brackenbury's dungeon-tower,
These silver mists shall melt away,
And dew the woods with glittering spray.
Then in broad lustre shall be shown
That mighty trench of living stone,
And each huge trunk that, from the side,
Reclines him o'er the darksome tide,
Where Tees, full many a fathom low,
Wears with his rage no common foe;
For pebbly bank, nor sand-bed here,
Nor clay-mound, checks his fierce career,
Condemned to mine a channelled way,
O'er solid sheets of marble grey.

Even more romantic than the Tees is its tributary the Greta, which passes close by Rokeby and won from Scott one of his most spirited descriptions of natural scenery:

The cliffs that rear their haughty head
High o'er the river's darksome bed,
Were now all naked, wild, and grey,
Now waving all with greenwood spray;
Here trees to every crevice clung,
And o'er the dell their branches hung;
And there, all splintered and uneven,
The shivered rocks ascend to heaven;
Oft, too, the ivy swathed their breast,
And wreathed its garland round their crest,
Or from the spires bade loosely flare
Its tendrils in the middle air.
As pennants wont to wave of old
O'er the high feast of Baron bold,
When revelled loud the feudal rout,
And the arched halls returned their shout;
Such and more wild is Greta's roar,
And such the echoes from her shore.
And so the ivied banners gleam,
Waved idly o'er the brawling stream.

Close by Rokeby Park the two rivers unite in a more open and placid, but still lovely, scene, celebrated by Turner in his

RIVER TEES

MEETING OF GRETA AND TEES

famous picture "The Meeting of the Greta and Tees." Scott's tribute is paid from the point of view of still another castle, Mortham, which also figures prominently in his story; it was an old border tower, but is now only a farmhouse:

> 'Twas a fair scene! the sunbeam lay
> On battled tower and portal grey:
> And from the grassy slope he sees
> The Greta flow to meet the Tees;
> Where, issuing from her darksome bed,
> She caught the morning's eastern red,
> And through the softening vale below
> Rolled her bright waves, in rosy glow,
> All blushing to her bridal bed,
> Like some shy maid in convent bred;
> While linnet, lark, and blackbird gay,
> Sing forth her nuptial roundelay.

Scott paid two visits to the neighborhood, in 1809 and 1812, and left few of its many beauties unsung. He explored

> each cataract and spring
> Where Tees in tumult leaves his source,
> Thundering o'er Caldron and High Force.

The waterfalls are even more numerous than the castles, and one of them, High Force, is said to be "the noblest in England," though the height of its fall is only 72 feet. But the woods below are very beautiful, and Caldron Snout, a few miles higher up the Tees Valley, is a still wilder combination of rock and fell.

The descriptions in *Rokeby* are the making of the poem; the story itself, cast in the times of the Cavaliers and Roundheads— the former commanded Scott's sympathies, and the latter supply all the villainous parts—is negligible, in spite of its sensational elements of kidnapping, piracy, and murder. Nor was he more successful in his later rhymed story of the northern wilds, *The Bridal of Triermain,* of which the scene is cast in the Vale of St. John, among the foothills of Helvellyn. It is an Arthurian legend of magic and mystery, and lacks the descriptive power

HIGH FORCE

of *Rokeby*. Tom Moore expressed a fear that Scott would travel
"by long quarto-stages" south from the Border, writing a
rhymed romance about every gentleman's seat he came across
by the way, and that the only way to get ahead of him was

> To start a new poet through Highgate to meet him;
> Who by means of quick proofs—no revises, long coaches—
> May do a few villas before Scott approaches.

With the proceeds of *Rokeby* Scott bought the estate of Abbots-
ford, upon which he built a turreted castle of his own, but he
wrote only one more long poem of adventure about the lands of
Wear and Tyne, *Harold the Dauntless*. After this he left the
field of metrical romance to Byron and devoted himself to his
new-found domain of prose fiction, in which he reigned—and
still reigns—without a rival.

Scott's first literary achievement of note was the publication
in 1802-3 of three volumes of *Minstrelsy of the Scottish Border*.
One of his delights as a child and his first purchase as a boy was
Bishop Percy's *Reliques of Ancient English Poetry, consisting
of Old Heroic Ballads, Songs, and other Pieces of our Earlier
Poets,* published in 1765 and founded mainly on a folio manuscript written about the middle of the previous century. In the
learned "Essay on the Ancient Minstrels in England," prefixed
to the first of his three volumes, Bishop Percy remarks that "they
are most of them represented to have been of the north of England. There is scarce an old historical song or ballad wherein a
minstrel or harper appears, but he is characterized by way of
eminence to have been 'of the north countrye'; and indeed the
prevalence of the northern dialect in such compositions shows
that this representation is real. On the other hand the scene of
the finest Scottish ballads is laid in the south of Scotland; which
should seem to have been peculiarly the nursery of Scottish
minstrels. In the old song of Maggy Lawder, a piper is asked,
by way of distinction, Come ye frae the Border? The martial
spirit constantly kept up and exercised near the frontier of the

BISHOP PERCY

two kingdoms, as it furnished continual subjects for their songs, so it inspired the inhabitants of the adjacent counties on both sides with the powers of poetry . . . Whoever is acquainted with that part of England knows that on the English frontier, rude mountains and barren wastes reach almost across the island, scarcely inhabited by any but solitary shepherds; many of whom durst not venture into the opposite border on account of the ancient feuds and subsequent disputes concerning the debatable lands which separated the boundaries of the two kingdoms, as well as the estates of the two great families of Percy and Douglas, till these disputes were settled, not many years since, by arbitration between the present Lord Douglas and the late Duke and Duchess of Northumberland."

THE PERCIES, who obtained the earldom of Northumberland in the fourteenth century, had many clashes with the Douglases, who were the leading family on the other side of the Border. These sometimes were of the nature of international warfare, for the Percies were appointed Lords of the Marches for the English realm, sometimes they partook rather of the character of a personal conflict, and sometimes both motives were united. Thus in August 1388 James Earl of Douglas made a raid with 40,000 men into the counties of Cumberland, Northumberland, and Durham, returning home by way of Newcastle, where in a skirmish he captured a pennon or banner belonging to Henry Percy, son of the Earl of Northumberland. Percy raised a force to pursue them and caught up to them at Otterburn, now a little village on the motor highway from Newcastle to Edinburgh, less than twenty miles from the Border. The first onset of the English archers threw the Scots into confusion, but Douglas rallied his men, and a fierce battle ensued in which Douglas was killed during a mêlée and Percy was carried off prisoner to Scotland. So far Froissart, who says he got his information from two squires of England and a knight and squire of Scotland, soon after the event. Both sides claimed the victory, and the English and Scottish ballads arrange the issue, the number of combatants and survivors on each side, and the incidents of the fight according to national predilections. The earliest ballad in date which has survived, *The Battle of Otterburn,* makes the death of Douglas the outcome of a personal encounter with Percy, who had challenged him to single combat from the walls of Newcastle after the manner of a Homeric warrior or a knight of medieval chivalry:

> The Percy and the Douglas met
>   The either of other was fain;
> They swapped together while that they sweat
>   With swords, of fine collain. [Cologne steel]
>
> They swapped together while that they sweat
>   With swordës sharp and long;
> Each on other so fast they beat
>   Till their helms came in pieces down.
>
> The Percy was a man of strength
>   I tell you in this stound;
> He smote the Douglas at the swordës length
>   That he fell to the ground.
>
> The sword was sharp and sore can bite
>   I tell you in certain;
> To the heart he did him smite
>   Thus was the Douglas slain.

Percy was ransomed and became a national hero under the name of "Hotspur." He lived to fight (in 1402) another battle with the Scots under another Douglas, son of his former antagonist, at Homildon Hill in Northumberland, on the northeastern edge of the Cheviots. Archibald, Earl of Douglas, became Hotspur's prisoner and afterwards his ally when the Percies revolted against Henry IV, whom they had helped to the throne. So Hotspur and Douglas, one slain and the other taken prisoner in the battle of Shrewsbury, became familiar to subsequent generations of Englishmen, first in the pages of the historians, Hall and Holinshed, and then in Shakespeare's *1 Henry IV*. But the ballads also did a great deal to win them enduring fame. "I never heard the old song of Percy and Douglas," wrote Sir Philip Sidney in his *Defence of Poesie*, "that I found not my heart moved more than with a trumpet." It is not certain whether Sidney had in mind the ballad quoted above, or one of the later versions known as *The Hunting of the Cheviot* or *The Ballad of Chevy Chase*, which borrow from the *Battle of Otter-burn*, but add some picturesque details probably of the writers' own invention. Sir Richard Witherington, a squire of North-umberland, who is not mentioned in the earlier ballad, becomes in a later version a kind of subordinate hero:

> For Witherington my heart was woe
> That ever he slain should be;
> For when his legs were hewn in two
> Yet he kneeled and fought on his knee.

In a still later version this degenerates almost to burlesque:

> For Witherington needs must I wail
> As one in doleful dumps;
> For when his legs were smitten off,
> He fought upon his stumps.

But by the time these lines were written, England and Scotland were united under one Crown, and the Percies and the Doug-lases were reduced to the less romantic struggles of legal dis-putes as to the boundaries of their estates; the last battle of the Border was the Raid of the Redeswire in 1575, fought at Carter Bar, where the visiting motorist now crosses the frontier between England and Scotland.

THE ROMAN WALL. When Scott made the hero of *Guy Man-nering* visit the Border, the excuse was "a desire to view the remains of the celebrated Roman Wall, which are more visible in that direction than in any other part of its extent. His educa-tion had been imperfect and desultory; but neither the busy scenes in which he had been engaged, nor the pleasures of youth, nor the precarious state of his own circumstances, had diverted him from the task of mental improvement. 'And this, then, is the Roman Wall,' he said, scrambling up to a height which commanded the course of that celebrated work of antiquity: 'What a people! whose labors, even at this extremity of their empire, comprehended such space, and were executed upon a scale of such grandeur! In future ages, when the science of war shall have changed, how few traces will exist of the labors of Vauban and Coehorn, while this wonderful people's remains will even then continue to interest and astonish posterity! Their fortifications, their aqueducts, their theatres, their fountains, all their public works, bear the grave, solid, and majestic character of their language; while our modern labors, like our modern tongues, seem but constructed out of their fragments.' "

John Wesley, on his visit to the Roman Wall, was moved to an altogether different meditation. He writes in his Diary under date May 21, 1755: "I preached at Nafferton, near Horsley, about 13 miles from Newcastle. We rode chiefly on the new western road, which lies on the old Roman Wall. Some part of this is still to be seen, as are the remains of most of the towers, which were built a mile distant from each other, quite from sea to sea. But where are the men of renown who built them and who once made all the land tremble? Crumbled into dust! Gone hence, to be no more seen, till the earth shall give up her dead."

Jessie Mothersole, who wrote the latest book on the Roman Wall, received from it a totally different impression. In her walk along its entire length, she found many subjects for pencil and brush, but the main theme of her book is the character of the two men who were responsible for its building—Agricola and Hadrian. The former especially appeals to her, and she begins and ends her *Hadrian's Wall* with the final paragraph from the biography of Agricola written by his son-in-law, the historian Tacitus. "Vain and transitory is the face of man and the likenesses thereof; only the fashion of the soul is eternal, to be preserved and expressed not by means of alien material and the art of another but by the character of the man himself. Whatever we loved and admired in Agricola abides and will abide, in the minds of men and the records of history, for all time. Many of the ancients have been engulfed in an inglorious and ignoble oblivion. The memory of Agricola, recorded and handed down to posterity, will survive."

Agricola was not unworthy of this magnificent eulogy. "Unassuming, tactful, patient, incorruptible; kind and affectionate; brave and energetic, and yet modest; strictly just, and yet merciful; so great that it would be an insult to dwell upon his probity and self-control"—this is the portrait of the man brought before us in the pages of Tacitus and justified by the events he relates. Born in Provence of a family distinguished for its public spirit, Agricola was educated at Marseilles, and did his first military service in Britain during the unhappy period of the revolt of Boadicea. When Vespasian became Emperor, Agricola was sent to Britain to command the Twentieth legion, and later was appointed to be governor of the province. He was at once faced with a rebellion in North Wales, which he put down with a firm hand, and reduced also the Isle of Anglesey which had hitherto resisted the Roman power. For the next year or two he devoted his efforts to reconciling the Britons to Roman government, encouraging their leaders to take part in the administration and to enjoy the advantages of Roman civilization. Colonies of Roman veterans were settled in the country as far north as York, which became the capital in succession to Lincoln and Colchester, and the inhabitants accustomed themselves to the peace, order, comfort and even to the luxury of Roman life. To secure the northern frontier, Agricola built a line of forts from the Solway to the Tyne, supported by connecting roads and with carefully planned communications with the south. In the following years he pushed the frontier further north to the isthmus between the Clyde and the Forth, and even defeated the tribes as far north as the Grampian Hills. He would undoubtedly have reduced all of Great Britain (his fleet sailed around it) and have under-

HADRIAN

taken the conquest of Ireland if he had not realized that his
success had aroused the jealousy of the Emperor Domitian, who
called him back to Rome. Agricola obeyed the summons, retired
quietly into private life, and died at the age of fifty-four, not
without suspicion of poison administered at the Emperor's in-
stigation.

Soon after Hadrian came to the throne, he visited Britain
and determined to consolidate the province by elaborate works
at the line of defense Agricola had already fortified between the
Solway and the Tyne. The works which he planned and which
were carried out after his return to Rome, were elaborate and
must have been costly even with the forced labor by which they
were doubtless built under military direction. They consisted
of (1) a stone wall over 73 miles long; (2) some twenty stations
or stationary camps, adjacent to the Wall, three or four miles
apart, to provide accommodation for the garrisons along its
course; (3) *castella* or mile-castles, connected with the Wall on
its south side at intervals of a Roman mile (about 1500 yards);
(4) between every pair of *castella,* two watch towers or sentry
boxes for look-outs. All these were of stone. To take the last
first, they measured about twelve feet long by ten wide, and
their walls were three feet thick. The mile-castles were quad-
rangular buildings, usually sixty feet from east to west and fifty
from north to south; their masonry was of the same character
as the Wall, which formed their north side; through the middle
of the north and south sides they were provided with massive
gates. The stations were permanent camps built on the model of
the temporary camps which the Roman legionaries built for
even a night's sojourn, protected with a *vallum* or rampart of
earth, dug out of the *fossa* or ditch running on the outside. The
permanent stations varied from less than an acre in size to more
than five; they were enclosed by stone walls from five to eight
feet thick, and were probably protected also by a rampart and a
fosse. The main wall was from seven to ten feet thick, usually
about eight feet. The height is more difficult to ascertain, owing
to the ruin of the higher parts. The Venerable Bede, writing

COINS OF ROMAN EMPERORS FOUND IN BRITAIN

some twelve centuries ago from personal observation, for his monastery was at Jarrow on the Tyne, wrote of the Wall in his day: "It is eight feet in breadth, and twelve in height, in a straight line from east to west, as is still visible to beholders." The height seems to be underestimated, probably because Bede left out of count the watch towers, for Elizabethan observers (including Camden) speak of its height as fifteen or sixteen feet or even higher; modern estimates put it at eighteen feet in some places. The Reverend John Collingwood Bruce, who was the great nineteenth century authority on the Wall, estimated that the masonry of the main structure, apart from stations, mile-castles, and turrets, would amount to over 1,700,000 cubic yards, and at $3 a cubic yard would cost over five million dollars.

But this was not all. Along the north side of the Wall ran a fosse, thirty-six feet wide and fifteen feet deep, dug or cut through soil, bog, or rock throughout its entire length, except where a precipice or a river made it superfluous. This would amount to the excavation of 5,585,072 cubic yards and would involve 698,134 days' labor.

On the south side of the Wall a military road was constructed of rubble stone, eighteen feet wide, elevated a foot or more above the surface, and protected by stout curbs; it connected the stations, and crossed the roads running north and south.

Beyond this again, probably to protect the approach from the south, was a set of supplementary earthworks, consisting of a ditch, rather smaller than that on the north of the Wall, flanked on each side by ramparts six or seven feet above the level of the ground. This *Vallum,* as it is called, has withstood the ravages of time better than the stone Wall (*murus*), which has been mercilessly pillaged during the centuries to provide building material for churches, inns, farmhouses, cottages, and what not, so that in many places the Wall has disappeared altogether, especially at its two extremities, where the country is more cultivated and more thickly populated. In the middle of its course, where the scenery is wild and desolate, the works survive with

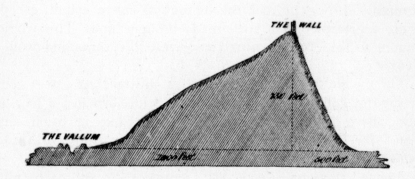

THE WALL

THE VALLUM

330 feet

1800 feet

500 feet

SOUTH.

B

A

NORTH.

SECTIONS OF ROMAN WALL

something of their ancient grandeur. The transverse sections, shown on the opposite page (with the Wall restored to its full height), were taken, the first near the eighteenth milestone west of Newcastle, and the second near Currawburgh, about seven miles further west; these two are reproduced from Bruce's *Roman Wall*. The third is a similar section after Warburton, of the works in the hill country further west, near Bradley farmhouse, where a stone was found built into the kitchen doorway, bearing the fragment of an inscription; the other fragment was found elsewhere and the two were pieced together by Dr. Bruce as shown below. Near a neighboring farmhouse were discovered traces of a mile-castle from the foundations of which was dug up a precisely similar tablet, proving (with others of the same kind discovered since) that the Wall was the work of Hadrian and not, as had long been supposed, of a later Emperor, Severus:

IMP[ERATORIS] CAES[ARIS] TRAIAN[I]

HADRIAN[I] AUG[USTI]

LEG[IO] SECUNDA AUG[USTA]

A[ULO] PLATORIO NEPOTE LEG[ATO]

PR[O]P[RÆTORE]

Of the Emperor Cæsar Trajanus
Hadrianus Augustus
The second legion, styled the August,
Aulus Platorius Nepos, being legate and proprætor

ROMAN WALL AT HOUSESTEADS

"The most striking feature in the plan both of the *Murus* and the *Vallum*," says Dr. Bruce, "is the determinate manner in which they pursue their straight-forward course. The *Vallum* makes fewer deviations from a right line than the stone Wall; but as the Wall traverses higher ground, this remarkable tendency is more easily detected in it than in the other. Shooting over the country in its onward course, it only swerves from a straight line to take in its route the boldest elevations. So far from declining a hill, it uniformly selects it. For nineteen miles out of Newcastle, the road to Carlisle runs upon the foundation of the Wall, and during the summer months its dusty surface contrasts well with the surrounding verdure. Often will the traveler, after attaining some of the steep acclivities of his path, observe the road stretching for miles in an undeviating course to the east and the west of him, resembling, as Hutton expresses it, a white ribbon on a green ground. But if it never moves from a right line, except to occupy the highest points, it never fails to seize them, as they occur, no matter how often it is compelled, with this view, to change its direction. It never bends in a curve, but always at an angle. Hence, along the craggy precipices between Sewingshields and Thirlwall, it is obliged to pursue a remarkably zig-zag course; for it takes in its range, with the utmost pertinacity, every projecting rock.

"This mode of proceeding involves another peculiarity. It is compelled to accommodate itself to the depressions of the mountainous region over which it passes. Without flinching, it sinks into the 'gap', or pass, which ever and anon occurs, and having crossed the narrow valley, ascends unfalteringly the steep acclivity on the other side. The antiquary, in following it into these ravines, is often compelled to step with the utmost caution, and in clambering up the opposite ascent, he is as frequently constrained to pause for breath. After crossing the river Irthing, in Cumberland, the Wall is opposed in its course westward by a precipice of upwards of one hundred feet in height. It cannot now be ascertained, whether or not the Wall was taken up the edge of this cliff, for the stratum is of a soft and yielding nature,

RUINS OF CILURNUM, ROMAN WALL

and is continually being removed by the river below. Certain, however, it is, that the Wall, accompanied by its ditch, is still to be seen on the very brink of its summit. If it did not climb this steep, it is the only one which, in the course of the line from sea to sea, it refused—and if it did ascend it, it would more nearly resemble a leaning tower than a barrier wall."

In these desolate regions, still unredeemed from their native wildness, life was very different from the ordered round of existence in a Roman villa south of York or Chester. Tacitus, describing the serious and energetic life led by Agricola on his first military service in Britain, tells us: "He did not imitate the usual practice of young men, who make the camp a scene of licentiousness, and waste their time in pleasures and idle excursions." Kipling in *Puck of Pook's Hill* ("On the Great Wall") draws a lively picture of what Britain was like toward the end of the fourth century. "Of course, the farther North you go the emptier are the roads. At last you fetch clear of the forests and climb bare hills, where wolves howl in the ruins of our cities that have been. No more pretty girls; no more jolly magistrates who knew your father when he was young, and invite you to stay with them; no news at the temples and way-stations except bad news of wild beasts. There's where you meet hunters, and trappers for the circuses, prodding along chained bears and muzzled wolves . . . Just when you think you are at the world's end, you see a smoke from East to West as far as the eye can turn, and then, under it, also as far as the eye can stretch, houses and temples, shops and theatres, barracks, and granaries, trickling along like dice behind—always behind—one long, low, rising and falling, and hiding and showing line of towers. And that is the Wall!" All along the south side of the Wall is "one roaring, rioting, cock-fighting, wolf-baiting, horse-racing town." The soldiers' liking for hunting deer, boars, bears and wolves in the forests and on the hills near the Wall is borne out by the remains of bones and teeth found in the ruins, and by the temples they erected to gods of the chase and of the woods. But in the stationary camps, the officers, at any rate, led comfortable lives, with heated rooms and baths.

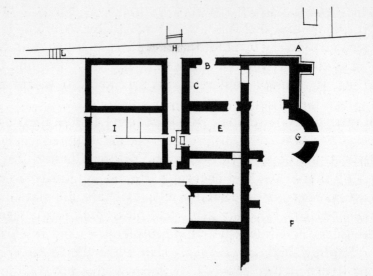

PLAN OF CHESTERS (CILURNUM)

SKETCH OF RUINS OF FORT

The ground-plan of the ruins of the fort at Chesters (Cilurnum), about twenty miles west of Newcastle, drawn by Dr. Bruce, gives a good idea of how the heating system worked. Descending a few steps (marked L in the plan on the opposite page) we pass along a street widening out from three feet to four at the other end. At H a street at rightangles leads south to D, the grand entrance to the main building, where the commander of the station presumably transacted business and administered justice (E). In the adjoining room (C) there was a bath, and at B a statue of a river god, presumably the presiding deity of the North Tyne, close by. Under the rooms beyond were pillars with flags about two inches thick resting upon them; above the flags a layer, five inches thick, composed of lime, sand, gravel and burned clay or pounded tile, and over this a floor of thin flagstones. At G there was a semicircular recess providing an alcove similar to one found in the baths at Halton Chesters (Hunnum) six miles nearer to Newcastle and at other stations on the Wall. In the recess there is an opening in the Wall to regulate the current of air from the hypocaust or furnace at F. An arched and tiled passage at X took the hot air from the furnace into the rooms west of the party-wall. The rooms (I) on the other side of the cross-street HD (probably the commander's residence) were heated separately by a hot air system, passing by underground flues and through hollow tiles in the walls. In this way the "scorching" of the air produced by some modern heating systems was avoided.

At Great Chesters (Aesica), 35 miles west of Newcastle, the plan of the ruins of the baths (excavated by Gibson and Hodgkin in 1897) illustrates the system very clearly. This plan is reproduced on the next page, where it may be scanned in detail.

The water to supply these baths was conveyed from a neighboring stream by an aqueduct dug into the hillside, three or four feet deep and proportionately wide, six miles in length; it was a clever piece of engineering, for in order to get a steady and even flow of water it was necessary to manage the gradients skilfully, the fall in the direct line being a little over two miles.

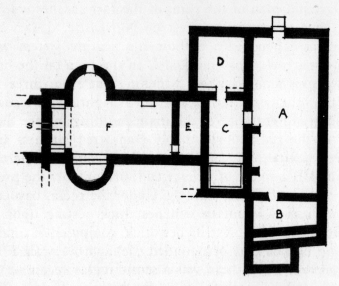

PLAN OF BATHS AT GREAT CHESTERS (ÆSICA)

The above diagram needs some explanation. A was a yard, 45 feet by 21; at the north end was the entrance, at the south end the latrines; midway on the east side was a door to the *frigidarium* with a cold water bath at the south end of the room. Adjoining this was (D) a square room with a stone seat against its south wall—probably a dressing room. E was a small room with a concrete floor resting upon a pillared hypocaust—the *tepidarium*. The last room (F) was probably the hot room, with alcoves, one on the south with a bath let into the floor, the other with a window opening, below which pieces of broken glass were found. Underneath this large room were heating arrangements and the main furnace lay beyond it (S).

The evidences of care for the spiritual welfare of the garrisons are less impressive. There are altars with inscriptions to various deities, and some without any inscription, ready for sale to the devout. There is an underground temple to Mithras at Housesteads (Borcovicus) and indications of another *mithræum* at Rutchester (Vindobala), but the most interesting remains are

THREE NYMPHS OF THE DEA COVENTINA

about a spring near Carrawburgh (Procolitia), consisting of a
massive stone structure 7 feet deep and measuring about eight
feet each way inside. Within it were over sixteen thousand coins
(mostly copper), a human skull, altars, bowls of Samian ware,
glass, bones of animals, a sculptured stone representing three
Naiads or water-nymphs, vases, brooches, rings, beads, dice,
votive tablets and altars. The last-mentioned made it clear that
it was not a Roman bath, as had been first supposed, but a shrine
to a nymph or goddess, by name Coventina, a local river deity
otherwise unknown to Roman mythology. Further excavation
revealed the stone walls of a temple or enclosure 40 feet square,
and it was conjectured that the shrine had been abandoned and
the coins and other objects thrown into the spring from fear of
attack, either by reforming Christians (for some of the coins
are of later date than the adoption of Christianity by Constantine) or of resurging barbarians, against whom the Britons were
unable to defend themselves after the withdrawal of the Roman
legionaries and the Roman fleet. Sorry as the Britons were to see

the Romans come, they were even sorrier to see them go. From the arrival of Julius Cæsar until the Emperor Honorius in 410 informed the Britons that they would have to look after themselves, more time had elapsed than from the discovery of America by Columbus to the present day.

INDEX OF ILLUSTRATIONS

PORTRAITS

INDEX OF PLACES AND THINGS ILLUSTRATED

Date Due

MAR 1 2 '54	OCT 24 '74	OCT 2 '84	
MAR 1 9 '54	F	OCT 2 8 '86	
MAR 3 4	OC 1 1 '78		
APR 4	OC 2 6 '78		
APR 30 '57	NO 9 '78		
APR 15 '57	DE 1 3 '78		
MAR 1 2 '58	DE 1 3 '78		
JUL 3 '60	OC 1 6 '79		
MAR 2 5 '63	NO 1 '79		
FEB 22 '66	JE 30 '80		
	NO 13 '80		
OCT 27 '67	DE 7 '80		
OCT 27 '67	DE 8 '80		
DEC 4 '69			
MAR 31 '72	OC 1 6 '81		
NOV 15 '72	NO 7 '81		
APR 2 0 '73	DE 4 '81		
MAY 8 '73	NO 1 5 '82		